How the
Stock Market
Works

John M. Dalton is a practicing attorney with the firm of Dalton & Dalton and an instructor at the New York Institute of Finance. Formerly with the American Stock Exchange, Inc., he was the Assistant Director of the Floor Rules Department, Director of the Trading Analysis Department, and a Senior Compliance Attorney. Mr. Dalton has often been called upon to appear at trials and arbitration hearings to explain Wall Street practices and procedures.

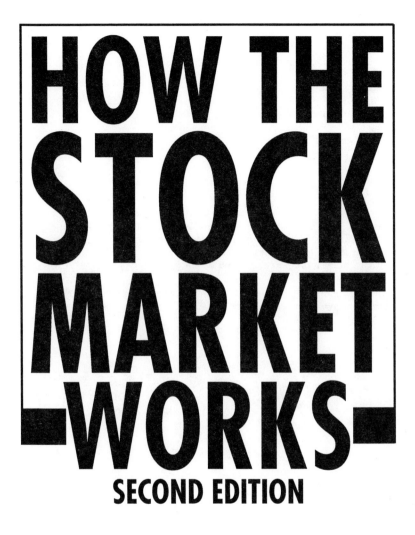

HOW THE STOCK MARKET WORKS

SECOND EDITION

EDITED BY JOHN M. DALTON, ESQ.

THE NEW YORK INSTITUTE OF FINANCE

Library of Congress Cataloging-in-Publication Data

Dalton, John
   How the stock market works / John M. Dalton.—2nd ed.
     p. cm.
   Includes index.
   ISBN 0-13-097866-3
   1. Stock-exchange.   2. Stocks.   I. Title.
   HG4551. D29 1993
   332.64′273—dc20   93-36063
                                       CIP

This publication is designed to provide accurate and authoritative information in regard to the subject matter covered. It is sold with the understanding that the publisher is not engaged in rendering legal, accounting, or other professional service. If legal advice or other expert assistance is required, the services of a competent professional person should be sought.

From a Declaration of Principles Jointly Adopted by a Committee of the American Bar Association and a Committee of Publishers and Associations

10 9 8 7 6

New York Institute of Finance
(NYIF Corp.)
2 Broadway
New York, NY 10004-2207

For the participants of my market,
Rosemary, John, Danielle and Steven

Contents

CHAPTER 1
The Stock Market:
What the Stock Market Has to Offer, 1

> Why stocks are offered ... The size of the stock market ...
> A word about bonds ... Why individuals and institutions
> buy stocks ... Dividends ... Capital gains ... Short selling ...
> Risks and rewards of investing ... Common stocks ...
> Preferred stocks ... Stock rights ... Stock warrants ...
> Summary

CHAPTER 2
Reading the Financial Press:
Determining Share Value—Determining Your Investment Return, 21

> Cash accounts ... Margin accounts ... Security positions:
> long, short, flat ... Pricing stocks: points and fractions ...
> The figuration of current yield ... Newspaper listings

CHAPTER 3
The Initial Public Offering:
Getting the Stocks to the Marketplace, 33

> The primary market—how businesses are capitalized ...
> Incorporating the business ... The initial public offering
> (IPO) ... After the offering is completed

CHAPTER 4
Inside the Brokerage Firm:
Who Does What? 61

> Full service versus discount ... Selecting a brokerage firm
> and an account executive ... The sales assistant

CHAPTER 5
The Secondary Market:
Executing Orders on the Exchange Floor, 75

> The New York Stock Exchange ... The auction system ...
> How orders are executed in the crowd ... Additional
> instructions on orders

CHAPTER 6
The Specialist:
Riding the Bulls and Bears, 97

> The specialist's role: as dealer, as broker ... How
> automation and telecommunication affect the role of the
> specialist ... Other duties of the specialist ... Odd-lot
> trading ... Assigning securities to the specialist

CHAPTER 7
The Secondary Market:
Over-the-Counter-Trading, 115

> Following an order being executed OTC ... Types of
> orders ... The National Association of Security (NASD) ...
> NASD rules of fair practice

CHAPTER 8
Investment Companies
Closed-End and Open-End Funds—the "Package-Plan"
Approach, 131

> Closed-end and open-end funds ... Pricing a closed-end
> fund ... Pricing an open-end fund

CHAPTER 9
Stock Options:
Multipurpose Instruments, 139

> Puts and calls ... Time value and intrinsic value ...
> Options as a hedging tool ... Call options ... Options to
> increase portfolio income

CHAPTER 10
The Back Offices:
Following the Long Paper Trail, 147

> The depository and clearing house ... The order
> department ... P&S department ... Margin department ...
> Stock record department ... Accounting department ...
> Dividend department ... Proxy department

CHAPTER 11
Stock Market Theories:
Can Prices Really Be Predicted? 175

> The first American analyst ... The analysts ... The
> technical approach

Introduction

Most people are involved with the stock market. It is not necessary to purchase stocks directly to be so involved—it is almost inescapable. The insurance companies that accept our premiums in exchange for protecting our lives and assets—the banks with which we are involved as borrower or saver—our pension funds and profit-sharing arrangements—are all intimately concerned with the stock market.

The"market" is an important part of all our lives. It is the principal means through which companies raise capital to expand their operations—and the medium used by millions of investors to protect their savings from the ravages of inflation. The stock market reflects a country's prosperity and prospects. Most developing nations give top priority to the development of a stock exchange and think of it as a symbol that they have truly entered the modern age. The world's stock exchanges, old and new, will ultimately be linked together, providing the means for both individuals and institutions to purchase and sell securities, at fair prices, almost instantaneously.

The mechanism for trading stocks is truly remarkable. Investments in any dollar amount can be made from a "menu" of over 30,000 different stocks. This text describes this mechanism and the products that are traded. Six new chapters have been added to this edition. The new material includes information on mutual funds, options, taxation, reading the financial press, and other topics of interest to those interested in an overview of the investment world.

Whether you are interested in "playing" the market, either as an investor, hedger, or speculator, or merely interested in the fascinating world of bulls, bears, and Dow Jones averages—this book will provide you with the basics.

How the Stock Market Works

CHAPTER 1

The Stock Market

What the Stock Market Has to Offer

"Businesses" usually evolve, over time, from one-man operations (sole proprietorships) to partnerships and ultimately to full-fledged corporations. Corporations traditionally meet their short-term cash requirements, for carrying inventory or for similar reasons, by borrowing from banks. When corporations need long-term financing, they may sell ownership interests in the company (common stocks and preferred stocks) to the public—or borrow from the public by selling bonds.

There are two major subdivisions to the stock market: the primary market and the secondary market. The *primary market* involves only new issues, while the *secondary market* handles "used" items. Chapter 3 explains the primary market; Chapters 5 and 7 describe the secondary market. In this text we refer to this entire market, both primary and secondary, as the well-functioning "stock market."

WHY STOCKS ARE OFFERED

Stocks exist to enable companies in need of long-term financing to "sell" pieces of the business—stocks (equity securities)—in exchange for cash. This is the principal method of raising business capital other than by issuing bonds. When the stocks of these corporations, which all corporations *must* issue, are owned by the public at large—including both private investors and institutions—they are said to be *publicly held.* These publicly held shares can be easily traded (sold) to other investors in the stock market, and are thus said to be *liquid,* or readily converted to cash.

The primary stock market, described in Chapter 3, is for newly issued shares, both common stock and preferred stock, which are sold by the issuer (the corporation in need of capital) to the investing public. Stock brokerage firms usually serve as intermediaries in these transactions, buying the new securities at wholesale prices from the issuer and then reselling them to the investing public at retail prices. This is, effectively, what happens when you buy a new car. General Motors produces the car, a "new issue," and then sells it to you through a dealer. You exchange cash for the car, General Motors gets the bulk of the cash, and the dealer earns a commission for his efforts in arranging the transaction.

THE SIZE OF THE STOCK MARKET

Approximately 4,000 different stock issues are currently traded on stock exchanges throughout the United States, (so-called *listed* securities) and about 25,000 other issues are traded over the counter. Generally speaking, the older, better established companies opt for listing on one or more exchanges, while the over-the-counter (OTC) market is where newer and smaller companies are traded. There are some notable exceptions to this, and quite a few companies that are able to meet the most exacting exchange listing requirements prefer to stay OTC.

The stock market also includes thousands of different mutual funds and thousands of different options to purchase stocks. All mutual funds and some stock options trade OTC. The New York Stock Exchange—this nation's largest exchange— handles an average daily trading volume of over 200 million shares. It is an extremely efficient marketplace where accurate quotations are instantly available, and buy and sell orders can be effected in a matter of moments.

A WORD ABOUT BONDS

This text covers the stock market. There are several other securities markets including the money market (debt instruments with less than one year to maturity) and the bond market. The bond market, where debt instruments of longer maturities are traded, is even bigger than the stock market. Unlike stocks, which represent ownership— a piece of the action—bonds represent a loan by the bondholder of the issuing company. The bondholder usually receives interest payments rather than dividends, does not have the right to vote, and is promised that, at maturity, the loan value will be repaid. A bond is a fixed-income security, a "senior" security, and its interest payments must be in full before shareholders in that same company can receive any dividends.

Investors generally purchase bonds for the stream of relatively safe, stable income. Bonds are priced differently from stocks, and the vast majority are traded OTC. Stocks are equity (ownership) securities; bonds are debt securities. Most investment portfolios contain both stocks and bonds. Determining the proper "mix" of these investment instruments, for various investment purposes and degrees of risk, is known as *asset allocation*. (For further information on debt securities refer to the *How the Bond Market Works* in this same series.)

WHY INDIVIDUALS AND INSTITUTIONS BUY STOCKS

Stocks are purchased as investments, to make additional money on the money invested. There are many other investment vehicles including real estate, precious metals, and rare paintings, but investing in stocks offers a great number of advantages. Among these advantages are the relatively low commission costs, the ease with which purchased securities can be safeguarded (brokerage firms will hold them for clients upon request), the speed at which they can be bought and sold, the ability to determine your investments' exact market value in a matter of minutes, and, most importantly, their "track record." Over the long term, investments in stocks have proven to be an excellent way to more than keep pace with the erosive effects of inflation.

DIVIDENDS

Many common stocks and all preferred stocks pay dividends. Most dividend-paying stocks make their distributions on a quarterly basis (four times a year). That schedule is not a legal requirement, but most companies stick to it. The amount and timing of dividend payments are at the discretion of the corporation's board of directors. Most profitable corporations share their profits with their investors by paying them a cash dividend. A very general rule is that one-half the profit gets paid to the shareholders, and the remaining half gets reinvested in the company. Companies in an aggressive growth period might elect to reinvest most, or even all, of their profits to fuel expansion, paying only token cash dividends or even none at all.

There is no law that states that a company *must* pay a dividend on its common shares, even if the company is profitable. The board of directors can raise, reduce, or eliminate a company's dividend rate. Dividends on common stock are flexible, therefore, but companies try to maintain a fairly even flow of dividends, increasing the dividend when the company enjoys a growth in net earnings. A company with an annual dividend rate of $1.20 would most probably be paying out $0.30 per quarter. In this instance the annual rate would be $1.20; the quarterly rate would be $0.30. (Dividends may also be paid in additional shares of stock *(stock dividends)* in lieu of, or in addition to, cash.)

The expected receipt of dividend income is sometimes justification enough for investing in a given stock, particularly if the yield on the investment exceeds the return afforded by savings accounts or CDs. Stocks that pay out a fairly generous dividend are known as *income stocks.* These are generally popular with individuals or institutions that are satisfied with the rate of return in and of itself. Such dependable income producers are usually in stable industries such as utilities and food stocks. While the receipt of income is important to many investors and, as stated previously, sometimes the *only* reason for purchasing a stock, most investors hope to gain an additional return in the form of *capital gains.*

CAPITAL GAINS

When a stock is purchased at a given price, then subsequently sold at a higher price, the resultant profit is known as a *capital gain.* Trying for such "buy-low, sell-high" profits over a short time span is a speculative activity known as *short-term trading.* Often the securities are held only for a single day, sometimes for as little as several hours! Most individual and institutional investors, however, have a much longer time horizon and will hold stocks for many years.

Companies that are expected to grow over time are known as *growth stocks.* Investors buy such stocks in anticipation that their per-share value will increase over time as the company prospers, and as its per-share earnings and dividends increase. When stocks that have been held for more than a year are sold at a profit, the profit is *long-term. Short-term* profits are the result of profitable trades on securities that have been held for one year or less. Chapter 13 deals with this subject in greater detail. A capital gain will also result from a *short sale* that is subsequently purchased (covered) at a lower price.

Investors sometimes purchase securities only for their capital gains potential. Many growth stocks pay out very little in dividends, sometimes not at all. It is probably fair to say that relatively conservative investors are attracted to income stocks, while those who are more adventurous, and more willing to take risks, gravitate toward growth stocks. While certain stocks are dividend payers with little chance for speculator growth in price (cash cows), and others offer small dividend potential but a chance for capital gains *(venture capital, special situations)*, many stocks—probably *most* stocks—offer possible rewards both through dividends *and* capital gains.

Ultimately, that is why stocks are purchased: for dividends and/or capital gains—for *investment.* Most well-rounded portfolios have a balance between income situations and stocks with capital gains potential. Some investors achieve this aim by buying a package of securities with such a mix, typically exemplified by growth-income mutual funds. (Investments such as these are described at length in Chapter 8.)

SHORT SELLING

Most of us think of making a "killing" by buying something at a low price and subsequently selling it at a much higher price. With most investment vehicles (undeveloped real estate, rare paintings and coins, art treasures), this is the only way to profit. Such investments rarely produce income while they are held, unlike stocks, and one's only hope for gain is to be astute enough to buy at the right time—at a low price—and to sell later at a higher price. The "buy-low, sell-high" principle is, after all, the essence of making capital gains. The stock market affords another method for striving for capital gains, and that is through the medium of the *short sale.*

Investors (and speculators) who believe a stock is selling at a bargain price will purchase it in anticipation of later selling the security at a higher price. They are *bullish* on the stock and expect it to increase in price. But what about investors who believe a security is *overpriced?* Such situations also offer the opportunity for capital gains through the medium of the short sale. Someone who thinks that a stock is selling at too high a price, and that it will decline, is said to be *bearish* on the stock. As unlikely as it sounds, it is possible (at least in the stock market) to sell this supposedly overpriced item first, and to buy it later! That's right; first sell at the high price and then buy at the low price. The difference between the sale price and the purchase price represents the investor's profit or loss. Naturally she wishes the stock to *decline* in value after she sells it, so that the purchase (the *covering* transaction) will be at a lower price.

Let's look at an example. John Bear believes that XYZ stock overpriced at $89 per share and that it is due for a fall. He *shorts* (sells short) 100 shares at $89 and then keeps his fingers crossed. XYZ does decline in price, and Mr. Bear covers the short position by buying 100 shares of XYZ at $76 per share. He first *sold* for $8,900 and then *purchased* for $7,600, making a profit of $1,300. Instead of buying at a low price and then selling at a high price, Mr. Bear first sold at a high price and then bought at a low price. It's backwards, but it works!

The mechanics of selling something you don't own are quite interesting. When you sell the stock short, where does the stock come from? Since you don't own the stock being sold, it must come from someone who owns it. This borrowed stock is then used to complete the sale transaction. Since you have sold borrowed stock, you are obligated to return that borrowed stock eventually. "He who sells what isn't his'n, must buy it back or go to prison."

Short selling is very different from "investing." Individual and institutional investors purchase stocks for their investment potential. They hope to make money on their invested capital through the receipt of dividends and/or capital gains. But capital gains profits may result from both long sales and short sales. As will be demonstrated, short selling is a very risky undertaking and is normally not practiced by the average individual investor. Short selling is usually best left to the institutional traders and arbitragers.

RISKS AND REWARDS OF INVESTING

When we buy a lottery ticket, we know that our maximum loss will be the price of the ticket. The same thing is true when we buy a stock; the most we can lose is what we paid for the stock. While the lottery offers a grand prize, there is no definitive "prize" when you purchase a stock for investment. But how high can a stock price go? Some have been going up for years—and are still going up! Stocks therefore (at least in theory) have unlimited profit potential. Investing in the stock market has proven to be extremely rewarding over time. Although stocks go up and down, sometimes rather dramatically, they generally have been in an uptrend for more than 60 years. Historically stocks have "returned" (dividends and capital gains) more than 10 percent annually, more than keeping pace with inflation. That's probably their greatest attraction; they are a proven investment medium that outpaces inflation.

There is no magic formula for making money in the stock market, but *patience* probably comes closest. Five years generally "bridges" most market declines, and, for those prepared to wait out a bear market, the market is *comparatively* safe. There have been only six losing five-year periods in the last 60 such periods. Patient investors who hold a well diversified portfolio of stocks have been rewarded handsomely. Most financial advisors consider stocks a *must* investment for virtually all investors.

Brokerage accounts are insured, by SIPC, for $500,000. This is *not* insurance against bad judgment in the selection and/or timing of stock purchases, but purely protection against the failure (bankruptcy) of brokerage firms. It is always a possibility that you will lose everything you have invested in an individual stock. Even if you don't lose everything, substantial losses can—and too often do—occur. The market does *fluctuate,* and that is both the good news and the bad news. One can profit from an upward move (selling long) and from a downward move (selling short). Guess incorrectly and you can certainly lose with either approach.

For investors who own securities, their potential loss is their entire investment, while there is no limit (theoretically) to the amount they can make. Short sellers have very different risks and rewards. Since the short seller makes his maximum profit from a downward movement in a stock's price, he is hoping that the stock falls in price as far as possible. In effect, he is hoping that the stock goes bankrupt so that he can "cover" for zero and thus make a profit equal to the proceeds of the original short sale. That's as far down as a stock can go—to zero—so that's the short seller's maximum profit potential.

The short seller is a bear who wants the stock's price to decline. What the short seller *doesn't* want is for the stock to go up! Remember, he has sold the stock at what he believes is too high a price and hopes to buy it back more cheaply. He doesn't want to have to buy it back at a higher price since this will result in a loss. There is no limit to the amount the short seller can lose. That's the inherent danger in short selling—the specter of unlimited losses.

While the short seller's profit is limited, the buyer has an unlimited profit potential—but can lose his entire investment. A further consideration for the short seller is that the stock he sold was borrowed from someone else and that it must ultimately be returned. If he shorts a dividend-paying stock, he will not receive the dividends but will have to pay them out! Since he has borrowed the stock, he must make good the dividends to the one he borrowed the stock from. This results in a negative cash flow for the short seller.

In a broad sense, bonds and money market funds are safest, while preferred stocks have slightly more risk and common stocks are the riskiest of all. The offset is that the high-risk situations offer the most potential reward. In general, the higher the potential risk is, the higher the potential reward. While stocks are generally risky, they have outperformed all other financial instruments over the long term. For all but the most ultraconservative investors, one of the greatest risks might be to *not* invest in stocks!

COMMON STOCKS

All corporations *must* issue common stock. These shares of common stock represent ownership in the corporation. The total number of shares that investors (both individuals and institutions) own at any one time is known as the *outstanding shares.*

An owner of common stock has, in effect, a "piece of the action." Common stocks are a type of *equity* (ownership) security. If a company has 1,000 shares of common stock outstanding, and you own 100 of those shares, then you are a 10 percent *owner* of the corporation (100 ÷ 1,000 = 10 percent).

The rights of the common stockholder vary from company to company, but normally they include the following:

1. The right to vote.
2. The right to dividends.
3. Residual rights.

The Right to Vote

Almost all common stocks carry the right to vote. Occasionally a company will issue several different classes of common stock, only some of which may be voting stock. This is comparatively rare. Shareholders vote for, among other things, the selection of directors who are elected to see that the company is operated in accordance with the terms of the corporate charter. The directors attend to day-to-day operations, sometimes directly and sometimes with or through a slate of officers. Shareholders are also asked to vote on extraordinary events such as mergers and acquisitions, changes in the company's capitalization, stock splits, and other unusual actions.

Voting is usually conducted either on a statutory basis or a cumulative basis. Under *statutory voting* (the most common method), if four different directorships are up for election and you own 100 voting common shares, then you can cast up to 100 votes for your favorite for each of the four seats. If you favor Mary, John, Lucy, and Pete, then you may give each of those candidates a maximum of 100 votes. Under this method, holders of more than half the voting shares have absolute control over the directorships since they will always outvote everyone else. Fifty-one-percent ownership thus assures 100 percent control. Under *cumulative voting,* you may "save" your votes and split them up any way you wish. Given the same four directorships, you might opt to vote none of your 100 shares for Mary, John, or Lucy, but instead vote 400 shares for Pete. Cumulative voting thus gives minority shareholders their best chance at gaining representation on the board of directors.

The Right to Receive Dividends

Common stockholders have the right to receive dividends *when, as, and if* declared by the board of directors. The dividend is under their absolute control and is not vested in the corporation's officers. Generally, while bonds pay a fixed amount of interest and preferred stocks pay a fixed amount of dividend, the dividend on common stock varies, usually in direct proportion to the company's earnings. Growth stocks usually exhibit a long-term pattern of increasing dividends through the years.

Residual Rights

When a company is dissolved, either voluntarily or involuntarily, many claims must be satisfied before the common stockholders can claim any "salvage" rights. Even though they are the owners of the company, their claims come dead last. All salaries and taxes must first be satisfied, then general creditors and bondholders are paid, then preferred shareholders. And *then* common shareholders get to share whatever may be left. Usually there is nothing left for the common stockholder since even the bondholders and holders of the preferred issues rarely get paid in full. Some rare exceptions to this occur when a company is overly rich in assets. In such cases the company may be "worth more dead than alive," and the common shareholders benefit when the company is dissolved.

The *par value* of a common stock is *not* an important consideration. Par value bears no direct relationship to a common stock's initial price, its dividend rate, or what it is worth in the current marketplace or in dissolution (book value). A company's par value is of use only to accountants. For most U.S. corporations, a par value of between $0.01 and $1.00 is usually assigned, and sometimes a common stock is listed as having *no* par value!

PREFERRED STOCKS

Many corporations issue preferred stock, although they are under no legal obligation to do so. Preferred shares generally pay a fixed dividend which is announced when the shares are first offered in the marketplace. Most corporations have only one class of common stock outstanding, but, for corporations that do elect to issue preferred stock, they usually issue several different such issues over time. When we say that someone owns "XYZ," it is understood that we are referring to common stock. Just "XYZ" is description enough; we don't have to say "XYZ common stock." When referring to preferred stocks, however, we must add something to the description of the preferred stock to distinguish it from the *other* issues of preferred stock that that same company probably issued. To avoid confusion, companies elect to name their different preferred issues in several ways. Here are some:

Method 1	Method 2	Method 3
ABC $8.00 preferred	CYA 7 percent preferred	RFQ A preferred
ABC $10.00 preferred	CYA 11 percent preferred	RFQ B preferred
ABC $12.60 preferred	CYA 13.2 percent preferred	RFQ C preferred

Method 1. ABC company preferred issues are distinguished, one from the other, by the dollar amount of the *annual* dividend. Note that preferred stocks, like most dividend-paying common stocks, pay their dividends every three months (quarterly), or four times each year. ABC $8.00 preferred has a fixed dividend rate of $8.00 per year ($2.00 per quarter). The ABC $10.00 preferred pays an annual dividend of $10.00 ($2.50 per quarter). The $12.60 preferred pays that amount annually ($3.15 quarterly).

Method 2. The different CYA company preferred issues show a percent (%) rather than a dollar amount. This is the percent of each preferred stock's par value that the company has agreed to pay annually as the dividend on that particular issue. While many preferred stocks have a $100 par value, some do not.

Preferred issue par values, unlike common stock par values, are important to know. Most preferred issues are originally offered at their par values. If the company is dissolved, the preferred shareholders are entitled to their issue's par value. When a preferred issue is callable (more on this later), the shareowner is entitled to par, and sometimes a small premium over par.

In this method, then, when the preferred dividend is expressed as a percent, the par value must be known so that you can figure out exactly how much of a dividend will be paid. If the issuer is saying that you will receive a certain percent, you must ask, "Percent of what?" The *what* is the preferred stock's par value. Presuming that all the CYA issues had a $100 par value, you would calculate 7 percent of $100 ($7.00), 11 percent of $100 ($11.00), and 13.2 percent of $100 ($13.20). These issues' annual dividend rates would be, in order, $7.00, $11.00, $13.20. Their quarterly rates would be, respectively, $1.75, $2.75, $3.30. If the 7 percent preferred had a par value of $50, its annual dividend would be $3.50 (7 percent of $50). If the 11 percent preferred had a par value of $38, its annual dividend would be $4.18 (11 percent of $38).

Method 3. RFG company uses only letters of the alphabet rather than dollar values or percentages. Now there is no way you can figure the amount of the dividend just from the security's name. You will have to look it up in one of the security industry's information service manuals such as Moody's, Value Line, or Standard and Poor's.

The Senior Aspects of Preferred Stock

This type of equity security is called "preferred" for several reasons. For one, a company must pay dividends on all its preferred stock issues, in full, before it can pay anything to the common shareholders. The preferred stockholder also comes before the common stockholder with respect to salvage rights. When the company is dissolved, either voluntarily or involuntarily, the preferred stockholders must receive their issue's par value and accrued cash dividends before anything may be distributed to the common stockholders. Within a given company, its preferred issues are certainly "safer" than the company's common stock, with respect to both dividends and salvage value. In a broad sense, preferred issues are purchased for fairly safe income and not for capital gain possibilities. They are "preferred" by the more conservative investor over common stocks.

Types of Preferred Stock

Cumulative Preferred. Virtually all preferred issues are *cumulative.* This means that, if the company skips a quarterly dividend, it is still owed to the preferred shareholder. If the company is struggling through bad times, they will almost certainly reduce or even eliminate the dividend on the common stock. If they get in a real cash bind, they will also skip the preferred stock dividend. While the "skipped" common stock dividend is gone forever, the preferred dividend becomes an arrearage and is still owed to the preferred shareholders. When the company ultimately recovers, all such passed-over preferred dividends must be paid before dividend payments to the common shareholders may resume. This is another example of the preferred stock's relative safety.

Callable Preferred. Some preferred issues are *callable.* This means that the issuing corporation reserves the right to retire the preferred issue by paying the stockholders a certain amount of cash. When a preferred issue is called, the shareholder has no other option than to surrender the stock. The minimum call price is par, which is the amount for which the issue was originally sold to the investing public. Callability is an undesirable trait for a preferred stock, at least insofar as the *shareholder is concerned.*

New preferred stocks are issued at the then-prevailing rates of return. If interest rates are high, then new preferred issues will also have a high return. If, sometime after a callable preferred issue is sold to the public, interest rates fall dramatically, then the company will refinance the existing issue by "calling" it and issuing other securities at a cheaper rate of interest. This saves the company money since they are replacing a high dividend rate with a lower rate, just as a homeowner refinances a mortgage when rates decline below the original mortgage rate. A shareholder who purchased a callable preferred when interest rates were high will have it called away from her just when things are getting good—when her return on the preferred she purchased is higher than newly issued preferreds. Thus, with a callable preferred, an investor cannot "lock up" a high rate of return.

Callable preferreds are usually not callable immediately after issuance. There is traditionally a grace period during which the issue is not callable, the first five years after issuance being fairly standard. When the issue ultimately becomes subject to call, the company usually offers a few "extra" dollars over par as compensation.

Let's look at how a typical situation for a $100 par callable preferred might be. NFW 14 percent preferred ($100 par) is offered at $100 per share in August of 1993. It is not callable until August of 1998, at which time the call price will be $106 per share. Beginning in 2000 the call price will be $104, reducing to $102 in 2002, and $100 beginning in 2004. The callable feature of this preferred stock might then be described as "noncallable for first five years, initially callable at a 6-point premium, scaled down to par in 2004." The issue may then be called, at the company's discretion, anytime after August of 1998. If interest rates remain at the same level as they were when the preferred was issued, or go even higher, than the company will probably not elect to call the issue.

Convertible Preferred. Some preferred issues are *convertible.* This option permits the shareholder to exchange preferred shares for other securities, usually common stock of the same corporation. The preferred shareowner has complete control over when, or if, he converts. You cannot convert back into preferred once you have exchanged your shares for common stock. It's a one-time deal.

The number of shares of common stock that you will receive for each exchanged share of preferred is known as the *conversion ratio*. Financial publications usually express the exchange feature as a *conversion price*. A conversion price can be changed to a conversion ratio simply by dividing the issue's par value by the conversion price. Thus a convertible preferred ($50 par) with a conversion price of $25 has a conversion ratio of 2. In other words, each preferred share can be exchanged for two shares of common stock ($50 ÷ $25). Most investors find it easier to work with the conversion ratio.

Nonconvertible preferred stocks (known as *straight* preferreds) move up and down with changes in interest rates. They go up in price when interest rates fall, and down in price when interest rates rise. Bonds exhibit the same trait; it's a feature of all fixed income securities. These straight preferreds, while sensitive to interest rate changes, are relatively impervious to other market forces such as reported earnings and the general business outlook.

That's both the good news and the bad news! Straight preferreds go their merry way, pricewise, even though the company's business falls off. They are "safe" in this respect. But what if the company does fabulously well? The common stock's dividend, which is unfixed, may be raised dramatically and the market price of the common stock may skyrocket. The straight preferred stockholder is normally denied the opportunity for large capital gain profits (other than by buying noncallable preferreds just before interest rates fall sharply). The capital gains game is the province of the common stockholder, while the preferred stockholder is normally only interested in yield.

Don't *convertible* preferreds thus permit you to play both games? If the common stock doesn't rise greatly in price, you simply hold the preferred and enjoy its relatively safe yield and price stability. If the common stock does rise dramatically in price, the convertible preferred will keep pace with this rise. If, for example, a preferred stock has a conversion ratio of 4, then it will always sell for at least four times the value of the underlying common shares. Therefore a convertible preferred stock offers capital gain possibilities as well as being a fairly sure income producer.

Isn't this the best of all possible worlds? A corporation issues convertible rather than straight preferred shares for a good reason: to save money! When issued, convertibles pay less of a dividend than do straight preferreds. That's the "price" you pay for the convertibility feature—the lower return you must accept.

STOCK RIGHTS

Some common stocks have a *preemptive rights* feature. This means that existing shareholders will be given the first opportunity to buy any new common shares that are sold to the public. The general rule is that "old" shareholders are issued one right for each share they own. These rights may be surrendered, with a cash payment known as the *subscription price,* for the new shares. Shareholders not wishing to subscribe for the new shares may sell their rights in the open market. This feature permits shareholders to maintain their same proportion of ownership in the company, should they choose to do so. For example, Ms. Claudette Morgan owns 100 shares of XYZ. Since a total of 10,000 shares of XYZ are outstanding, she owns 1 percent of the company (100 ÷ 10,000). If another 10,000 shares were issued, and Claudette did *not* purchase any of these new shares, her ownership would be reduced to only 0.5 percent (100 ÷ 20,000). If the company had a preemptive rights feature, and Ms. Morgan chose to use her rights and subscribe to 1 percent of the new shares, she would then own 200 shares and would remain a 1 percent owner (200 ÷ 20,000). A rights offering lasts about one month. During this time the rights are traded on the same exchange or marketplace as are the old shares of stock.

Since the subscription price is set somewhat under the current market price for the old shares, the rights have value. After all, using them gives you the ability to buy stock at a discount, and so save some money. It's similar to the value of a discount coupon. When a shareholder receives rights, she must determine whether to subscribe to the new shares. If the rights are *not* used, they should definitely be sold for their intrinsic value. It would be foolish neither to use nor to sell rights.

STOCK WARRANTS

While rights are usually issued on old shares, warrants are normally issued as a feature of new offerings. Warrants are, essentially, long-term rights. Typically, they offer holders the right to purchase common shares at a fixed price (the subscription price) for periods of up to ten years, sometimes even longer. They are often issued as a "sweetener" on a new issue of bonds to make the new offering more attractive to the investing public. While rights are issued with a positive value (they allow the purchase of stock at a price *less* than the stock's current market price), warrants are "out of the money" at the time they are issued. They permit the purchase of the company's stock at a *higher*-than-current price so that, at least at the time of the issuance, they have no value. What's their attraction? Since they have so long to run (up to 10 years or more), investors believe that *sometime* during their long life the underlying common stock's market price might rise to well above the subscription price, and thus the warrants would then have real value. Warrants are generally considered to be speculative. As we shall see in Chapter 9, they are very similar to a "deep out-of-the-money call." Warrants do not necessarily trade on the same exchange or marketplace as does their underlying common stock.

SUMMARY

In this chapter we have examined several of the investment products available in the stock market. Common and preferred shares are both equity securities. Common and preferred shareholders are considered owners of the corporation, even though only common shareholders ordinarily have the right to vote. The preferred share has many of the features of a bond: a fixed annual payment, a superior position over the common stock with respect to dividend payments, and possibly a call feature and/or a convertibility feature.

Most people think of common stocks when they speak about the "stock" market. Preferred issues are also stocks, although they don't enjoy the same press coverage. There are many more common stock issues outstanding than there are preferred issues. Common stocks are not callable and not convertible. Also mentioned were two financial instruments that are not *quite* stocks, at least not when they are purchased. Rather, they represent the right to *buy stocks. These are short-term (rights) or long-term (warrants). They don't vote, nor do they receive dividends, but rights and warrants are also part of the "stock" market.*

Several later chapters will be devoted to other instruments of the stock market: closed-end and open-end funds in Chapter 8, and stock options in Chapter 9. The former represent a "package-plan" approach to investing, the latter a sophisticated way of investing in, speculating with, and hedging common stocks.

CHAPTER 2

Reading the Financial Press

Determining Share Value—
Determining Your Investment Return

CASH ACCOUNTS

Individuals who purchase securities through a brokerage firm normally do so either in a cash account or in a margin account. Some customers utilize only one of these types of accounts; other clients have both.

Settlement Date—Regular Way

The *cash* account, by far the most common, calls for the customer to pay for any purchases, in full, on or before the transaction's *settlement date.* The settlement date (also known as the *due date*) for most transactions falls five business days after the trade date (T+5). This is known as *regular way settlement,* used for the majority of all trades. Trades done on a Monday, for example, settle on the Monday following, Tuesday's trades settle the following Tuesday, and so on. If any of the five business days after the trade date is a holiday, delivery is extended one day because five *business* days must be counted to establish the settlement date. This five-day settlement is used for almost all transactions except those in options and government securities. Trades in these investment products normally settle on the *next* business day after the trade (T+1). This is regular way settlement for trades in options and governments.

When clients sell securities in a cash account, they are entitled to be *paid* by the brokerage firm on the settlement date, provided they have made *good delivery* of the securities sold. If the security that was sold is long in the customer's account (almost certainly in *street name)* at the time of the sale, there will be no problem with the delivery since the security is already in the firm's possession. If the security is not long in the customer's account, it must be delivered to the selling firm, in good form, on or before the settlement date.

The brokerage firm cannot pay out the proceeds of the sale before they have possession of the securities sold. A customer cannot demand payment unless the securities sold have been received into the account, in negotiable form (good delivery). Under unusual circumstances the customer may be unable to deliver on or before the settlement date. If the security hasn't been received by the tenth day after settlement (T+15), then the brokerage firm may have to *buy in* the security, thus flattening the account, and charge the customer for any resultant debit. This doesn't happen very often.

Many cash account clients leave their securities with their brokerage firm to avoid having to safeguard them in a safety deposit box. They are also saved the bother of sending their securities to their broker when they are selling, and thus they can always be paid on the settlement date. Since SIPC insures accounts for $500,000, there is very little reason for clients to be concerned about the safekeeping of their securities.

MARGIN ACCOUNTS

Just as you can purchase a home or an automobile by putting up only a portion of the purchase price and borrowing the remainder from a bank or other financial institution, you can also purchase most securities in the same manner. When investors make a down payment on securities and borrow the balance of the purchase price from the stock brokerage firm buying the securities for them, they are said to be buying *on margin* (in a margin account). You can therefore purchase twice as much market value of stock on margin as you can for cash.

However, even though this affords the opportunity to make more money for a given amount of invested dollars, it also means that you will *lose* twice as much if a margin investment goes sour. Another consideration is that you must pay interest on the amount owed to the broker (the *debit balance*). This interest, charged monthly, is usually more than the amount of dividends and interest coming into the account from the securities purchased.

Although trading on margin provides *leverage*, it is considered a relatively sophisticated technique and is definitely not for the faint of heart. If the market value of your margined securities drops dramatically, the brokerage firm will demand that you deposit more money (a *maintenance call*). If you cannot (or choose not to) meet the call, then some or all of your securities will be sold to bring the account to a properly margined status. Unfortunately, such forced sales are normally executed in rapidly falling markets that are near their low point.

Stocks purchased on margin cannot be sent to you. They must remain with the brokerage firm as collateral for your debit balance. Such securities will be in the broker's name, even though you are the true owner. You are the *beneficial owner,* but the brokerage firm is the *owner of record* (registered owner). Such securities, owned by you but held by the brokerage firm, are said to be in *street name.* When you own stocks held for you by a brokerage firm, in cash and/or margin accounts, that firm will send to you, monthly, a statement of your account showing the securities and cash that they are holding for you. They will refer to your "positions" as either *long* or *short.* Interestingly, trades will be posted to your account on their *settlement* date rather than their trade date. You are considered the owner of the securities on the trade date, but the trades aren't posted to your account until settlement date. Some brokerage firms will show "pending" trades for securities with a trade date in a given month that do not settle until the following month. This avoids the anxiety of those customers who, for instance, buy or sell in late April but don't see the trades appear on their April monthly statement. Those late April trades won't be posted until early May.

SECURITY POSITIONS: LONG, SHORT, FLAT

A customer's security positions at the brokerage firm are said to be "long" in his account. To be *long* means to *own,* to have a positive (+) position. You are thus long any securities that your broker is holding for you. Should you order your broker to buy 100 shares of IBM for you, you "go long" immediately after the trade is executed for you. Your account will remain "long 100 IBM" until such time as you ask the broker to send you the stock certificate, or until you ask him to sell the shares.

If you sell the shares while they are with the broker, your account will then be *flat* (a zero position). The sell trade "flattens" the position. The position will also become flat if you, the customer, ask for physical delivery of the shares. The shares will be transferred to your name and shipped to you. Your account will say "delivered 100 IBM" (or simply "100 IBM del"), and this will also flatten the position. The word *flat* will not appear on your statement; it is simply the brokers' way of designating that they don't "owe" you any shares.

A partial reduction of the shares held by the brokerage house does not flatten the account. If you are long 250 XYZ and you sell only 100 XYZ, your long position will be reduced to 150 shares. If you are long 1,000 NFW and your broker delivers 300 shares to you, then your long position is reduced to 700 shares. Your long position reflects only your standing with the brokerage firm, since, they have no way of knowing what shares you might have at home, with other brokerages, or with banks. Only if you sell all your shares does your account go flat.

Should you send stock to your broker to be held in your account, the transaction will be posted as a *receive.* Purchases and receives will create or increase long positions; sales and delivers will reduce or eliminate long positions.

Your broker keeps all your positions separate. Should you own 300 shares of ABC, 400 shares of DEF, and 500 shares of GHI (a total of 1,200 shares of the three different stocks), your broker will show you not "long 1,200," but rather "long 300 ABC, long 400 DEF, long 500 GHI." When, as a customer, you wish to know which securities the broker is holding for you, you are most likely to ask, "What's my long position?"

After a short sale the customer's account will be *short* the stock borrowed to complete the sale. Since a short sale is the sale of something that you *don't* own, after the sale you *owe* (not *own)* the stock to the person it was borrowed from. This is a negative (–) position. The stock was borrowed and, until you return it (by a covering buy transaction), you will remain short. Some active trading accounts have both long positions (the customer is bullish and expects the long stocks to go up in price) and short positions (the customer is bearish on the short stocks and expects them to go down in price). Short sales may be executed only in a margin account!

Sometimes a short position is the result of an error. If you own 300 shares of XYZ that are long in your account, and you ask your broker to sell them, he should enter an order to sell 300 shares. But suppose he makes an error and instead sells 3,000 shares! After the incorrect trade is posted, the account will show a short position of 2,700 shares of XYZ. (You were long only 300 shares but 3,000 shares were sold, resulting in a short position of 2,700 shares.) The error will, of course, be corrected by the removal of the oversale of 2,700 XYZ and your account will then be, correctly, flat with respect to XYZ. Short positions may also result from the sale of the wrong security (ABC instead of ACB), an incorrect delivery (CAY instead of CYA), or other errors on the part of the brokerage firm's staff or the client herself. A short position that is not the result of a deliberate short sale is an indication of trouble in an account. The account should be researched immediately to find the source of the error so that it can be fixed as soon as possible.

To be *long* means to *own* (+), to be *short* means to owe (–), to be *flat* means to neither own nor owe (0). We have all heard such expressions as, "Don't sell him short!" or "That's the long and short of it." Now you know how such expressions came into use.

PRICING STOCKS: POINTS AND FRACTIONS

Stocks, both common and preferred, are priced in dollars and in eighths of dollars. A stock trading at "26" is selling for $26.00 per share. The next higher price is 26⅛ ($26.125 per share), the next lower price is 25⅞ ($25.875 per share). The full range of prices for a stock trading between 17 and 18 would be: 17, 17⅛, 17¼, 17⅜, 17½, 17⅝, 17¾, 17⅞, 18. It is comparatively simple to memorize these fractional values;

Stock Fraction		Per-Share Value
⅛	=	$0.125
¼	=	$0.25
⅜	=	$0.375
½	=	$0.50
⅝	=	$0.625
¾	=	$0.75
⅞	=	$0.875

A *point* on a stock means one dollar per share. If a stock is trading at 94 ($94 per share) and it goes up 2 "points," the price will then be 96 ($96 per share). A stock at 46½ ($46.50 per share) that goes down 3 "points" will decline to 43½ ($43.50 per share). A price change of "one and one-half points" translates to a difference of $1.50 in the per-share price of the stock.

Most investors buy stocks in 100-share lots (*round lots*). Amounts of shares between 1 and 99 are referred to as *odd lots.* Here are some examples of the dollar values of various stock prices, both on a per-share basis (1 share) and on a 100-share basis:

Share Price	Dollar Value of 1 Share	Dollar Value of 100 Shares
13¾	$13.75	$1,375.00
5⅛	$5.125	$512.50
88	$88.00	$8,800.00
46½	$46.50	$4,650.00
128⅝	$128.625	$12,862.50
1¼	$1.25	$125.00
22⅜	$22.375	$2,237.50
39⅞	$39.875	$3,987.50
7	$7.00	$700.00

Many lower-priced stocks (and stock options) trade in sixteenths (¹⁄₁₆) or thirty-seconds (¹⁄₃₂) rather than eighths. Rights, warrants, and closed-end funds also trade in eighths. Mutual funds (discussed in Chapter 8) trade in dollars and cents!

THE FIGURATION OF CURRENT YIELD

A stock's *current yield* is calculated by dividing its annual dividend per share by its current market price per share. It shows the percent of the current market price that is expected to be returned to a shareholder, as cash dividends, during the coming year. This is known as the investor's return. It takes into account only the anticipated dividend and does not reflect any possible changes in the per-share price during the year. (A security's *total return* would reflect both dividend income and per-share price changes.)

For example, ABC common stock is currently trading at 46⅜ and has an annual dividend rate of $2.60 (a *quarterly* rate of $0.65 per share). ABC's current yield would be 5.6 percent. The annual dividend is divided by the current price: 2.60 ÷ 46.375 = 0.056 or 5.6 percent.

Current yields on preferred stocks are figured in the same manner. Rights, warrants, and stock options do not pay dividends and so do not have a current yield. *The Wall Street Journal,* among other newspapers, shows each stock's current yield on a daily basis, figured on the "closing" price each trading day, adjusted for changing dividend rates on an ongoing basis.

NEWSPAPER LISTINGS

Investors can track the value of their stockholdings through the financial press, of which *The Wall Street Journal* is the most widely known and most widely utilized. Figure 2–1 shows a portion of the New York Stock Exchange stock

Figure 2–1.

Quotations as of 5 p.m. Eastern Time
Friday, June 4, 1993

	52 Weeks Hi	Lo	Stock	Sym	Div	Yld %	PE	Vol 100s	Hi	Lo	Close	Net Chg
			-A-A-A-									
	14⅝	10¾	AAR	AIR	.48	3.5	...	515	14	13¾	13⅞	– ⅛
	11¾	10¾	ACM Gvt Fd	ACG	.96e	8.2	...	371	11¾	11⅝	11¾	...
	10	9	ACM OppFd	AOF	.80	8.2	...	300	10	9¾	9¾	– ⅛
	11⅞	9⅞	ACM SecFd	GSF	.96	8.7	...	410	11⅛	11	11	...
	9¾	8⅝	ACM SpctmFd	SI	.80	8.4	...	377	9⅝	9⅜	9½	+ ⅛
	11	9¼	ACM MgdIncFd	AMF	1.08	9.9	...	234	10⅞	10¾	10⅞	+ ⅛
	11¾	8⅝	ACM MgdMultFd	MMF	.85e	9.4	...	240	9⅛	9	9	...
n	15⅛	14⅝	ACM MuniSec	AMU		...	...	423	14¾	14⅝	14⅝	...
	9⅞	6⅜	ADT	ADT		...	...	1965	9¾	9⅜	9⅝	+ ⅛
	2½	⅞	ADT wt			...	...	155	1¾	1⅝	1⅝	...
	40¼	27⅛	AFLAC	AFL	.50f	1.3	16	960	38⅞	38½	38⅝	– ⅛
	29⅜	18	AL Labs A	BMD	.18	.7	34	397	28¼	27½	27½	– ½
	65⅞	52⅝	AMP	AMP	1.60	2.6	22	978	61⅜	60¾	61¼	+ ¼
	72⅞	54⅜	AMR	AMR		...	dd	2732	71⅞	70⅝	70¾	– ⅝
	47¼	39¼	ARCO Chm	RCM	2.50	5.5	23	162	45⅝	45	45⅜	– ½
	2¼	**1⅜**	**ARX**	**ARX**	·	**...**	**13**	**42**	**2⅛**	**2**	**2**	**– ⅛**
	51½	29¾	ASA	ASA	2.00	4.1	...	476	49⅝	49	49¼	+ ¼
	33	22⅝	AbbotLab	ABT	.68f	2.6	17	16925	26⅞	25½	25⅞	–1⅛
n	9⅞	3⅝	Abex	ABE		...	dd	222	4½	4⅜	4⅜	...
	13¾	10¼	Abitibi g	ABY	.50	...	...	11	11⅝	11½	11½	– ¼
s	15	6	AcceptIns	AIF		...	dd	21	13½	13⅜	13½	+ ⅛
n	4⅝	2¼	AcceptIns wt			...	...	95	4	4	4	...
n	32	27½	ACE Ltd	ACL	.10p	.4	...	801	28¼	27¾	27¾	– ¼
	11	4¾	AcmeCleve	AMT	.40	3.7	14	227	11	10¾	10¾	– ⅛
	9¼	**3¾**	**AcmeElec**	**ACE**		**...**	**dd**	**122**	**8⅜**	**7¾**	**8⅜**	**+ ½**
n	24¾	15⅛	Acordia	ACO	.29e	1.5	...	184	19⅜	19	19⅜	+ ¼
	22¼	10⅜	Acuson	ACN		...	12	620	10⅞	10¾	10¾	...
	22¼	18⅜	AdamsExp	ADX	1.62e	7.6	...	195	21½	21¼	21⅜	...
	32⅞	7⅜	AdvMicro	AMD		...	12	3565	28⅝	28	28	– ½
	66	29½	AdvMicro pf		3.00	5.2	...	27	58¾	58¼	58¼	–1
	7¾	4⅞	Advest	ADV		...	dd	52	6⅛	6	6	– ¼
s	24¾	12⅜	Advo	AD	.02p	.1	21	193	20¾	20	20¾	+ ¾
s	49⅜	34	Aegon	AEG	2.15e	4.7	...	82	45⅝	45¼	45⅝	– ⅞
	55⅞	37¼	AetnaLife	AET	2.76	5.2	56	1521	54⅝	53½	53½	–1⅜
	14½	9⅞	AffilPub	AFP	.26f	2.0	31	551	13⅜	13	13⅛	– ⅛
	25	20⅝	AgriMinl	AMC	2.42	10.8	9	121	22⅝	22⅜	22½	– ⅛
	22⅛	13	Ahmanson	AHM	.88	4.9	14	850	18⅜	18	18⅛	– ¼

price tables published in *The Journal* on Monday, June 7. It shows prices for the previous trading day, Friday, June 4.

In the figure, there are 12 headings across the width of each column. (They are shown with numbers in parentheses, which do not appear in the listings.)

(1)	(2)	(3)	(4)	(5)	(6)	(7)	(8)	(9)	(10)	(11)	(12)
52 Weeks					Yld		Vol				Net
Hi	Lo	Stock	Sym	Div	%	PE	100s	Hi	Lo	Close	Chg

(1) The *52 Weeks Hi* lists the highest price at which a round lot (100 shares or more) of that particular stock has traded during the previous 52 weeks, plus the current week, excepting only the trading day shown.

(2) The *52 Weeks lo* shows the lowest round lot trade recorded during the same period, plus the current week, again excepting the trading day shown.

(3) The *Stock* column shows the security, with its name abbreviated to fit into the small space allotted. Also shown, if necessary, is whether the stock is a preferred issue or a different class of common stock. Enough information will be given, even if cryptically, to distinguish the security from all the other issues on that exchange.

(4) The *Sym* column lists the security's trading symbol. Every stock is assigned a symbol consisting of 1, 2, or 3 letters of the alphabet. Each security's symbol is listed as a convenience to those who "watch the tape" and want to follow the price movements of their favorite stocks. Registered representatives enter customers' orders by stock symbol rather than by spelling out the entire name of the security they are buying or selling.

(5) The *Div* column shows the company's estimated *annual* dividend rate. Irregular payments, as well as special or extra dividends, are identified with footnotes.

(6) The *Yld %* column shows the stock's current yield, based on the dividend rate shown and the closing price, just as we described in the preceding section of this chapter.

(7) The *PE* column shows the stock's *price-earnings ratio.* This is calculated by dividing the closing price by the company's primary per-share earnings during the previous four quarters.

(8) The *Vol 100s* column shows the total number of shares of that security traded that day, in hundreds.

(9) The *Hi* column shows the highest price at which the stock traded that day.

(10) The *Lo* column shows the lowest intraday price.

(11) The *Close* column lists the price at which the last reported trade took place on that day.

(12) The *Net Chg* column shows how the day's closing price compared with the previous day's closing price—how much the stock went up, or down, compared with the previous day.

Let's follow a complete line of information, from left to right, across the entire "New York Stock Exchange Composite Transactions" listing. We'll use AbbotLab (about in the middle of Figure 2–1):

(1) The first figure, 33, signifies that AbbotLab sold at that price, and no higher, sometime during the previous year. $33.00 per share was the "high for the previous year."

(2) The next figure, 22⅝ ($22.625 per share) was the stock's yearly low. That gives us a trading "range" for the stock of 33 high-22⅝ low, a variance of 10⅜ points.

(3) Next is an abbreviation for the name of the corporation. Its full name is, of course, Abbott Laboratories.

(4) The ticker symbol assigned to Abbott Laboratories is ABT.

(5) The annual dividend is $0.68 per share. The *f* after the dividend indicates that it was recently increased.

(6) The current yield is shown as 2.6 percent. We can check this out by dividing the annual dividend ($0.68) by the stock's closing price (25⅞): $0.68 ÷ 25.875 = 2.6 percent. It checks out!

(7) The price/earnings ratio is 17. This means that the stock is selling for about 17 times its earnings over the last four quarters. This indicates that Abbott Laboratories' per-share earnings over the previous four quarters were about $1.50! Using a little algebra: if P/E = 17 and P = 25.875, then E = 25.875 ÷ 17, which is 1.52.

(8) The trading volume for the day was 1,692,500 shares (16925 × 100). It was a very active stock that day!

(9) The day's highest trading price was 26⅞ ($26.875 per share).

(10) The intraday low price was 25½ ($25.50 per share). Its "trading range" during the day was 1⅜ points.

(11) The last trade of the day was at 25⅞ ($25.875 per share).

(12) The price change from the previous closing price was down 1⅛. This indicates that the previous closing price was 27! If it closed at 25⅞ on the day indicated, and that price was −1⅛ from the previous close, then that previous close was 1⅛ higher than the current close. The stock lost a "point and an eighth" on the day shown.

Note that ADT (not A *B* T, but A *D* T) does not pay a dividend and does not appear to have any net earnings: the "Yld %" and "PE" columns are blank.

See the ADT warrants listed just after ADT? The name of the security is shown as ADT wt. No dividend or earnings are indicated for this security either.

See the letters to the extreme left of the figure? The "n" means that the stock has only been listed on the exchange within the previous year. The "s" indicates that the stock has had a split, or a 10 percent or greater stock dividend, within the previous year.

The exhibit shows at least one preferred stock. Can you find it?

The Initial Public Offering:

Getting the Stocks to the Marketplace

Some 250 years ago, Wall Street was nothing more than a dirt path that started in front of Trinity Church and ran downhill toward the dockyards of Manhattan's East River.

There, on the piers, is where the stock market began. The original securities were actually bills of lading for the cargoes loaded off the inbound ships. No paper money was exchanged. The international unit of trade was silver, since gold was hard to come by. Bars of silver were cut into pieces and "doubloons" of eight, when necessary, to purchase shares in the cargo, which is why stocks are traded in eighths in the United States to this very day.

From such beginnings, securities trading flourished in this East river shipping center. In 1789, as a result of mounting war debts, Congress authorized the issue of $80 million in government bonds. A few years later, bank stocks were offered as a result of the establishment of the nation's first bank. Insurance companies began to appear, and an organized pattern of trading emerged. Although no formal stock market existed, there were securities to be traded. As they became more and more plentiful, securities were sold literally over the counter like any other product. This is how the so-called "over-the-counter" market of today initially developed.

In the spring of 1792, 24 men signed an agreement on Wall Street that, in effect, was the beginning of the New York Exchange (NYSE). They agreed to sell securities only among themselves and established fixed commission rates—a policy that did not change until May of 1975, when rates were made negotiable. In the early 1800s, the members of this group— the New York Stock and Exchange Board— moved into what is now 40 Wall Street. In 1863, they moved again to the present site of the New York Stock Exchange, although the building occupied today was not completed until 1903.

Figure 3–1. Wall Street in the Early 1800s.

With the advent of the Industrial Revolution, Wall Street exploded with activity. Issues that were deemed too speculative to trade by the Board were eagerly traded by non members, often right in the street since few non members could afford office space. These traders became known as "curbstone brokers" and the market as "The Curb." By the early 1900s the Curb had grown considerably and its brokers occupied offices on Broad Street. The system of trading by hand signals was developed by brokers in an attempt to communicate over all the curbside shouting and confusion with their shouting clerks leaning out of upper-story windows. In fact, it came to be the exchange's trademark. In the early 1920s, the Curb Market moved indoors into its present location of 86 Trinity Place, Manhattan. Many years later, in 1952 the so-called New York Curb Exchange adopted its present name, the American Stock Exchange (AMEX).

Today the stock market is worldwide. In addition to the New York and American exchanges, there are regional exchanges across the United States, as well as in London, Tokyo, Paris, and elsewhere around the globe. The American over-the-counter (OTC) market, which began as the "outsiders" trading circle, compares favorably with the exchanges in terms of the volume and quality of the securities traded.

The exchanges and the OTC market, together, make up what is known as the "secondary market." We will talk about the secondary market in Chapter 7. In this chapter, we will look at the primary market.

THE PRIMARY MARKET—HOW BUSINESSES ARE CAPITALIZED

There are several ways to buy ownership in a business. Perhaps the simplest way is to negotiate a one-on-one agreement with the business owner. For example, suppose your friend is opening up a small plant that manufactures candle figurines. He calculates that the money he intends to invest is not enough to cover the start-up period, when expenses typically outweigh revenues. To make up the difference, he asks you to invest in his business. You decide to do so, and a business agreement is drawn up, stating the terms and nature of your profit-sharing ownership. Since you know nothing about manufacturing candle figurines, the agreement stipulates that you do not become involved in the day-to-day affairs of the business. You have just become a part owner—a partner—in the business.

Although you share ownership, you will never see a stock certificate, because the business is not a corporation. When your friend owned it by himself, it was a proprietorship. When you invested, it became a partnership. But neither form of business is permitted by law to issue stock. To do that, the business must become a distinct legal corporate entity

As time goes by, you and your friend might want to incorporate for one or more of several reasons. Suppose, over the first three to five years of the business, the candle · figurines are so well accepted that it is time to expand. You want to open at least two more plants in different parts of the country and start a national marketing and sales campaign. To do this, you need far more money than you could hope to borrow from friends or relatives.

There are several possible sources of funds.

One source is a commercial bank, such as Citibank, Chase, Chemical, and others. Any money you get from such a source would be borrowed and only on a short-term basis. The bank would become a creditor of yours, not an owner.

Another possibility is a venture capital firm, whose sole purpose is to invest in young, promising companies. To secure funds from such a firm, you would have to prepare a convincing business plan for the expanded operation, showing the return you expect on the investment—and how you intend to make it. Among other requirements, the venture capital firm will expect you to incorporate. What does the venture capitalist get out of investing in your company? A sizable percentage of ownership.

A third source of funds is the investment banker, who can help you raise the money through the sale of securities, *only* if the company is incorporated.

Before explaining what the investment baker, or underwriter, does for the company, let's see how the business becomes incorporated.

INCORPORATING THE BUSINESS

A corporation is a legal "person," separate and distinct from its owners. As a sole proprietor, or partner, an individual could lose his personal assets—the house, the car—if someone sued the business, and business assets were insufficient to satisfy the claim. When the business is incorporated, however, it becomes an entity on its own. If someone sues the business, only its assets are subject to loss. Your liability as a corporate shareholder is limited. Similarly, anyone who buys stock in a corporation (and who becomes a part owner) enjoys this same limited liability; owners may lose only what they invest, nothing more.

The Certificate of Incorporation (or Charter)

The first step in forming a corporation is drafting a certificate of incorporation, or charter. This document contains all the information necessary to identify the corporation distinctly in the eyes of the law. One such piece of information, of course, is the company's name; no two corporations may have the same name. For example, if the company's name is Maxwell Manufacturing, no other company may incorporate under that name. Conversely, if another corporation has already incorporated under that name, Maxwell Manufacturing must incorporate and do business under another name.

The charter contains, among other clauses, several elements of interest.

The purpose statement. This clause states what the corporation does for a business. In Maxwell's charter, the business could be as specific as the manufacture of candle figurines. This information is important to prospective shareholders, who need to know how the company is going to use their money. They might support the idea of candle figurines, but what happens if the acceptance of this new idea weakens in the marketplace? Maxwell might see an opportunity to make great profits by diversifying and making plastic chess pieces, but stockholders could take action—even sue—because the company is violating its original purpose statement of making candle figurines.

To avoid such situations, many states, led by Delaware, permit charters to have "general purpose clauses," that is, business as a corporation. This type of statement gives the company's management, that is the Board of Directors, the flexibility to diversify without fear of action from the shareholders.

The capital statement. This clause states the number of shares authorized for sale in order to raise capital. It also stipulates whether the company will issue common or preferred stock—or both. New companies preparing to go public usually issue common stock for several reasons. Common stock gives its owners equity through the use of voting rights, as well as the right to share in appreciation in value as the company prospers. But it does not obligate the company to pay regular fixed cash dividends, as does preferred stock—payments that a young company may not always be able to make, in as much as dividends may be paid only if there is sufficient surplus of earnings and profits. In addition, common stock can be priced lower than preferred stock when it is offered to the public and it therefore has a larger potential market.

The capital statement also states how many of the authorized shares the company will be issuing, that is, offering for sale. For example, if Maxwell's capital statement says that it has authorized 1 million shares of common stock for sale it may offer part or all of them in the primary offering. Let's say that you and your friend decide to issue about half—600,000 shares. The other 400,000 shares you decide to save for some future time when you might need additional capital. The 1 million shares are the "authorized stock." The 600,000 are classified for sale, and they are said to be "issued and outstanding," once they are sold. The "rainy-day" stock of 400,000 shares is said to be "authorized but unissued."

You and your friend, of course, would retain major percentages of the issued shares. If one or more of your employees made key contributions to the company's success during start-up and you want to reward them—keep them in the company—perhaps you would give them a percentage of the issued shares as well.

Or you might grant them an option to buy company stock at a specified low price at any time in the future. For instance, suppose that in the past three years Bill Wilson was a key person in figuring out ways to meet production quotas and deadlines. Without him your success would be doubtful. You grant Bill an option to buy Maxwell stock any time over the next ten years for $10 a share. Although you plan to publicly offer the stock at $15 a share in the primary offering, its value should increase steadily in the years to come. Should the stock's market value increase to $20, $30, $40, or more, Bill need only exercise his option to buy at $10, and he has a built-in profit.

When the charter is filed with the secretary of the state in which you wish to incorporate, and all other legal requirements are met, Maxwell Manufacturing becomes Maxwell Manufacturing, *Inc.*

Glass-Steagall Act

Now that Maxwell is incorporated, it has established the foundation for selling securities in the public market, referred to as the "issuance" or "underwriting" of securities.

But how is the actual underwriting of securities to take place and the needed capital raised through the sale? Can either a brokerage firm or a commercial bank assist in this process?

Prior to the Crash in 1929, banks were heavily engaged in the stock market. As the market plummeted, may banks went under. As a result, the Great Depression began. As President Franklin D. Roosevelt took office, Congress declared that the federal government should have regulatory powers over the financial securities markets (specifically the stock market) and, further, that commercial banks may not provide brokerage services involving corporate securities. This is the essence of the Glass-Steagall Act of 1933: Commercial banks may take deposits and issue loans; investment banks may be involved in the buying and selling of securities.

This dividing line was a clear one until the 1980s, when commercial banks began to successfully challenge the law. Nowadays, commercial banks offer discount brokerage services and have time deposits whose rate of interest is pegged to a market index. Correspondingly, many brokerage houses offer the equivalent of checking and money market accounts to their investing clients.

Nevertheless, the line is still there, albeit not as distinct as in the past. Banks can sell and buy stocks, but no one in the bank may give you any investment advice related to securities. All they can do is take your order. This type of service is called "discount brokerage." Banks can, however, deal in U.S. government bond and municipal bond securities in the primary market (bonds are debt instruments, unlike stocks); in this case, they do what investment bankers normally do for corporations issuing stock. In fact, many banks, such as Citicorp and Bankers Trust, are bigger than most brokerage houses in the business of selling municipal bonds.

Governmental bonds were not a factor in the great crash of 1929. Recently, commercial banks were granted permission by the Federal Reserve to act as investment bankers, for example, to underwrite corporate bonds.

With banks in brokerage, with brokerage firms financing mortgages and maintaining checking accounts, how reasonable is it to maintain this line of demarcation between commercial and investment banking? The Great Depression is long over, and banks are continuing to vigorously push for the Glass-Steagall Act to fall, once and for all.

What all this means to Maxwell Manufacturing is that the company may borrow short-term funds from a commercial bank, but the loans have to be ruled out for four main reasons.

1. Banks are often unable to lend a potential start-up business venture borrower the amount of money that it needs to borrow.

2. Banks are often unable to provide the terms that such a borrower wants. For instance, a company might want to borrow money at a fixed rate for 20 years, whereas most banks will not make fixed-rate commercial loans for longer than seven years.

3. Banks are often unable to lend to companies with low credit ratings, and a potential for great risk. New companies often do not have enough collateral to secure bank financing. Because banks have a duty to their depositors not to take excessive risks with their deposits, there is some truth to the adage that "the only way to get a bank to make a loan is to have so much money that you don't need one." Individual investors, on the other hand, are often willing to invest in risky situations if they feel the potential reward justifies the risk.

4. Banks often charge interest rates that translate into more dollars paid out than the company has to pay if it raises capital directly from investors.

The alternative to a commercial bank loan is to turn to an investment banker to help in offering shares of the company to the investing public. Companies that cannot be served adequately by commercial banks often turn to investment bankers for such help. These firms serve as intermediaries between potential investors and the companies wishing to raise capital. Because such firms, through their brokers, are in contact with thousands of investors, they can match issuers of securities with investors for whom the securities are appropriate.

For example, if a small growth company like Maxwell needs money for its new plants and inventory, an investment baking firm can line up the investors interested in the high-risk/high-reward stock like Maxwell's.

THE INITIAL PUBLIC OFFERING (IPO)

The first step to going public is to engage the services of an investment banking firm in order to sell (underwrite) the securities. The investment banker will have the necessary marketing contacts and skills, as well as the legal expertise to sell the securities in compliance with US securities laws. When the terms of such an arrangement between the issuer and the banker are negotiated one on one, the underwriting is called just that—negotiated. This is in contrast to a "competitive" underwriting, in which a number of investment bankers may compete for the privilege of conducting the offering. Competition occurs for offerings by Coca-Cola, IBM, or Holiday Inns. For a company like Maxwell, the deal is negotiated.

For a start-up company like Maxwell, the investment banker will probably distribute the stock on a "best-efforts" basis. The role of the investment banker, or underwriter, is simply to make the best effort it can to sell the stock. The risk remains with the issuer, and the underwriter takes a commission on whatever it sells. If the firm's investors do not express enough interest in the issue, the issuer has the right to call the whole thing off if it has reserved an all-or-none requirement. Hence, the name "all or none": the underwriter will sell all of the issue or none of it.

This type of underwriting contrasts with one that is conducted on a "firm" commitment basis. In this case, the underwriter actually buys the stock from the issuer at one price and resells it to the public at another, slightly higher price. The profit to the underwriter is in the spread between the buy and sell price.

Given Maxwell's lack of track record, the underwriter will very likely offer management a best-efforts deal. And Maxwell would probably be wise to accept it.

The Registration Process

After the Crash of 1929, investigations led to the uncovering of a number of abuses in the securities industry. Prior to 1929, no law prohibited companies from issuing stock at liberty, without regard for the effect of unlimited issues on shareholders' interests, on the value of the stock itself, or, for that matter, on the economic system of the country. The Securities Act of 1933 was enacted, with the chief purpose of protecting the public in the primary, or new issue, market. Enforcement of the law is delegated to the Securities and Exchange Commission (SEC).

The chief tool of the SEC in this area is the "full disclosure statement," which is required for any IPO of $5 million or more. This document is prepared jointly by the issuer and underwriter, and it tells everything there is to know about the issuer. (See Figure 3–2.) The Act—a lawyer's dream—runs about 80 pages with another 400 pages in regulations. Yet it can be basically summed up in three words—"Tell it all." If you need capital and are going public, tell it all—everything—in the disclosure statement. Some of the main items are:

* Management aims and goals

* How many shares the company is selling

* What the issuer intends to do with the money

Figure 3–2. Some of the Information Required in the Full Disclosure Statement.

1. The name of the issuer.

2. The name of the state or sovereign power under which the issuer is organized.

3. The location of the issuer's principal office.

4. The names and addresses of the directors and other senior officials.

5. The names and addresses of the underwriters (if any).

6. The names and addresses of persons owning 10 percent or more of any class of the issuer's stock.

7. The quantities of securities owned by the directors, senior officials, underwriters, and 10 percent or greater holders

8. The general character of the issuer's business.

9. A statement of the issuer's capitalization.

10. A statement of securities reserved for options outstanding, with names and addresses of persons allotted 10 percent or more of these options.

11. The amount of capital stock of each class included in the offer.

12. The issuer's funded debt.

13. The purposes to which the proceeds of this offering will be applied.

14. Remuneration payable to the issuers directly, naming them specifically when annual payments exceed $25,000.

15. The estimated net proceeds to be derived from the offering.

16. The price at which the public offering will be attempted.

17. Commissions, fees and so on, to be paid to the underwriters.

18. An itemized detail of expenses incurred by the issuer in connection with this offering.

19. The net proceeds derived from any securities sold by the issuer in the preceding two years and pertinent details of those sales.

20. Any consideration paid to a promoter in the preceding two years.

21. The names and addresses of any vendors of property or goodwill to be acquired with the proceeds of this offering.

22. Full particulars of any dealings between the issuer and its officers, directors, and holders of 10 percent or more of its stock that transpired in the preceding two years.

23. The names and addresses of counsel passing upon the legality of the issue.

24. The dates and details of material contracts created outside the issuer's ordinary course of business within the preceding two years.

25. Certified financial statements of any issuer or business to be acquired with proceeds of this offering.

26. A copy of the underwriting contract or agreement.

27. A copy of the law firm's written opinion attesting to the legality of the issue.

28. A copy of all material contracts referred to in item 24.

29. A copy of the issuer's charter, bylaws, trust agreement, partnership agreement, and so forth, as the case may be.

30. A copy of the underlying agreement or indenture affecting any security offered or to be offered by the issuer.

* The corporation's tax status

* Fallback plans in the event things don't go as expected

* The company's legal standing, such as any lawsuits

* Its income and expenses—its profit and loss

* Inherent risks of its enterprise

If something is held back in this statement, severe civil and criminal penalties can result, with the civil monetary damages often worse than the criminal consequences.

The disclosure statement cannot be used to sell securities; the firm's sales force may not show it to clients to get an order. The reason is that the statement has to be accepted by the SEC. Until it is, it cannot be considered as having met legal requirements. To denote that the statement is printed, in red ink, on the side of the statement. With this red blurb, the registration statement is called the "red herring." (See Figure 3–3.)

The SEC does not "approve" the statement. The SEC may send the statement back to the underwriter more than once, requesting additional information or clarification. Once all the information required by law is included, the SEC may accept the statement and declare the offering effective. By accepting it, the Commission merely affirms that the statement now meets legal requirements. It does *not* affirm that the company is well managed, that it will

Figure 3–3. The Standard Statement on a "Red Herring."

A registration statement relation to these securities has been filed with the Securities and Exchange Commission, but has not yet become effective. Information contained herein is subject to completion or amendment. These securities may not be sold nor may offers to buy be accepted prior to the time the registration statement becomes effective. This prospectus shall not constitute an offer to seal or the solicitation of an offer to buy nor shall there be any sale of these securities in any state in which such offer, solicitation, or sale would be unlawful prior to the registration or qualification under the securities laws of any such state.

be successful, or that the stock will rise in value. All that remains for the individual investor to determine.

Conversely, a rejection of a registration statement is not a condemnation of the company or the stock. It is only an indication that, for some reason, the underwriter cannot supply the information required by law

Once the statement is accepted, the "red herring" statement comes off, and the statement becomes a "final prospectus." *Now* it may be used to solicit orders from the investing public. The prospectus offers investors the basic information they need at least to know that the company offering is in compliance with federal securities laws.

Finalizing agreements. Once the terms of the offering are settled among the underwriters, they have an agreement drawn up and sign it. This is the agreement among underwriters, which stipulates:

* Members of the underwriting group

* Members of the selling group

* Size of the underwriters' retention (the pot)

* How group sales will be conducted

* What the lead manager must do if the stock's price climbs or drops quickly in the after market

The next agreement is made between the underwriting group and the issuer—the "underwriting agreement" or "purchase agreement." This formalizes the negotiations leading up to this point. It is filed with the SEC and becomes part of the registration statement by amendment.

The Cooling-Off Period

While the SEC is reviewing the statement, the IPO is said to be in the "cooling-off period," usually about 20 days. During this period, the underwriter's staff is busy doing several things.

Circling the stock. Stockbrokers (account executives registered representatives, stockbrokers) are busy calling the firm's present clients to solicit "indications of interest." The salespeople will speak about the stock in general, both risks and benefits, but cannot ask for an order in as much as the SEC has not declared the offering effective and a final price has not been established. Instead, they simply ask whether the client would be interested in buying such a stock and, if so, about how much. This is called "circling the stock."

The information gathered in this process is a solid indication of how successful the offering is likely to be.

Forming the syndicate. After the underwriting agreement is entered into in principle, between the investment banker and the issuing corporation, the investment banking group creates a syndicate, which is a temporary group of investment bankers, formed for the express purpose of underwriting the offering. Most firms do not try to sell an entire issue by themselves (unless it is a small one). Instead, they solicit the help of other firms. All of the firms involved in selling the new offering, acting as a group, form the syndicate. The firm that puts the deal together is called the "lead manager." In building a syndicate, a brokerage firm can play three different roles:

1. If the firm puts the deal together, it is the "lead manager" and runs the books.

2. If the firm does not put the deal together but is willing to commit its capital by buying some of the issue for resale (in a firm offering), the firm is simply called an "underwriter."

3. If it does not commit its capital but helps only to sell the securities, the firm is referred to as a member of the "selling group."

Each of these three types of participants shares differently in the spread, depending on the capital at risk and the responsibility undertaken.

Example: Brokerage firm A takes on an offering of some 1 million shares and, assuming responsibility as lead manager, builds a small syndicate and selling group. Brokerage A pays the issuer $9.50 per share. It plans to resell the shares to investors for $10 a piece. The spread between $9.50 and $10.00 of 50¢ represents a 5 percent profit on the deal. Here's how the spread, per share, is split among the lead manager, underwriters, and selling group members:

* $0.05 per share goes to the lead manager just for putting the deal together.

* $0.20 per share goes to each underwriting firm per share sold, to compensate it for risking its capital.

* $0.25 goes to the firm that sells a share—a selling group member—to compensate it for the sales effort.

Thus, if Brokerage A both underwrites and sells a share, it is entitled to the full 50¢ spread.

If another syndicate member both underwrites and sells a share, it is entitled to 45¢ (20¢ for capital risk and 25¢ for the selling effort).

If a firm underwrites only but does not sell a share, it gets 20¢.

If a member of the selling group sells but does not underwrite a share, it receives 25¢ for the sale.

Let's suppose that the sales go as follows:

Firm	No. of Shares in Offering	No. of Shares Underwritten	No. of Shares Sold
Brokerage A	1,000,000	250,000	200,000
Underwriter B		250,000	200,000
Underwriter C		250,000	200,000
Underwriter D		250,000	200,000
Selling Group A			100,000
Selling Group B			100,000
	1,000,000	1,000,000	1,000,000

Brokerage A, the lead manager, underwrites 250,000 shares and
sells 200,000 shares. In this case, firm A earns:
250,000 underwritten × $0.05 = $12,500.00
200,000 shares sold × $0.20 = $40,000.00
Selling Group member B sells 100,000 shares and earns:
100,000 shares sold × $0.25 = $25,000
And so on.

Given Maxwell's size and relative newness as a corporation, perhaps only one investment banker is interested in
it. In this case, management would negotiate directly with
the one underwriter over the price that Maxwell receives for
the stock. If Maxwell cannot get what it thinks is a fair price
in a firm offering, it simply does not sell its shares.

If no investment banking firm will make it a firm offer,
Maxwell can resort to accepting a best-efforts offering. The
disadvantage is that an offering is an expensive proposition. If it does not go through to completion and success,
the corporation can lose tens and sometimes hundreds of
thousands of dollars in expenses.

Blue-skying. In the 1900s, the Kansas state legisla-
ture passed the country's first state securities law. One of
the state lawmakers quipped, "Now Kansas citizens will
have more of a basis for making investment decisions than
merely by the shade of the blue sky."

Today every state has its own securities laws, and, to
do business in a state, the brokerage house has to comply
with these laws. When a new issue of stock is coming to
the market, the underwriter's legal staff gets to work on
meeting such requirements—state by state. They are said
to be "blue-skying" the issue.

The Due Diligence Meeting

Some time during the cooling-off period, the lead manager assembles representatives from all the firms in the
syndicate. This, the due diligence meeting, has a couple of
purposes, in addition to ironing out any last-minute details.

Allocating the issue. Each underwriting firm indicates how much it will sell of the issue, depending on the information from the salespeople who circled the stock. This can be a ticklish job for the lead manager, who ultimately decides which firm gets what. The firms now have to make good on their commitments. The manager does the best job possible in allocating the issue, but holds back a portion, usually about 25 percent, for allocation to the selling group and sale to institutional clients. The held-back portion is known as "the pot."

Group sales are made out of the pot. If an institutional investor, such as a pension fund or a mutual fund, wants 50,000 shares, the manager will take those shares out of the pot, rather than glean them a little here and a little there from the underwriters. In turn, each member of the syndicate shares in the proceeds according to its percentage of sales in the overall issue.

When the members hear, "The pot is clean!" they know that institutional investors consider the stock a worthwhile one and their selling efforts get easier.

Setting the price. The new issue has no market value, since it has not yet traded on the open market. What price, therefore, is the "right" one?

To determine its fair value, the underwrites ask at a pricing meeting:

* How strong is the company fundamentally?

* How much demand will there be for the stock?

* How strong, or weak, is the market right now?

Setting the price is a tightrope walk. The issuing firm, of course, wants as high a price as possible, and investors want as low a price as they can get. The underwriting firm, whose profit comes from the spread, has to set a price that is fair to the issuer but attractive to investors. Historically, a stock that is "priced right" rises slightly in value as it hits the market. If the market price drops slightly, the price was set too high. If the price skyrockets, investors win big, the issuer watches additional capital fly out the window, and the underwriter is left wearing only a sheepish grin.

By the end of the meeting, the syndicate has its price, and the lead manager notifies the printing company that it can start printing the final prospectuses with the price fixed.

The Effective Date

The SEC has accepted the registration statement by declaring the offering effective and announcing an effective date. The time has come to see how the public receives the offering.

The salespeople now have a document that can be used to solicit and accept orders for the stock. The final prospectus has a consolidation of the information in the registration statement and *must* be given to anyone who buys the stock no later than with the customer confirmation statement. This is a customer's receipt of purchase and it occurs on the "effective date," the date on which the stock may be sold. (See Figure 3-4.)

The salespeople start calling clients with the price information. As the orders are finalized, the underwriting firms keep the lead manager abreast of sales. The manager, whose job is to "keep the books" for the group, knows how the offering is going.

Stabilizing the market. As the issue is distributed, the reception among investors is sometimes not as great as expected. Maybe the price was set too high; maybe the company is just not strong enough in the eyes of the investing public. Whatever the reason, the offering is "weak." If new owners of the stock see the price drop in the marketplace, the danger is that they will start getting rid of their shares and start a sell-off. In such a case, the stock's price would drop sharply and the underwriters would stand to lose a bundle because they would own a substantial quantity at a lower price.

This is the one time the law allows a brokerage firm acting as underwriter to "fix" a market price. It may place a standing bid on behalf of the syndicate in the secondary

Figure 3–4. A Final Prospectus.

PROSPECTUS

$75,000,000

DynaFlow Technology, Inc.

7¾% Convertible Subordinated Debentures Due 1998

(Interest Payable February 1 and August 1)

The Debentures are convertible at any time prior to maturity, unless previously redeemed, into shares of Common Stock of the Company at a conversion price of $46.43 per share, subject to adjustment under certain conditions. On January 26, 1983, the last reported sale price of the Company's Common Stock on the American Stock Exchange was $40⅜ per share.

The Debentures are redeemable at any time on not less than thirty days' notice at the option of the Company, in whole or in part, at the redemption prices set forth herein, including interest accrued to the date of redemption, provided that the Debentures may not be redeemed prior to February 1, 1985, unless prior to the mailing of the notice of redemption the price of the Company's Common Stock has been at least 150% of the conversion price for 30 successive trading days. Mandatory sinking fund payments sufficient to retire $7,500,000 principal amount of Debentures annually commencing February 1, 1991 are calculated to retire 70% of the issue prior to maturity. The Company may credit against mandatory sinking fund payments Debentures previously acquired, converted or redeemed other than through the mandatory sinking fund.

The Debentures will be subordinated to all Senior Indebtedness (as defined) of the Company. As of December 31, 1982, after giving effect to the application of the estimated net proceeds from the sale of the Debentures, the Company's Senior Indebtedness would have been approximately $2,193,000. There will be no restrictions in the Indenture upon the creation of Senior Indebtedness.

Application will be made to list the Debentures on the American Stock Exchange.

THESE SECURITIES HAVE NOT BEEN APPROVED OR DISAPPROVED BY THE SECURITIES AND EXCHANGE COMMISSION NOR HAS THE COMMISSION PASSED UPON THE ACCURACY OR ADEQUACY OF THIS PROSPECTUS. ANY REPRESENTATION TO THE CONTRARY IS A CRIMINAL OFFENSE.

	Price to Public (1)	Underwriting Discounts and Commissions (2)	Proceeds to Company (1)(3)
Per Debenture	100%	2.75%	97.25%
Total	$75,000,000	$2,062,500	$72,937,500

(1) Plus accrued interest, if any, from February 1, 1983 to the date of delivery.

(2) The Company has agreed to indemnify the Underwriters against certain liabilities, including liabilities under the Securities Act of 1933.

(3) Before deducting expenses of the Company estimated at $260,000.

The Debentures are being offered by the several Underwriters named herein, subject to prior sale, and when, as and if delivered to and accepted by the Underwriters, and subject to approval of certain legal matters by counsel. It is expected that delivery of the Debentures will be made against payment therefor on or about February 3, 1983, at the offices of **Stone, Forrest & Rivers**
160 Wall Street
New York, NY 10041

Securities Brokerage
INCORPORATED

Giant, Recker & Crane

over-the-counter or stock exchange market to buy the new stock at or slightly below the offering price. It may not be higher. The effect of this standing bid is that it prevents the market value of the stock from dropping far below the offering price. New stock owners are assured that speculators will not step in and render the market for the stock unstable. This measure taken by the lead manager is known as "stabilizing the market."

Hot issues. At other times, the issue sells vigorously—customers cannot get enough of them. The issue is "hot"! The syndicate members have no problem distributing the portions allocated to them. In fact, they want more.

Managers may deal with a hot issue in a couple of ways. They can oversell the issue by as much as 15 percent—legally—because historically they get that much in cancellations. If they are still short, they can go into the market and buy the stock back. This is not considered a stabilization measure because the manager is paying at least the offering price and probably more.

The manager can also ask for a "green shoe privilege." With the offering selling out quickly and customers asking for more, the lead manager asks the corporate issuer for an option to buy more of the stock at a price below the original offering price, and usually within 30 days after the effective date. Once the agreement is signed and filed by amendment with the SEC as part of the registration statement, the manager exercises the option, buys the additional shares, and uses them to cover the short positions created when they oversold the issue.

There's a downside to a hot issue. With demand for the stock so great, the aftermarket value is likely to increase sharply, as investors who could not purchase them in the offering seek them out in the secondary market. For this reason, anyone who is in a position to buy stock in the initial public offering is often guaranteed an instantaneous profit. Insiders could easily cash in on a hot issue. To prevent such an abuse, no one who works for one of the underwriters or who is related to an employee of the firms may buy these issues during the offering. That's the law.

The Tombstone

No doubt you have seen television advertisements for major brokerage houses. Shearson [Lehman Brothers] creates imaginative 30-second spots centering around a glass half-full or a setting sun. Investors smilingly thank Paine Webber [Dean Witter]. Smith Barney earns money the old-fashioned way. And Charles Schwab tells you why it's a lot smarter to place your orders with a discount firm. Securities firms are allowed to advertise their services and names with all the sophistication that Procter & Gamble uses to sell its soap.

But they are *not* allowed to use such techniques to sell securities. Securities may be sold only by prospectus—the final prospectus. The brokerage firm may not, by law, conduct a commercial ad campaign on behalf of a new issue of IBM debentures or of a high-tech stock.

What they are allowed to do is to place a somber ad in the financial news on the effective day of the offering. This ad does nothing more than convey basic information about the issue, the issuer, and the underwriting group. It is so understated an ad that it is called a "tombstone" and in fact looks like one. The double irony is that, by the time the ad appears and is read, the issue is very often sold out or nearly so since the indications of interest converted into orders on the effective date usually deplete the amount of available stock.

If the ad does not sell any stock and if it's too late to serve that purpose anyway, what reason does the syndicate have for placing it? Why spend the tens of thousands of dollars required to have it appear in the *Wall Street Journal* and/or *New York Times*, or other financial publications?

The reason is prestige. Investment bankers work according to an informal but very visible pecking order. Some syndicates are made up of firms that have done underwritings together for years. They are used to working together, and each firm knows where it stands in relation to the others. In other cases, the political maneuvering and dickering that go into the arrangement of the firms' names on the tombstone can be fierce.

Look at the tombstone in Figure 3–5, focusing for now on just the underwriters' names. The top two names, Dean Witter Reynolds Inc. and Merrill Lynch Capital Markets, are the two lead managers. How do you know that? Their names are at the top and on a separate line.

Syndicate members are arranged alphabetically by groups, and the alphabetical rule carries throughout the listing. In Figure 3–5, read from the next line—Bear Stearns & Co. Inc.—down to Wertheim Schroder & Co. If you look at the "last" names of these firms, you will see that they are listed across each line alphabetically: Bear, Boston, Brown, Dillon, and so on. The alphabetization starts all over again with Advest, Inc. because the next group represents a different bracket of underwriters, one that has lesser standing in the investment banking community. While Bear, Stearns and that group are in the "major" bracket (handling large portions of the underwriting), Advest and the others up to Thomson McKinnon are in a "submajor" bracket. They handle less than the firms in the major bracket.

Handling still less per firm is the bracket that includes Tucker, Anthony through Wheat. And again of still lesser presence in the syndicate are Barclay through Williams.

The urgency with which higher standings are pursued arises from something other than prestige. As it is with most issues in the securities industry, the underlying motivation is to make money. The lesser-bracketed firms stand to make less money than the higher ones because they are generally allocated last and the least.

In the $1.1 billion Citicorp stock offering, for example, Merrill Lynch organized a syndicate of 110 underwriters and took 2 million of the 20 million shares in the offering. Institutional investor orders ran high, the pot was cleaned

Figure 3–5. A Typical Tombstone.

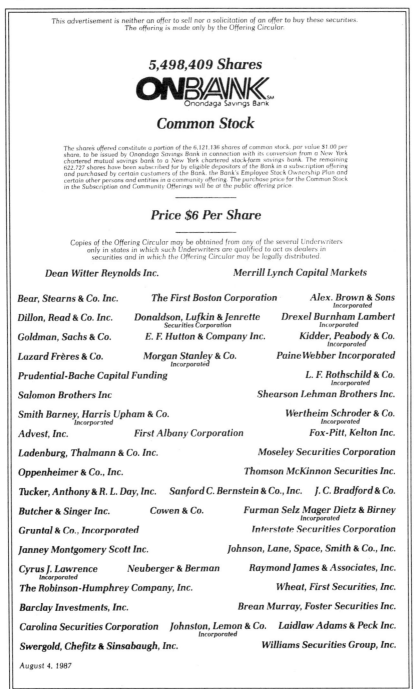

This advertisement is neither an offer to sell nor a solicitation of an offer to buy these securities.
The offering is made only by the Offering Circular.

5,498,409 Shares

ONBANK℠
Onondaga Savings Bank

Common Stock

The shares offered constitute a portion of the 6,121,136 shares of common stock, par value $1.00 per share, to be issued by Onondaga Savings Bank in connection with its conversion from a New York chartered mutual savings bank to a New York chartered stock-form savings bank. The remaining 622,727 shares have been subscribed for by eligible depositors of the Bank in a subscription offering and purchased by certain customers of the Bank, the Bank's Employee Stock Ownership Plan and certain other persons and entities in a community offering. The purchase price for the Common Stock in the Subscription and Community Offerings will be at the public offering price.

Price $6 Per Share

Copies of the Offering Circular may be obtained from any of the several Underwriters
only in states in which such Underwriters are qualified to act as dealers in
securities and in which the Offering Circular may be legally distributed.

Dean Witter Reynolds Inc.   **Merrill Lynch Capital Markets**

Bear, Stearns & Co. Inc.   **The First Boston Corporation**   **Alex. Brown & Sons**
Incorporated

Dillon, Read & Co. Inc.   **Donaldson, Lufkin & Jenrette**   **Drexel Burnham Lambert**
Securities Corporation   Incorporated

Goldman, Sachs & Co.   **E. F. Hutton & Company Inc.**   **Kidder, Peabody & Co.**
Incorporated

Lazard Frères & Co.   **Morgan Stanley & Co.**   **PaineWebber Incorporated**
Incorporated

Prudential-Bache Capital Funding   **L. F. Rothschild & Co.**
Incorporated

Salomon Brothers Inc   **Shearson Lehman Brothers Inc.**

Smith Barney, Harris Upham & Co.   **Wertheim Schroder & Co.**
Incorporated   Incorporated

Advest, Inc.   **First Albany Corporation**   **Fox-Pitt, Kelton Inc.**

Ladenburg, Thalmann & Co. Inc.   **Moseley Securities Corporation**

Oppenheimer & Co., Inc.   **Thomson McKinnon Securities Inc.**

Tucker, Anthony & R. L. Day, Inc.   **Sanford C. Bernstein & Co., Inc.**   **J. C. Bradford & Co.**

Butcher & Singer Inc.   **Cowen & Co.**   **Furman Selz Mager Dietz & Birney**
Incorporated

Gruntal & Co., Incorporated   **Interstate Securities Corporation**

Janney Montgomery Scott Inc.   **Johnson, Lane, Space, Smith & Co., Inc.**

Cyrus J. Lawrence   **Neuberger & Berman**   **Raymond James & Associates, Inc.**
Incorporated

The Robinson-Humphrey Company, Inc.   **Wheat, First Securities, Inc.**

Barclay Investments, Inc.   **Brean Murray, Foster Securities Inc.**

Carolina Securities Corporation   **Johnston, Lemon & Co.**   **Laidlaw Adams & Peck Inc.**
Incorporated

Swergold, Chefitz & Sinsabaugh, Inc.   **Williams Securities Group, Inc.**

August 4, 1987

quickly, and four of the lowest-bracketed firms never received any stock at all to sell. At best, they were credited to their portion (however small) of the institutional sales.

In the words of a syndicate department manager at a major investment banking firm, "Tombstones have been, and remain, Wall Street's scoreboard. They provide a subjective measurement of a firm's strengths."

And that's not all they do. They also provide investors with some idea of the investment value of the issue. For example, Salomon Brothers will not underwrite a new company's issue unless the corporation has a sound financial track record and structure. It is not in the business of selling medium- or low-quality issues. If Salomon Brothers is part of the offering, you may assume that the issuer has met fairly stringent financial requirements.

Neither will you find a company like Salomon underwriting two-cent stocks, so-called "penny stocks." Such stocks are low-priced because they are *very* high-risk with little to no economic fundamentals, and a tremendous quality of stock authorized for sale available. Selling for less than a dollar, they even require special market making requirements.

This is the type of gamble you take when you invest in penny stocks. The potential is certainly there to win big, if the Company is successful and the demand for the stock continues. But the success stores are few and far between, and you have to be willing to take your losses as part of the penny stock game. Before moving on, let's look at a few other items in the tombstone in Figure 3–5.

* At the very top is a notice, as prescribed by law, indicating that the ad is "neither an offer to sell nor a solicitation of an offer to buy." It also makes reference to the "Offering Circular," another name for the final prospectus.

* Immediately below the advisory is the number of shares being offered If you multiply that number by

the offering price ($6, just a little farther down in the ad), you come up with the size of the offering: $3.3 billion.

* The issuer is Onbank, short for Onondaga Savings Bank.

* The details of the issue are set forth in the paragraph below the issuer's name.

* Copies of the offering circular (final prospectus) may be obtained only in the states where the issue has been blue-skyed and where the underwriting firm is licensed to do business. In the case of the larger firms, that's all the states. For the smaller, regional firms, it might be just some.

* Down in the lower left-hand corner is the effective date, in this case August 4, 1987, the date on which the stock was first offered.

AFTER THE OFFERING IS COMPLETED

When the offering is completely distributed, the syndicate is disbanded, and the deal is said to have "broken syndicate." The stock may now be bought and sold in the secondary market, along with the thousands of other securities already there.

Some issues will begin trading immediately on an exchange, if the issuer is already listed—AT&T, Reynolds, General Motors, and the like, or if the Company has completed its filing for listing on a national securities exchange.

If the issuer is not listed, the stock may begin trading in the over-the-counter market, and brokerage firms—most of them the original underwriters—may elect to become "market makers" in the stock. (I will explain more about market makers in Chapter 7.)

Whether the stock trades on an exchange or in the OTC market, the underwriters relinquish their intermediary role between issuer and investor. The issuer has the capital it sought, and the investor can watch the stock's quotations every day in the financial news.

CHAPTER 4

Inside the Brokerage Firm:

Who Does What?

In a brokerage firm, the only person who takes an order from you, the customer, is the registered representative, also known as an account executive (AE) or, more commonly, a stockbroker. AEs are "registered" because the law requires them to pass an examination prepared by the New York Stock Exchange and administered by the National Association of Securities Dealers (NASD, about which we will say more later). This examination contains questions on every aspect of the securities industry—the markets, the products, the back office operations, and the regulatory requirements. Having passed the exam. AEs are legally qualified to give clients investment advice and to take orders.

Investors should remember, however, that account executives are *sales* professionals. As such, their compensation is earned from commissions (that is, charges for the execution of transactions), not from fees. Here's how account executives earn their money. A client enters an order with the AE to buy 100 shares of Pinhole Enterprises. The broker then sends the order to the order room (or wire room, see Figure 4–1), whose staff forwards the order to the appropriate market where Pinhole is traded. If the order is executed—that is, the stock is purchased—at $17 per share, the client has just spent $1,700 (100 shares × $17). And the firm has just earned a commission. If the brokerage firm charges 1.96 percent on transactions, then the customer will be charged an additional $33.32 on the purchase ($1,700 × 0.0196). Of that $33.32, a percentage, usually between 20 percent and 40 percent, goes to

Figure 4–1. Some of the Interdepartmental Relationships within a Brokerage Firm.

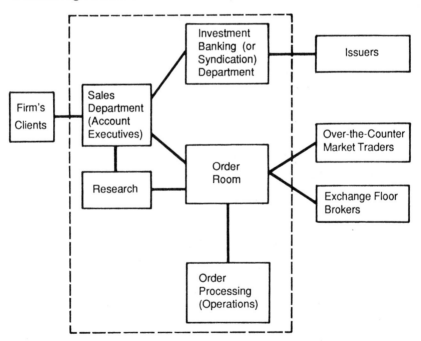

the AE: the balance goes to the firm itself. This is one way in which brokerage houses earn profits.

A couple of things become clear from this example. One is that both the AE and the firm make money on every purchase or sales transaction, whether or not it turns out to be a profitable one for the client. This is not to say that AEs do not care about the profitability of transactions. With few exceptions (which we read about in the papers), AEs *do* care very much for an easily understandable reason: As long as the AE continues to make profitable recommendations to clients, they will remain customers. Nevertheless, registered representatives—unlike other professionals, such as doctors or lawyers—must be regarded as *sales*-oriented. Their compensation increases in direct proportion to (a) the number of times a client places an order to buy or to sell and (b) the size of the order. The AEs who last in the business are the ones who make well-reasoned, suitable recommendations to their clients. Others sometimes let the sales orientation dominate their thinking. These seldom last in the business, which is why over 60 percent of all account executives have been in the business for less than five years.

Another question that arises from our example is, how does an AE, much less a large brokerage house, make money on small, single transactions? The answer is that it is very difficult. The "retail" portion of the securities business—the portion coming from individual investors—has shrunk over the years to a very small percentage of the total dollar volume traded in the stock market, approximating 20 percent. The other 80 percent comes from "institutional investors," such as pension funds, mutual funds, insurance companies, and other "big" players in the market. Obviously the commission on 5,000 or 10,000 shares of a blue-chip stock selling around the $100 mark is going to make the brokerage firm a great deal more money than the 100-share retail order.

Still another way that brokerage houses earn money is by buying and selling securities for their own inventory proprietary trading account. Professional traders employed in the trading department of the firm will buy and sell the stock and other securities.

How do the traders know what to buy and what to sell? They rely on their intuition and judgment, as well as on the reports and recommendations of the company's research department, which supplies reports and other information to both the sales and trading areas. (See Figure 4–1.) In the research department are highly skilled financial professionals who follow the ups and downs of the market, analyze specific stocks, weigh the effects of outside influences on the market (interest rates, inflation, deficit reports, and the like), and ultimately make calculated projections as to what and when to buy and sell. Traders act on the information on behalf of the firm; account executives use the information to make recommendations to their clients.

For most of the U.S. stock market's history, a brokerage firm's commission was fixed. No firm could charge more or less than the industry-wide minimum. On May 1, 1975, sometimes called "May Day," this all changed when commission rates became negotiable. Competition among brokerage houses became keener than ever, and not long thereafter "discount houses" appeared on the scene.

FULL SERVICE VERSUS DISCOUNT

As the name "full service" implies, full-service brokerage firms supply clients with a wide range of service, including:

* *Investment research.* The brokerage firm's research department analysts watch market trends, search out future investment possibilities, and supply research reports.

* *Asset management.* A number of brokerage firms offer customers what are known as "management accounts," which serve as savings accounts, check-

ing accounts, and investment accounts—all in one. For example, if you sold some stock but did not wish to immediately take or reinvest the proceeds, you could "park" the money in the firm's money market account until you made up your mind, as opposed to transferring it to demand or time deposit in a bank. You earn interest (probably more than you could from a demand deposit), and the brokerage firm maintains control of your assets.

* *Investment advice.* While many investors do their own investment analysis, it cannot be compared to the millions of dollars spent on research by a full-service brokerage firm. For example, Dean Witter has spent up to $20 million per year on stock research alone! Spending that kind of money on research does not make the professional analysts right all the time, but if they were not right often enough, either they would not be employed by the firm or the firm would be out of business. When the AE makes a recommendation to a client, it is based on the same information given to the traders—who use the firm's money to buy and sell.

* *Order execution.* How would you buy or sell stock without the services of a broker? To sell stock, for example, you would have to locate a buyer who is willing to make the purchase at the price you want. You would have to certify to the buyer that you are the legal owner, and then you would have to make arrangements to transfer ownership. The brokerage house does all this for you.

* *Clearing.* After the order is executed, there is a long paper trail, in which each step meets a legal or regulatory requirement. (See Figure 4–1; we will explain clearing further in Chapter 10.).

Firms that offer this full range of services fall into a number of categories.

"Wire houses" are large, diversified firms that are generally known to investors and noninvestors alike: Merril Lynch, Dean Witter Reynolds, Shearson/Hutton, Prudential Bache, Smith Barney, and so on. They offer a wide array of investment vehicles and are very retail-oriented. They seek the individual investor's account.

While wire houses handle institutional accounts and trade for their own inventories, they also make money on the retail side by handling large volumes of transactions *efficiently*. In fact, their name derives from the fact that orders are entered, from all over the country, over the "wire"—that is, by means of highly automated systems that keep the cost of processing and clearing order transactions very low.

"Specialized" firms, unlike the wire houses, deal in only one investment vehicle, or a very few, such as government bonds. One widely known specialized firm is Lebenthal & Co., specializing in municipal bonds.

The "carriage trade house" is essentially a New York-based firm whose clients are well-heeled and select. Some traditional examples are Morgan Stanley, Donaldson Lufkin, or Bear Stearns. Their service is highly personalized and their research exceptional.

If you feel you would like to open an account with such a firm, you may find that you do not meet their customer requirements. These houses are very selective. Most new accounts are opened only on the recommendation of existing clients. More often than not, references are required.

"Boutique firms" also offer personalized service, but to the middle-income-bracket investor. They are also fairly diversified, and they therefore can offer the benefits of both a wire house and carriage trade firm. Such firms are Grunthal, Butcher and Singer, F.S. Mosely, and the like.

All these types of firms are considered "full service."

Discount firms offer fewer services and charge lower commissions. When you place an order with a discount firm, you may receive only two services: order execution and clearance. You have to do your own research and analysis, pick your own stock, and decide on timing by yourself. Your AE, a person who probably works for a salary rather than a commission, takes your order and confirms its execution—without offering any investment advice, even upon request. Thereafter the discount firm's back office clears the transaction. Some discount houses go so far as to offer newsletters or possibly money markets, but that's all.

In return for sacrificing services, you get commissions that are anywhere from a quarter to two-thirds lower than those of full-service firms. For example, if you bought 5,000 shares of stock at $8 per share, you could pay as much as $860 to a full-service broker (if you are not a customer entitled to a volume discount), and as little as $170 to a discounter.

Discount commissions can take two forms:

* *A percentage of the share's price.* If you sell 100 shares at $20.50 (for proceeds of $2,050), and if the firm charges a 1.1 percent commission rate, the commission in dollars would be $22.55 (1.1 percent × $2,050).

* *A dollar amount based on the number of shares traded.* If you buy 100 shares, regardless of their price, the firm might charge a flat $0.20 per share for the transaction. You would pay $20 ($0.20 × 100 shares). Odd-lot transactions for less than 100 shares will probably cost you more; brokerage firms provide quantity discounts for higher-volume transactions.

Both full-service and discount firms offer benefits and have their drawbacks.

Which suits your purposes better? The real question is, how much help do you need in making your investment decisions? If you are confident in your investment choices, you can obviously save quite a bit in commission dollars with a discounter. However, if you do not have the time or resources to research a company thoroughly, you may wind up losing much more in poor investment choices than you would save by going with a discount house.

For example, suppose you buy 100 shares at $30 per share with a discount broker, and suppose the commission rate is 1.1 percent. You pay $33 in commission (100 shares x $30 x 0.011). If you bought the same stock through a full-service broker who charges 2.5 percent, you would pay $75 (100 shares x $30 x 0.025). That's a $42 saving if you go with the discounter—42¢ less per share.

If your stock is a good investment choice, it will rise in value, and your profit on it will be greater because of what you saved on commissions. As soon as the market value hits $30.33, you have broken even; any increase in value from that point is profit. If you had bought through a full-service firm, you would not break even until the stock hit $30.75.

On the other hand, if, without the benefit of investment advice from the AE, you buy a stock that turns out to be a poor investment choice, you could lose considerably more than 42¢ per share.

Another question to ask in deciding between discount and full service is, how frequently do you trade during the year? If you enter, say, a half-dozen orders over the course of a year, perhaps the savings do not represent enough to offset the risk of making investment decisions without expert advice. If you are an active buyer and seller of stock, the savings could be a considerable factor in your profits and losses over the year. (Of course, if you are an active trader, you are also probably an active analyst and don't need the advice as much as the "dabbler.")

Whether choosing discount or full service, always check into the firm's background and reputation.

SELECTING A BROKERAGE FIRM AND AN
ACCOUNT EXECUTIVE

Should you elect to do business with a discount house, there is no need to "select" an AE. The salesperson at the other end of the phone line is there for one thing: to take your order and get it executed. Again, don't expect any small talk or advice.

One way to find a broker is to give an order or open an account with an AE who "cold calls" you right out of the phone book. That salesperson may or may not turn out to be the right one for you and your investment objectives. It's also possible that the cold caller is looking for a quick order. *Never* commit to a cold-calling securities salesperson, unless you are satisfied that he or she is legitimate and sincere. For one thing, if all you hear and feel over the phone is pressure to place an order, hang up. If you are undecided about a caller's credentials, listen for the following signals:

* Does the caller ask leading questions? "As a provider, you *do* want the best for your family, don't you?"

* Is the appeal mainly to your "sense of greed" or "guilt" over missed past opportunities?

* Does the caller promise guaranteed results? "This stock is 100 percent guaranteed to double in value in less than six months!" (This type of selling is against the law.)

* Is the caller rushing you into making a decision without supplying you with answers to your questions? "If you wait for the prospectus or the annual report to arrive at your office, these valuable shares undoubtedly will be sold to other smart investors who are able to act quickly."

* Does the caller seem to care about whether the investment suits your financial means? "Don't worry about investing the money. You'll have it back *and more* within three months."

* Does the caller hedge when asked information about the brokerage firm or stock? "If you haven't heard of XYZ Securities, sir, you can't have been investing for very long. We're one of the biggest names in brokerage."

     * Is the cold caller looking for a substantial monetary commitment way beyond your budget.

Any legitimate, reputable account executive will be more than happy to answer your questions straightforwardly—because your questions represent a glimmer of interest on your part. Look at the call from the cold caller's point of view. An AE may make as many as one hundred calls before anyone expresses interest in opening an account. That's the normal "batting average" for telephone sales in securities. In making those hundred calls, prospects hang up abruptly, waste the caller's time with questions and then don't place an order, and say no scores of times. By the time someone shows some interest—enough to ask questions—the caller is primed to provide all the information you want.

Here are some legitimate questions to ask:

* Where did you get my name?

* Why is this stock suitable for me?

* What risks are involved?

* Will you speak to my lawyer and/or accountant?

* Where is the stock traded?

* What are the market making sources?

* Which regulatory agency governs your firm?

* What if I want to withdraw from this investment in the future? Am I locked in, or is there an adequate resale market?

* Where can I get references about your firm or you?

* When can we meet to discuss things further?

You at least know whether you are dealing with someone who is legitimate and who has a sense of professional expertise. You can take things from there.

You can be more active in selecting a broker. You may decide to open an account with a particular firm and then try to find an AE within the firm. Or you might simply look for a broker who seems to be able to meet your investment objectives. In either case, you can start by asking friends, relatives, and business associates about their brokers. Particularly, you might ask:

* Have you been pleased with your broker?

* Have the recommendations, on the whole, worked out well?

* What are your investment goals, growth (short term or long), yield, diversification, Blue Chip, safety of principal, and is your broker responsive to them?

* Does the broker respond to your calls? Call back promptly? Do you get requested information quickly?

* What about the firm? How are your accounts handled? Are mistakes corrected promptly? Do you get your monthly statement on time?

* Do you think your broker would be able to handle the account?

* Are there monthly carrying charges?

Again, look at it from the AE's point of view. Most successful brokers, who have endured in the business for any length of time, rely on word of mouth for references. Sometimes they even actively solicit references from their existing clients. A good AE knows that the best kind of "prospecting" is to provide quality service to present customers. This is the type of broker you should seek out—one who will work with you on a professional level.

Once you have the names of several AEs, phone each of them. They will be happy to answer your questions if you express interest in opening an account. Nevertheless, have your questions ready. Most AEs work in a hectic environment, many handling up to 200 accounts. Don't be surprised if the salesperson asks to meet with you after business hours.

Whether on the phone or face-to-face, here are some questions to have answered:

* How does the broker plan to handle your account, given your investment goals?

* Will you be notified promptly of favorable opportunities to buy and/or sell.

* Has the broker worked at any other firms? Which ones?

* What kind of services does the firm provide?

* What's the commission rate? When does an investor qualify for special rates? (Don't forget that rates are negotiable. You might be eligible for a special rate.)

And, if you wish, you can write the Securities and Exchange Commission (SEC) or National Association of Securities Dealers (NASD). These regulatory agencies will not endorse a person or an agency, but they can advise you as to whether a broker or firm is registered to do business and whether there have been any disciplinary proceedings. These addresses are:

U.S. Securities and Exchange Commission
Public Reference Room
Washington, DC 20549
202-272-7450

National Association of Securities Dealers
1735 K Street N.W.
Washington, DC 20006
202-728-8000

Once you get the right answers to your questions, determine your own investment objectives, and select an account executive, the salesperson will have some questions for you that probe your financial status. How much income you earn per year ... how much money you have in accounts or other investments ... how much you have to invest ... and so on. These are questions that people don't normally ask of one another. Yet the AE is required to know everything possible about your financial worth, as well as your personal tolerance of risk: Are you a risk taker or risk avoider? Be prepared to make full disclosure to the AE. Doing so is in the best interests of both of you.

THE SALES ASSISTANT

In most brokerage sales offices, one person serves as an assistant to every two or three account executives. This person handles routine calls from customers, follows up on paper work, takes messages, keeps the files, and in general does the office work and, when necessary, is the back office liaison connected with securities sales. This person is known as the "sales assistant," and although they typically are not registered, like AEs, they need to know a great deal about investment products, the markets, and regulations.

When the account executive calls a customer to say that the missing dividend check has been located, the sales assistant was probably the one who found it.

When the AE explains how a margin error has been corrected in a customer's account, the assistant likely straightened things out.

When the AE sends the client a corrected confirmation statement or monthly statement, the assistant made the call to the appropriate "back office" department to find out what happened.

These "behind the scenes" people can help you on many a routine matter. They may *not* help you with investment advice, express opinions on a particular stock, or take an order. They may, however, help you get mistakes corrected and answer questions about the firm's policies, procedures, and current quotes and prices.

Customer brokers and sales assistants are the brokerage firm employees that the investing public know best. The rep takes investors' orders and passes them on to the "marketplace," where they are logged in and, in turn, forwarded to other firm employees who actually participate in the stock market. These are the traders who get the clients' orders executed in the over-the-counter market or the floor members who get the job done on an exchange.

CHAPTER 5

The Secondary Market:

Executing Orders on the Exchange Floor

The client's order is passed from the sales desk to the order room, usually through a telecommunications link. From there, it is routed to one of two places for execution: an exchange floor or an over-the-counter trading desk. Although these markets share some characteristics, they are different in a number of ways. In this and the next chapter we will see how orders are executed on an exchange. Executing orders in the over-the-counter market is the subject of Chapter 7.

THE NEW YORK STOCK EXCHANGE

To visitors at the New York Stock Exchange, the trading floor may seem a study in confusion: people taking calls at banks of telephones along the walls, crowds milling at trading posts, pages pushing through clusters of brokers, great electronic ticker tape screens suspended from girders along the ceiling and flashing coded trading information. Tens of millions of transactions take place here every trading day. Yet despite the hectic pace and apparent chaos, an organized and effective system is in effect and orders can be executed here, accurately, in a matter of seconds.

While the New York Stock Exchange is not the only exchange in the country, it is certainly the oldest and, in terms of volume, the biggest. At the exchange are traded some of the largest corporations in the country: IBM, AT&T, General Motors, and the like. NYSE is therefore often regarded as the prototype of exchanges—the "Big Board." As such, it is used as the model of exchange trading for this chapter.

The NYSE Floor

The exchange floor consists of separate trading rooms, all connected by passageways that allow members to walk from room to room to execute orders. Each room contains mechanical and electronic equipment for use in the transaction of business:

1. Most of the stock securities listed on the exchange trade in the *main* room.

2. The *garage* is a nickname for a smaller trading area located next to the main room. It was built many years ago when a lack of space became a problem. Why the "garage"? Because that was what the room was once used as.

3. The *blue* room, even smaller than the garage, is on the other side of the main room. It was built in the late 1960s when the volume of activity on the floor increased rapidly. Why the "blue room"? That's the color of the walls.

Stocks are traded at specific locations on the floor called "trading posts." Each post is a horseshoe-shaped structure with an outside circumference of 26 to 31 feet. At each post a number of assigned stocks are traded in "round lots." (A round lot is 100 shares.) The only exception is that some stocks are traded in 10-share units at another trading post called "Post 30." At this large tablelike structure, located in a corner of the garage, most of the inactive preferred stocks listed on the NYSE are traded in lots of 10 shares. Because of their inactivity, the trading unit assigned is 10.

Around the edge of the trading rooms are telephone booths, used by member organizations to

* Receive orders from their offices

* Distribute orders to brokers for execution

* Transmit details of the executed orders and pertiment trading information back to their offices

The Players on the Floor

Only members are allowed to do business on the floor. Membership, or "seats on the exchange," may be transferred or sold subject to the approval of the governing body of the exchange. The price of a seat, like that of a stock, depends largely on the forces of supply and demand. New York Stock Exchange members are usually categorized according to their activities. There are

* Floor brokers

* Two-dollar brokers

* Competitive traders

* Competititve market makers

* Bond brokers

* Specialists

Each group is assigned a *primary* function.

Figure 5–1. Layout of the NYSE Floor.

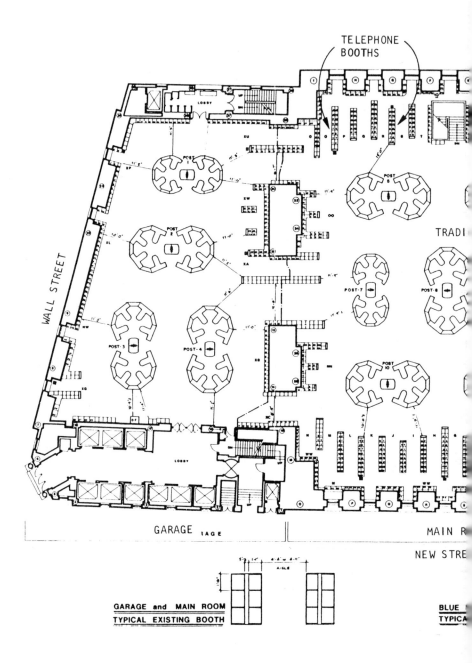

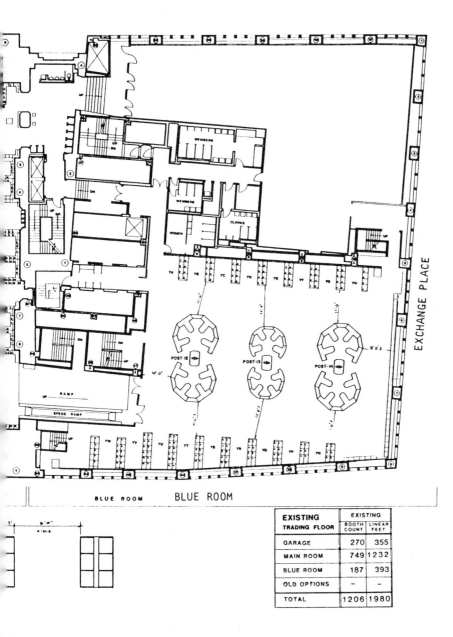

EXISTING TRADING FLOOR	EXISTING	
	BOOTH COUNT	LINEAR FEET
GARAGE	270	355
MAIN ROOM	749	1232
BLUE ROOM	187	393
OLD OPTIONS	–	–
TOTAL	1206	1980

Floor brokers, also known as commission house brokers, working on the exchange floor, execute the orders of public customers of their firm.

Very often, commission house brokers are unable to handle the volume of orders they receive. Even if these brokers receive only two orders they receive. Even if these brokers receive only two orders at the same time, there can be a problem if the orders are for different securities. If the brokers try to execute two orders at different trading posts, they may miss the market in one or both. In such a situation, brokers may call upon the two-dollar broker.

Two-dollar brokers execute orders in any security for any organization and are paid a commission known as "floor brokerage" for their services. At one time the fee for these services was a flat $2 for each 100-share order executed. Now, however, the fee is fully negotiable according to the difficulty of the execution, the size of the order, and, often, the price of the security. These brokers are also known as "independent brokers" or "agents." (Commission house brokers with available time can also act as two-dollar brokers.)

Competitive traders buy and sell stock for their personal accounts and risk on the floor. To be allowed to do so, they must meet certain financial, trading, and reporting requirements, and their transactions are regulated to prevent them from conflicting with transactions initiated by public customers of member organizations.

Although they attempt to buy and sell profitably for their accounts, competititve traders frequently act as buyers when customers want to sell and as sellers when customers want to buy. In this capacity, they enhance the liquidity of the market and, in so doing, assist the specialists, whose function will be described shortly. Competitive traders may also act as two-dollar brokers to earn brokerage fees, provided they have not traded the same stock for themselves on the same day.

Figure 5–2. The Floor of the American Stock Exchange.

Competitive market makers buy and/or sell stock in any NYSE-listed issue at the request of a floor official or another broker holding a customer's order. They can deal in any stock, which differentiates them from specialists who maintain markets in specific issues assigned to them.

Though competitive market makers may also act as two-dollar brokers for brokerage fees, they may accept only certain types of orders. Also, they may not act for themselves as principal and for others as a two-dollar broker in the same stock during the same trading day.

The *specialist* is the focal point of most of the activity on the exchange floor. Each stock listed on the NYSE is assigned to a specialist unit. For each stock assigned, specialists must maintain a "fair and orderly market" and an "orderly succession of prices." Specialists may not let the price of a stock "run wild." When supply (sellers) greatly exceeds demand (buyers), specialists must act as buyers; they buy the stock with their own money and for their own accounts. When there are more buyers than sellers, they must act as sellers, again for their own accounts. In general, although specialists do not participate in every transaction, they manage the activities of the trading crowd.

Specialists therefore furnish a vital service to the exchange, and to the entire stock market, by providing liquidity and saving it from violent price swings that typically work against the interests of the investing public.

Specialists strive to achieve two things:

* *Price continuity,* which is the degree of price change from one transaction to the next. For example, a stock that moves from 30 to 30¼ on one transaction has better continuity than one that moves quickly from 30 to 31.

* *Market depth,* which is the number of shares associated with the price movement between two or more transactions. As an example, a stock that

moves from 30 to 30½ in five transactions totaling 5,000 shares has greater depth than one that moves from 30 to 30½ in five transactions totaling 1,000 shares.

Specialists pool their financial resources and expertise to form "specialist units." Each unit is responsible for maintaining fair and orderly markets in the securities assigned to its members.

In the next chapter, the crucial duties of the specialist will be explained further.

THE AUCTION SYSTEM

The exchange market is known as an "auction market" because trading takes place by open outcry and prices are determined by exchange members who call out bids and offers. This is just another way of saying that trading takes place at prices determined by supply and demand.

Along the walls of the exchange are telephone clerks who are employed by member firms and who take orders from the order room or trading areas of the firm. They pass the orders along to the firm's commission house brokers who then take the order to the trading post, where the stock specified in the order is traded. At the trading post, the members of the exchange who are involved in the purchase and sale of the particular issue are referred to as the *trading crowd.*

Arriving at the post, the member broker first asks for the current market in the security but does not reveal the terms of the order. This request is actually for the *quote,* which consists of the bid and offer prices, as well as their *size* (that is, how many shares are being quoted). The size is always in round lots. The "bid" is the highest price that brokers are willing to pay for a number of shares. The "offer" is the lowest price at which brokers are willing to sell. The difference between the bid and offer prices is the "spread." Only the highest bid and the lowest offer may be quoted. It is the responsibility of the specialist acting as on-floor market maker to maintain the quote. Each and every stock is assigned to a specialist.

* 27½ bid—27¾ offered, 200 by 100. This quotation means that 2 lots, or 200 shares, are wanted at 27½, and 1 lot, or 100 shares, is being offered for sale at 27¾. The spread is ¼ point (27¾ less 27½) and is expressed as "twenty-seven-and-one-half to three-quarters, two by one."

* 63⅞ bid—64⅛ offered, 2 up. This quotation means that 200 shares are wanted at 63⅞ and 200 shares are offered at 64⅛. The spread is a quarter-point (64⅛ less 63⅞).

The specialist, acting as a market maker, supplies the quotation at the request of the broker. If the broker has an order that can't be executed at the specialist's bid or offer, he can (depending on the type of order he is holding) start bidding (if buying) or offering (if selling), as long as his prices are either equal to the price of the bid or offer, or better. This means bidding or offering "inside" the spread. For example, the specialist is quoting the market at 42½ bid and offered at 42¾. If a broker is holding an order to buy at 42⅝, he can start bidding in the trading crowd. The same rule applies to sellers. Brokers cannot offer stock for sale in the crowd unless their price is equal to or lower than the prevailing offer. Remember that the quote consists of the best (highest) bid and the best (lowest) offer.

The trading crowd uses a language all its own. To avoid confusion and misunderstandings, brokers must state their bids and offers as prescribed by the exchange. Bids are announced as "price for size." When bidding for a stock, a broker says something like,

* "35½ for 2...

* 12⅝ for 7...

* 54 for 3."

The word "for" indicates that the broker is buying. Similarly, an offer is announced as "size at price." The word "at" means that a broker is selling:

* "2 at 28...
* 10 at 15¾...
* 6 at 43½."

Notice again that size is quoted by lots and not by shares. Accepting a bid or offer also requires a certain wording. To accept, or "hit," the bid, the broker says "Sold!" This one word finalizes a transaction and can cause a change in the market through the entry of a new series of bids and offers in the stoic. To accept an offer, the broker says "Take it!" As long as brokers and traders accept bids and/or take offers, stock prices are constantly fluctuating.

HOW ORDERS ARE EXECUTED IN THE CROWD

Three basic types of orders are allowed on the exchange floor.

1. A *market order* is to be immediately executed as soon as the broker enters the trading crowd at the best available price. A market order to buy stock requires a purchase at the lowest, meaning the best, offering price available at the time the broker enters the crowd. A market order to sell stock that is owned by a customer (meaning "long stock") requires a sale at the highest "best" bid price available at the time of entry.

If brokers fail to carry out the instructions of a market order, they have "missed the market." Their firm may be required to reimburse the customer promptly for any loss resulting from the error. But brokers don't miss the market often. When they do, their error is usually caused by their misplacing the order after receiving it from the telephone clerk, or by accepting too many market orders in different securities at the same time.

2. A *limit order* sets the maximum price that the customer is willing to pay as a buyer, or the minimum price that he or she is willing to accept as a seller. A member cannot disobey the customer's instructions by paying more to buy or by selling for less than the specified price.

A price limitation, however, always includes an "or better" qualification. That is, if members can buy the stock below the limit or sell it for more, then they have to do so immediately. If brokers fail to finalize an order that can be carried out according to the customer's wishes, they may be held financially responsible for missing the market. If commission brokers get to the crowd and cannot execute a limit order right away because a customer's requested limit price is currently unavailable, they generally cannot wait at the post very long. Other orders may be coming in—maybe orders for other stocks trading at other posts. In these situations, the order is left with the specialist who puts the order "on the book" and executes it for a fee, called "floor brokerage," when the market permits. The broker is then free to get on to other business.

3. A *stop order* is a "memorandum" that becomes a market order only if a transaction takes place at or through the "stop" price stated in the memorandum. That transaction is called the *electing* or *activating sale.* Stop orders may be entered for a variety of reasons as "buy stop" or "sell stop," depending on their purpose.

A buy stop order is placed above the present market level for one of the following reasons:

* To reduce a loss on an existing short position. (This subject is discussed further later in the chapter.)

* To purchase a security if a transaction at the stated price creates a technical buy signal.

* To preserve a profit on a previously established short position.

For example, a customer sells a stock short at 28, anticipating a drop in value. (A short sale is a sale of stock that the seller does not own in the expectation of a drop in prices.) She can suffer a substantial loss if the price rises higher than 28 contrary to her original expectations. To protect herself against loss caused by an upward move in price, she can enter a buy stop order at a price higher than 28, for instance 28½. If the price rises to 28½ or above, the memorandum becomes a market order to buy, and the broker purchases the stock immediately the best available price. The best available price, however, is unknown until the stop order is activated and becomes a market order and is actually executed. It is therefore impossible to determine the exact loss until the purchase is carried out.

A sell stop order is placed at a price below the present market level for one of the following reasons:

* To preserve a profit for a stock previously purchased at a lower price.

* To initiate a short position by a short sale (but only if a transaction at the stated price creates a technical sell signal).

* To reduce a loss on a present stock holding.

Example: A customer purchases a stock at 35 and watches it rise to 43. As it continues to move higher, he will most likely want to hold onto that security. But if it begins to drop, the paper profit will soon disappear and a sharp decline could lead to a loss. So the investor enters a sell stop order at a price below 43, at 42½ for example, and tries to preserve most of his paper profits in the event of a rapid decline in price. If the price falls to 42½ or lower, his stop memorandum is activated and becomes a market order to sell at the best available price. The exact profit can be determined only when the actual sale takes place.

ADDITIONAL INSTRUCTIONS ON ORDERS

Limit and stop orders may be qualified by additional instructions that can affect the tactics and/or timing of the brokers in the trading crowd.

Day order. This is valid only for the trading day on which it is entered. All orders are automatically regarded as day orders, unless specified differently.

Good-till-canceled (GTC). A GTC order, or "Open order," remains valid until the customer cancels it or until it is executed.

Some brokerage firms accommodate their customers by accepting orders good through the week, through the month, or through a specified day. Because these orders may not be entered on the trading floor, they must be entered as straight GTC orders. The member firm assumes responsibility for canceling the order if it cannot be executed by the close of business on the specified date. If the firm fails to do so, it must accept any financial liability resulting from its error.

Not held (NH). This allows a floor broker to use personal judgment in determining the price and the time of execution of an order, although sometimes the discretion is for only a ⅛ or ¼ point. Brokers are "not held" responsible for missing the market if their judgment proves to be wrong. Specialists can never accept this instruction from a customer because their primary responsibility is to maintain a fair and orderly market, not to trade on behalf of customers.

Participate but do not initiate (PNI). Institutional customers may use the PNI instruction to buy or sell large orders of stock as long as such activity does not create a new price. This type of transaction allows buyers or sellers to accumulate or distribute shares without disturbing the market forces.

All or None (AON). This customer wants to buy (or sell) a sizable quantity of stock at one time and at a designated price. Brokers are prohitibed from announcing this instruction in the trading crowd. They must inquire about the quotation and quality and watch market conditions carefully, until *both* the price and quantity available can satisfy the order. It's all or none. Only then may the brokers execute the order. Normally, AON orders are left with the specialist, and are normally in large size and are used by institutions to test the available depth of the market.

Fill or Kill (FOK). This instruction calls for the immediate and complete purchase or sale of a specified amount of stock, or no execution at all. If the broker cannot fill the order immediately upon entering the crowd, the order is automatically canceled (that is, "killed"). The order is an immediate depth tester and often used to obtain a better price inside the spread on a here and now basis.

Immediate or Cancel (IOC). The customer wants all or part of the order executed promptly, as soon as it is entered in the trading crowd, with the unexecuted portion of the order canceled immediately. When the floor broker makes the bid (or offer):

* If someone responds but only partially fills the order, the broker accepts, cancels the unsatisfied portion of the bid (offer), withdraws from the trading area, and reports partial success to the customer.

* If no one responds, the broker withdraws the bid (offer), leaves the trading area, and reports to the customer that the order has been canceled. The order is similar to the Fill or Kill except that the customer is willing to accept less than all.

Scale order. Scale orders are multiple limit orders that are entered at various prices but at the same time. Multiples of round lots (100 shares) may be either bought at prices called down from a given value or sold at prices scaled up from a given value. Let's say that the customer places a scale order to buy 400 shares, the first 100 at 51, and then each 100 of the remaining shares at execution prices that are successively ⅛ point lower. This order means that 100 shares are to be bought at 51, 100 at 49⅞. 100 at 49¾, and 100 at 49⅝. This is an example of scaling down. Another customer places a scale order to sell 300 shares, 100 at 15½, "scaled up" ¼ point for the remaining 200 shares. With this order, 100 shares are sold at 15½, 100 at 15¾, and 100 at 16.

In either case, the purpose is to obtain a favorable "average" purchase or sale price. That's the advantage. The disadvantage is that the entire order may never be carried out unless the stock fluctuates in a wide enough price range.

At the close. On the stock exchange, this type of order is executed at the close of the trading day. The end of trading is signaled by the ringing of a bell for 30 seconds. However, this may not be the final trade in that security; another broker could have better timing during those last 30 seconds.

Alternative (either/or). The broker has been furnished with two alternatives: either to buy at a limit as soon as possible, or to buy the same security at market. Execution of one part of the order automatically cancels the other. With this type of order, a customer is trying to buy at a given price, if possible, and, if not, to purchase the security regardless.

Sell plus. The broker has either a market or a limit order to sell a security at a price higher than the previously priced transaction for the stock. For example, if the previous price was 36, then the current sale price for a sell plus order would be 36⅛.

Buy minus. The broker has a market or limit order to purchase a security at a price lower than the previously priced transaction for that stock. For instance, if the previous price was 54, then the current execution price for this order would be 53⅞.

Switch (contingent or swap) order. The customer enters a limit order to sell (or buy) one stock. When it is executed, he or she enters a limit or market order to buy (or sell) another stock. The transaction may also be called a "proceeds sale" if the proceeds of the sell order are used to make the purchase on the buy order.

Cancellation. Although a cancellation is not really an order, it can significantly influence floor trading activities. A cancellation is the revocation or modification of a buy or sell order, an action that is allowed at any time before the execution of an order.

Crossing Stock

To "cross stock," a broker combines, or pairs off, a purchase order with a sell order in the same security at the same time and same price but for different customers. Let's look at an example. Customer A enters a market order to buy 2,000 shares of Chrysler at the same time that customer B enters a market order to sell long 2,000 shares of Chrysler. Both orders are given to the same floor broker, who carries the orders to the Chrysler crowd. Each stock trades in its own designated location, at a post, referred to as "the crowd," which is of course managed by its assigned specialist. The broker, if market conditions permit, may cross the orders—that is, execute both orders at the same time—by having customer A buy from customer B. The purpose of the cross is to permit both A and B to obtain a better price. To cross stock, the broker must make certain of three things. First, the stock has to be crossed at its assigned trading post and within the quotation prevailing there. Second, the spread must be at least a ¼ point when the broker enters the trading area; an ⅛ point is not large enough for crossing within the spread. The broker must pair off the orders at a price within the quotation. If the stock were quoted 13–13¼, the intended cross would occur at 13⅛, not at 13. A quotation of 13–13⅛ doesn't leave any room between the bid and offer prices to arrange a cross, because the trade has to be made at either 13 or 13⅛; it cannot be made within the quotation. Third, the broker must give either customer a brief opportunity to improve on the price at which the orders are to be crossed or paired off. To do so, the crossing broker momentarily either bids ⅛ point lower or offers ⅛ point higher than the crossing price.

A short sale is the sale of a stock that the investor does not own. Accordingly, the seller is considered to be "short" the security. The principle of the successful short sale is to "sell high and buy low" at a later date, typically in anticipation of a price decline. The seller's brokerage firm borrows stock for delivery to the buyer's firm. The selling firm can arrange this "stock loan" by borrowing the stock from its own vault or from another firm. The selling investor pays interest on the borrowed stock, just as he or she would on the loan of money. When the customer closes the short position by buying the stock in the open market, the stock is given back to the lender. To insure that the stock borrowed is returned, a short sale can only be transacted in a margin account. Of all transactions, short sellers assume the most risk.

An example will clarify how a short sale works. Customer Patel sells 100 shares of Hitek short at 30⅛, expecting it to drop in price. Her brokerage firm, Langley and Bros., takes 100 shares of Hitek from its vault to make delivery to the buyer firm on settlement day.

A week later, Hitek's price has dropped to 27¼. Patel places a market order to buy 100 shares, which she uses to close the open short position. The shares are returned to the Langley vault. This order closes the short position profitably. Patel received $3,012.50 on the short sale, bought the stock at $2,725.00, and closed the position at a profit of $287.50. Even deducting commissions, fees, and interest charges, the short sale is a success.

Not all short sales are so successful. If the stock should rise in price after the short sale, the short position becomes more and more of a losing situation.

Again, all short sales must be executed in a margin account (which is explained in Chapter 10). Also, short sales may not be executed when they are likely to increase the momentum of a down trading market. The SEC requires that a short sale has to be executed on a "plus tick" or zero plus tick, referred to as "upticks." That is, the trade must be made at a price that is higher than the last different regular-way sale of the security.

For example, if the last transaction in Hitek was at 30, Patel's short sale order could not be executed at a lower price. A transaction at 30⅛ would, of course, constitute an uptick.

The short sale can also be made on "zero plus tick," which is a price equal to that of the preceding transaction but higher than the last different price. Let's say that two round lots of Hitek trade at 29⅞ and 30, in that order. A short sale may be executed on the next trade at 30 or higher. The first trade at 30 is a plus tick; it represents an advance in the price. The second trade at 30 is a zero plus tick, and the seller in that trade is permitted to have been a short seller.

You'll recall that stock from the vault was given to whoever bought it in Patel's short sale. A question might arise as to whether the lender is entitled to receive dividends that may be declared on the stock. The answer is yes. Securities lenders are still entitled to receive any dividends paid during the time the securities are loaned. The short seller is responsible for protecting the lender's interests, and paying dividends personally, even when the lender's certificates are reregistered into the name of the new buyer.

To ensure this protection, the lending firm must maintain accurate records of all securities loaned. If the issuing corporation declares a cash dividend, the borrowing firm sends the lending firm a check for the dividend amount. The customer whose certificates may have been loaned never realizes that the broker/dealer no longer possesses the security. The short seller's margin account is debited with the actual amount of the dividend or interest on the "record date," the day the short seller becomes liable for that payment. (More about dividends is to be found in Chapter 10.)

Institutional Trades

Selling or buying a large block of stock—such as 100,000 shares or more—by an institutional investor could be an upsetting influence on the market depending on the stock. In such a case, the brokerage firm may request permission from the NYSE to use one of the following special block procedures:

* Exchange distributions or acquisitions

* Special offerings or bids

* Secondary distributions

Let's use an example to explain an *exchange distribution.* An institutional client of a brokerage firm, a pension fund, intends to sell 100,000 shares of CNF. The seller certifies in writing to the NYSE that it owns all the shares and that the amount in question represents all of the security to be marketed for a reasonable period. The brokerage firm, rather than going directly to the floor, asks other firms (generally one or two) to canvass their clients for offsetting purchase orders (which are not binding). Once the selling member firm is assured of sufficient purchasing interest, the large sell order and all the buy orders are sent to the floor of the exchange, where they are officially "crossed at the current market price." The pension fund pays everyone's "special commission." The transaction is printed on the ticker tape and identified by the letters "DIST" preceding the security symbol and volume.

If the pension fund wanted to purchase a large block of stock, the transaction is called an *exchange acquisition*. The fund's brokerage firm would solicit buyers, the stock would be crossed, and the letters "ACQ" would identify the transaction on the ticker tape.

A *secondary distribution* involves an amount of listed stock so very large that it cannot be normally handled on the exchange. It is better handled "off the floor," that is, over the counter. Often the distribution is handled collectively by a number of brokerage firms, acting either as dealers (buying and then reselling the stock as in a firm underwriting) or as brokers (selling on behalf of the institutional customer and taking commissions). Since the block is sold off board by a group of firms, somewhat similar to a primary offering, the transaction is called a "secondary distribution."

Such an enormous transaction has to meet a number of requirements:

* The selling brokerage firm must obtain the permission of the exchange.

* The fixed price of the distribution may not be higher than the last security transaction on the exchange at the point that the offering commences.

* The seller absorbs all commissions.

* All buy orders on the exchange floor whose prices are equal to or higher than the offering's price must be satisfied first.

* If the offering starts (as is often the case) after exchange trading hours, the distributor must make the special price available for at least 30 minutes after the close.

Although the ticker tape does not show the actual transactions in such an offering (they are "off board"), it announces its completion or continuance from day to day, as the case may be.

All the rules and regulations—whether required by the SEC, the exchange, or the firms themselves—have one thing in common: to maintain just and equitable principles of trade. For the market to be *fair* for everyone in it, the forces of supply and demand have to be allowed to determine prices. But it's not a perfect world. Given the liberty, some market participants would orchestrate transactions so as to manipulate prices. Others, in sincere attempts to protect their interests, might place orders that would work against stability. Therefore, for even a free market to be orderly, you need rules and regulations.

But you also need something else. Every second of the trading day, the buy orders and sell orders exert pressures on the price of a stock to go up or down. What rule or regulation can dictate what is to be done in every fleeting situation? When, at any given moment, is the market stable and when is it threatening to become volatile? What is needed is someone on the trading floor whose primary duty is to watch each stock, moment to moment, and to do instantly whatever is necessary to maintain a fair and orderly market. That person is the specialist, who is the subject of the next chapter.

CHAPTER 6

The Specialist:

Riding the Bulls and Bears

On the exchange floor, the forces of supply and demand take the form of orders to sell and orders to buy, respectively. When the sell orders outnumber the buy orders, stock prices tend to go down. With more buy orders at the trading post, prices tend to rise. The greater the preponderance of one type of order over the other, the faster and farther prices can move. When there is excessive, one-sided buying or selling volume, this is when you see dramatic price fluctuations, that is, great volatility.

The psychology of buying and selling stock—of supply and demand—is such that lopsided volume spurs more volume. As holders of a stock see prices dropping sharply, they decide to sell—selling tends to cause more selling. As would-be owners of a stock see prices rising, they decide to buy—buying tends to cause more buying. Either way, as they enter their orders, they create more volume on one side of the market and increase the force of supply or demand. This increased volume draws more orders to sell or to buy, thus creating even faster price movements. It's a self-perpetuating cycle of more volume, bigger price movements, still more volume. This is when prices move too quickly for investors to react properly—to sell a stock that is losing value rapidly, for instance. And this is when investors get hurt in the stock market. Left unchecked, the cycle can lead to precariously high-priced stocks and, worse, to selling panics and crashes.

On the other hand, if a stock is not trading at all—that is, if volume is zero—it would draw very little investor interest. Such a lack of liquidity would cause prospective owners to buy at much higher-than-normal prices and to sell at much lower-than-normal levels. Many a stock would not trade at all under such conditions.

The role of the specialist is to eliminate the temporary disparities between supply and demand. When, for instance, sell orders outweigh buy orders, specialists must and will buy stock to absorb the sales. They'll also take the sell side, given a greater number of buy orders. Either way, they put a brake on the cycle. Similarly, if an order comes in for a stock that no one else is buying or selling, the specialist will become the "other party," or "contra," to the transaction, just to "make a market" in the stock. In either case, specialists do not dictate or change market direction. They simply allow the market value of a stock to rise or fall in reaction to the forces of supply and demand without large or unreasonable price fluctuations. Specialists maintain the "fair and orderly market" which is their responsibility at minimum to no change in price; this is referred to as market continuity.

THE SPECIALIST'S ROLE: AS DEALER, AS BROKER

Specialists on the NYSE fulfill their responsibilities in two capacities: To begin with, once a corporation lists its stock on either the NYSE, or the American Stock Exchange it is assigned to a specialist by the Allocations Committee of that Exchange. Specialists are registered broker-dealers, and the concept is a unique American institution practiced nowhere else.

Specialists provide two main functions:

* As *agents or brokers*, they execute orders on behalf of other floor members and charge a commission for this service, called "floor brokerage." In this capacity, they are acting as agents on behalf of the public customer orders that are left with them. Normally, orders left with the specialist are limit orders, stop orders and other nonmarket order types that are "away from market" and cannot be immediately filled. This process of entrusting an order to a specialist is referred to as placing an order "on the book."

* As *dealers* (or *principals* or *market makers*), they buy and sell stock for their own accounts and with their own money to provide liquidity to the marketplace. In this capacity, they take no commissions; instead, they expect to profit on what they buy and resell.

When floor brokers cannot execute an order immediately, such as in the handling of a limit order that is "away from" the current quote, they may leave the order with the specialist in that stock for execution at a later time. The specialists file all such orders in their book, which is a log of all limit and stop orders left with him for execution. When specialists eventually execute these orders, they do so as agents of the entering brokers on behalf of their customers, and they charge the brokers' firms a commission.

Even as agents, however, specialists must act in the best interests of the market. Given several limit orders for the stock, specialists are always checking the book and will quote the highest bid or lowest offer, as appropriate; that is, the highest price anyone is willing to pay for the stock or the lowest price at which anyone is willing to sell the stock. If these prices are no more than ⅛ or ¼ point from the last sale price when a floor broker enters the trading crowd with a market order to buy or sell a stock, then the specialist executes the limit order and tells the broker the name of the firm that entered the limit order in the book. If all the limit orders are more than ⅛ or ¼ point away from the last sale price, or if there are no limit orders logged in their books, then specialists may execute trades for their own accounts. Under no circumstances may specialists compete with orders in their books, that is, by selling at the same price ahead of orders entrusted with him.

When specialists buy or sell for their own accounts, they are acting as *dealers* or *market makers*. Although the specialists' passive role as brokers' agents is an important one, their active role as dealer/market makers is critical to the maintenance of a fair and orderly market and to the proper functioning of the auction market.

When a market order arrives at the post and none of the "book" orders is near the last sale, specialists are expected and are required to bid for or offer stock from their own accounts at a price variation reasonably close to, or at, the last sale. In so doing, specialists prevent wide price fluctuations and assure that each transaction bears a price relationship close to the prior transaction. Again this is referred to as maintaining price continuity. (Actual price variations will depend on the size or volume of the transaction.)

For example, the last sale in CMF stock was 50, the best public bid on the specialist's book is 49½, and the best public offer in the book is 50½. (Assume that there is no other broker in the crowd.) A broker who wants to buy 100 shares at the market in this instance without a specialist would purchase at 50½, the offer price. Similarly, a broker seeking to sell 100 shares without a specialist would receive 49½, the bid price. The specialist, who must provide price continuity with reasonable depth and limit price fluctuations, is expected to narrow the quote spread and is obligated to improve the market by making a better (higher) bid and/or a better (lower) offer for his own account. A one-point spread between 49½–50½ is excessively wide and will cause wide price variations. The narrowest spread is one-eighth. For a stock that is bid 49½, if the stock is reasonably active and liquid, the widest spread you should expect is one-quarter of a point.

The price and size of specialists' quotations, either for orders on the book or for their own accounts, must be firm. Again, specialists may not compete at the same price with public orders on their books.

Supply and demand cause price movements; specialists do not establish price. They adjust their bid and offer prices depending on the size, prices, and types of orders logged in their books and/or executed at the post. The aim of the specialists' trades is to "stabilize" the market by counterbalancing the force of supply and/or demand. In fact about 95 percent of all specialists' transactions as dealers (or "principals") are aimed at stabilizing the market trend. But how do specialists know the trend? They watch the rice of the last sale.

To stabilize a market:

* *They sell on a plus tick (+) or a zero plus tick (0+).* A "plus tick" is a sale made at a price higher than the previous sale. For example, if the last sale was at 50⅛ ($50.125), a plus tick sale would be at 50¼ ($50.25) *or higher.* A "zero plus tick" is a sale at the same price as that of the previous sale but higher than the last different price. For instance, let's say that sales occur at 50, 50⅛, and again at 50⅛. The second sale at 50⅛. The second sale at 50⅛ is a zero plus tick because it is the same as the prior sale but higher than the last different sale of 50.

* *They buy on a minus tick (–) or zero minus tick (0–).* A "minus tick" is a price lower than that of the last sale. If the price moves from 50⅛ to 50, the second sale is a minus tick. A "zero minus tick" is the same price as the last sale, but lower than the last different price. In a series of transactions at 50⅛, 50, and 50, the second sale at 50 is a zero minus tick.

Here is a series of transaction prices and the corresponding indicators:

50	Initial sale
50⅛ +	Plus
50⅛ +	Zero plus
50¼ +	Plus
50¼ +	Zero plus
50⅛ –	Minus
50⅛ –	Zero minus
50 –	Minus
50⅛ +	Plus

Accordingly, to counterbalance selling in the market, which will cause a price drop, the specialist is expected to purchase stock to stabilize the selling trend on downticks. Similarly, to stabilize an uptrend caused by buying, specialist dealer sales activity should be on upticks.

HOW AUTOMATION AND TELECOMMUNICATION AFFECT THE ROLE OF THE SPECIALIST

As a result of increased activity and volume over the years, all exchanges have had to speed up order handling to provide efficient and prompt execution. So the exchanges developed computer-assisted order routing systems, permitting member firms to transmit small orders directly to the specialist post without intervention by the floor broker.

These systems therefore enable member firms to use their floor brokers more efficiently to handle larger orders.

To accommodate small round-lot market orders, the NYSE makes use of an automated system known as *Designated Order Turnaround* (DOT). The American Stock Exchange uses a similar system called Post Execution Reporting (PER). This computerized, message-switching system connects subscribing member firms with the trading posts on the exchange floor. Orders of up to 5,099 shares can be entered through the system and be received within seconds at the appropriate trading post for immediate execution by the specialist. Bypassing the firm's telephone clerks, the DOT system eliminates the need for commission house brokers or two-dollar brokers to physically transport orders and execute them at the trading posts. The system thus saves precious time in processing small market orders. Transaction reports are routed back to the originating firm through the same system.

This system also handles odd-lot orders of up to 99 shares, either separately or simultaneously with round-lot orders. Over the years, more and more firms have come to use such systems, and technological enhancements have improved them. Gradually, the systems have been upgraded to accept larger market orders, limit orders, and odd-lot orders. Today, exchanges and their members can guarantee one-price executions up to certain limits on system-generated orders. Telecommunication is also having an effect on exchange floor activities, particularly those of the specialist. Congress saw the need to connect other market centers that traded the same securities as the NYSE or Amex, such as the Boston Cincinnati, the Midwest, Pacific, and Philadelphia Stock Exchanges, as well as NYSE-listed stocks that are traded also in the OTC market. The latter is referred to as the third market. The intent of Congress was to provide public customers with the best price regardless of the exchange and the OTC market on which a stock is traded. From this need evolved the *Intermarket Trading System* (ITS), a linkage of all exchanges that trade the same stocks.

While this system certainly benefits public customers by fostering competition, it has its complications. One is that professional market makers in other parts of the country can access the primary market on the floors of the NYSE and Amex, and NYSE and Amex specialists are afforded access to regional markets as well. Another complication is that the floor brokers and specialists on the NYSE or Amex are obligated to comply with additional rules and procedures.

Foremost among the rules is the one that requires *preopening notification*, whereby specialists must solicit interest, whether among public customers or principals, from other market centers when the opening price is an ITS stock is expected to exceed agreed-upon guidelines. Not to do so would cause wide variations between the exchanges in dually listed stocks. Other rules prohibit:

* Trading through and honoring better bids and/or offers that are away from the market.

* Causing a locked market, either by posting a bid in an ITS security at a price equal to or higher than a published offer on another market center, or by offering it at a price equal to or lower than a published bid on another market center.

The linkage of market centers within the United States has prompted some exchanges to explore international connections and continuous after hours trading. With the demand for increased order flow and volume, longer trading hours, and improved automation through computerization, the NYSE and Amex are continually seeking to tap underused resources and find other ways to expand business.

OTHER DUTIES OF THE SPECIALIST

It is fair to say that the specialist is involved, not always directly, but at least indirectly, in just about every kind of transaction on the exchange floor. To manage the crowd properly, specialists must be aware of every trade in the assigned stock. In addition to holding and executing limit and stop orders, and otherwise acting as a contra to the market, specialists are involved in

* Short sales

* Stopping stock

* Block sales

* Odd-lot trading

Short Sales

Specialists may sell stock short when necessary to maintain a fair and orderly market. Specialists must sell stock to meet demand whether they have a long or short position in the stock. But the same rule applies to them as to investors: Short sales may be executed only on plus or zero plus ticks. This rule prevents short sellers from driving the stock down, creating public sell interest, and then covering their positions at artificially depressed prices—thus reaping huge profits.

Although short selling seems like a negative force in the marketplace—a downward influence of a stock price—it may actually cause a stock to rise higher. This is called the "cushion" or "short interest" theory. Eventually, short sellers must become buyers to return the stock to the lender; they must reenter the marketplace to cover their initial short sales and realize their profit or limit their loss. In so doing, they exert demand pressure thereby causing upward influence on the stock price.

Stopping Stock

By "stopping stock," specialists guarantee a price on a customer's order, thereby allowing the broker to try to improve on the price without fear of missing the market.

Specialists may grant such a privilege (though they are not obligated to do so) under the following conditions:

* The buy or sell order must be for a public customer's account, not for an exchange member's account.

* The broker must ask for the stop. The specialist cannot solicit such requests from the broker.

* The spread must be at least a ¼ point when the request is made.

* The specialist must be willing and able to trade as principal if necessary to avoid defaulting on the guarantee.

Let's look at an example. Broker Quigley, entering the trading crowd with a market order to buy 100 shares of Hitek, is informed by the specialist that the quotation is 42 to 42½. Ordinarily, Quigley is obliged to buy Hitek at 42¼ or face the risk of having someone else take it, in which case she is guilty of missing the market.

To avoid missing the market, she asks the specialist to "stop" 100 shares at 42¼, which assures her a price no higher than that. If the specialist agrees to stop the stock, Quigley has a chance to acquire it more cheaply by trying to buy the stock at 42¼ inside the quote spread without potential financial liability. To improve the price for the customer and to narrow the spread in the quotation, she bids 42⅛ for the 100 shares. The market is now quoted 42⅛—42¼. If another broker brings a market order to sell into the crowd soon afterward, Quigley buys 100 shares at 42⅛ because her bid of 42⅛ is the highest prevailing bid.

If another broker with a buy order arrives and purchases the stock offered at 42¼ before the seller appears, then Quigley is "stopped out" and forced to pay the guaranteed price of 42¼, guaranteed by the specialist. But Quigley has not missed the market while trying to do better for her customer.

Block Sales

Specialists also act as a conduit for putting together buyers and sellers of large blocks of stock. A block is generally defined as a trade of 10000 shares, or more. As central figures in the marketplace, they usually are aware of selling and buying interest expressed to them in their specialty stocks. To minimize a large sell order's impact on the price of the stock, the specialist contacts other brokers who have expressed a buy interest. If unable to locate enough interest on the opposite side to handle the whole order, the specialist may negotiate a suitable purchase bid with the seller and buy the balance for his or her own account.

There are about 600 specialists on the floor of the exchange, each assigned two or three stocks. This kind of activity goes on in each of those 1,800–2000 trading crowds all day long.

ODD-LOT TRADING

An odd lot is an amount of stock smaller than the normal trading unit. The normal trading unit, or "round lot," is 100 shares. However, as previously mentioned, a relatively few inactive stocks have been assigned a trading unit of 10 shares. An odd lot is therefore a trade from one to 99 shares. Any trade of 100 shares is a round lot. A trade of multiple of 100 shares involves more than one round lot. For example, a 1,000-share trade in a stock would be considered to be ten round lots or trading units.

Although most odd-lot orders are processed through the exchange's computerized facilities, they are executed by specialists who are the designated odd-lot dealers in their stocks. In addition to maintaining an orderly round-lot market, specialists also accommodate odd-lot customers by acting as dealers and filling odd-lot orders. Broker-age firms, acting as agents for their customer, transmit the odd-lot orders to the specialists, who execute the orders as principals. Specialists must buy when a customer wants to sell, and sell when a customer wants to buy. And they must do so at the first possible opportunity after receiving the odd-lot order.

The customer pays two types of charges on odd-lot orders. One is the commission charged by the brokerage firm for its services for processing the order. The commission appears as a separate charge item on the customer's confirmation statement. The second charge is known as the "differential," which is paid to the specialist odd-lot dealer for executing the order.

Let's look at an example. Customer Jones enters a market order to buy 50 shares of B&D. Jones' brokerage firm telecommunicates the order directly to the trading post and charges a commission. When the specialist gets the order, he watches for the next sale in B&D, which is known as the "effective sale." If the next B&D trade takes place at, say, 30, the specialist sells Jones 50 shares of B&D, out of his own inventory, at 30⅛. The ⅛ point tacked on to the effective sale price is the differential and it goes to the specialist as compensation for filling the order. On Jones' confirmation statement, the execution price is "30⅛." The differential is not itemized. While the normal differential is ⅛ point, it may vary.

If Jones had put in an odd-lot sell order, the specialist would have deducted a ⅛ point from the effective sale price. Jones' confirmation would have read "29⅞" and the ⅛-point difference would, again, go to the specialist.

Specialists are not obligated to charge a differential, and often they do not. Usually, no differential is charged to odd-lot orders entered in the following ways:

* At the beginning of the trading day, on the opening transaction in the issue.

* Through the off-the-trading-floor facilities of a few large member organizations.

* Through the NYSE Designated Order Turnaround (DOT) system, if entered as part of a round-lot order.

Neither is the differential charged when a customer enters separate odd-lot orders, all with the same terms and conditions, which add up to a round lot. In such a case, the orders *must* be combined, or bunched, into the trading unit, thereby eliminating the odd-lot differential. Odd-lot orders for separate customers may be bunched as long as the consent of each customer is obtained.

Types of Odd-Lot Orders

All of the following may be entered as day or good-till-canceled orders.

Like round-lot market orders, *odd-lot market orders* require execution at the best available price. Because odd-lot orders may not be bid, offered, or used to initiate transactions, they must wait for an effective round-lot execution.

To sell short on a market order, the effective sale must be higher in value than the last round-lot transaction at a different price. For example, with the last sale on CMF at 40¼, trades occur at 40 and then 40⅛. Because the trade at 40⅛ is at a higher price than that of the previous price of 40, it qualifies as the effective sale for an odd-lot short seller. (This is basically the same requirement as for short sellers of round lots.)

Odd-lot limit orders must all be executed on the first eligible effective sale. Because odd lots are never repre-sented in the quotations, they do not have to wait their turn for execution. And they do not actively compete with one another, as do round-lot orders.

In an *odd-lot limit order to buy,* the effective sale is the first round-lot transaction in that stock that is *below* the limit. When the differential is added to the round-lot price, the execution price may not exceed the customer's maximum price limit. For example, an odd-lot limit order to buy Hitek Industries at 30 must be executed as soon as a round-lot trade in Hitek takes place at 29⅞ or less. When the ⅛-point differential is added to the execution price of 29⅞, the odd-lot trade appears on the customer's confirmation as 30, the same limit designated by the customer.

For a *limit order to sell long,* the effective sale is the first round-lot transaction *above* the limit. When the differential is subtracted from the round-lot price, the execution price may not be below the customer's designated minimum price. For example, an odd-lot order to sell Hitek at 31 must be executed as soon as a round-lot transaction takes place at 31⅛ or higher. When the ⅛-point differential is deducted from the execution price, the odd-lot trade appears on the confirmation as having been executed at a price of 31, as requested.

For a *limit order to sell short,* the effective sale is the first round-lot transaction that is both higher in value than the last different price (that is, an uptick) *and* above the limit stated in the order. Let's say that the last round-lot trade in Hitek was at 30¾, a minus tick, and a customer enters an odd-lot limit order to sell short at a price of 30⅝. If the next round-lot trade in Hitek is at 30¾, the broker may not execute the order. The sale is higher than the odd-lot limit but not higher than the last transaction. If the next round-lot trade is at 30⅞ or higher, the order may be executed because the price is higher than the limit *and* the previous trade. (This rule prevents a short sale from being executed on a downtick, that is, a lower effective sale price.)

The *odd-lot stop order* is a notice addressed to the specialist to buy or sell the odd lot at the market, if and when a round-lot transaction occurs at or through the stop price. The round-lot transaction that activates an odd-lot stop order is called the *electing sale,* and the effective sale is the first transaction following the electing sale. For example, the specialist has an odd-lot stop order to buy Hitek at 29½. The first round-lot transaction at 29½ is the electing (or activating) sale. The stop order is executed, however, on the next round-lot transaction, at *any* price, which becomes the effective sale. The differential is then added to the effective sale price.

The *stop limit order* is treated as normal limit order after the stop is elected, but the next round-lot transaction is not necessarily the effective sale. If the next round-lot transaction is not at least ⅛ point better than the customer's limit, the odd-lot order cannot be executed. If the market moves continuously away from the customer's price, the order may never be executed. As an example, with Hitek at 29⅝, the specialist has an odd-lot sell stop limit order for 29¾ stop, 29¾ limit. A round-lot trade at 29¾ or higher activates the order by electing the stop. If the market moves higher on the next trade, then the order may be executed. If it backs off to 29⅝ or lower, the order may not be executed—and it will not be executed as long as the market moves away from the limit in that direction.

The *on-the-quotation order* is for customers who insist that their odd-lot order be executed immediately. The price is based on the existing round-lot quotation, not the transaction, on the floor of the exchange. The customer can buy at the prevailing offering price plus the differential or sell long at the prevailing bid price minus the differential.

The *at-the-close order* is for customers who wish to buy or sell their stock as near the end of the trading day as possible. An at-the-close order to buy or sell is executed not on the last round-lot sale of the day but on the quotation prevailing when the closing bell stops ringing. Customers may buy at the offering price plus the differential, or sell long at the bid price minus the differential. With a *basis price order,* specialists may execute odd-lot orders at "basis" price, which is a fictitious round-lot price, somewhere within the prevailing bid and offering. This price is used when the issue doesn't trade throughout the day, and when the spread between bid and offering is at least two full points. Basis price executions are available only to customers who deal in stock that trades in 100-share units by the exchange, and they must enter their orders at least 30 minutes before the market closes.

ASSIGNING SECURITIES TO THE SPECIALIST

Specialists lose assigned stocks because issuing companies merge, acquire one another, or delist their stocks. As a result, the competitive environment among specialist units for new listings is fierce. Whenever a qualified company becomes listed on the NYSE, the Allocation Committee of the exchange decides which specialist unit can best service this newly listed corporate stock.

Of great importance in this decision are floor brokers' evaluations of the specialist unit and their past performance. The exchange requests floor brokers to quarterly evaluate specialists' performance in a number of critical categories, such as the quality of their principal market-maker activities, service, staffing, and brokerage function. On the basis of the floor brokers' evaluations and disciplinary actions in the specialist units' files, the Allocation Committee assigns a unit to specialize in the stock. While the committee considers other factors, such as the units' capital, manpower, and expertise, the decision is weighted heavily on performance: The better a particular unit's performance, the more likely it is to be selected by the Allocation Committee.

Given the competition among market centers to attract new listings, listed companies have tremendous input into the selection of its specialist unit. The company may be given a list of units that are performing equally well, along with the opportunity to interview them. The persistent fact remains that the only way for a business—and a specialist unit is a business—to survive and grow is to involve itself with new listings.

The specialist system is unique and is used on the Amex and on the regional exchanges across the country. The Chicago Board Options Exchange (CBOE) also employs a market-maker system. Unlike the specialist on the CBOE, members classified as "market makers" are charged with maintaining a fair and orderly options market. (Other exchange employees, called "board brokers," maintain the public order book.) On the floor of the CBOE, screens display the book market and the market maker's market. Through their competitive bids and offers, the best available market is displayed.

Market makers, whose activities must be conducted at least partially in person, may trade in other than their assigned options—unlike specialists, who are restricted to their assigned stocks. As a result, market makers compete among themselves for executions, and the board brokers make sure that executable book orders are satisfied.

The fact is that in any market in which supply and demand determine prices a moderating influence is needed. In the over-the-counter market, that influence is exerted by the market makers, whom we will meet in the next chapter.

CHAPTER 7

The Secondary Market:

Over-the-Counter Trading

Forty, fifty stories or more above the sidewalks of Manhattan, an open office floor covers the area of half a city block. Inside are paneled and carpeted offices, whose windows command views that extend for miles. Outside these offices are first the assistants' desks and then banks of desks whose main features are computer terminals. Clerks hurry amid the desks, dropping off orders and picking up execution slips.

This is a trading room for a major brokerage firm.

In the middle of the floor, a clerk drops off an order ticket at one of the traders' desks to buy 100 shares of Safeco, Inc.

The trader calls a market maker in Safeco. He obtained the name and telephone number of the market maker from the "pink sheets." Named for their color, these sheets contain an alphabetical list of stocks traded over the counter. They include the names of market-maker brokerage firms in each stock and, of course, the telephone numbers. The pink sheets are published daily.

The trader first attempts to obtain a quote from the market maker, since all trading in every market begins with a quote. The quote consists of the bid, the offer, the size of the bid, and the size of the offer. The bid is the highest purchase price; the offer, the lowest selling price.

"How are you quoting Safeco?" the trader asks, or "What's the market in Safeco?" The inquiry could be as simple as, "How's Safeco?" The market maker on the other end of the phone responds. "Twenty-four and one-half bid, twenty-four and three-quarters offered, five by five."

Figure 7–1. A NASDAQ Screen.

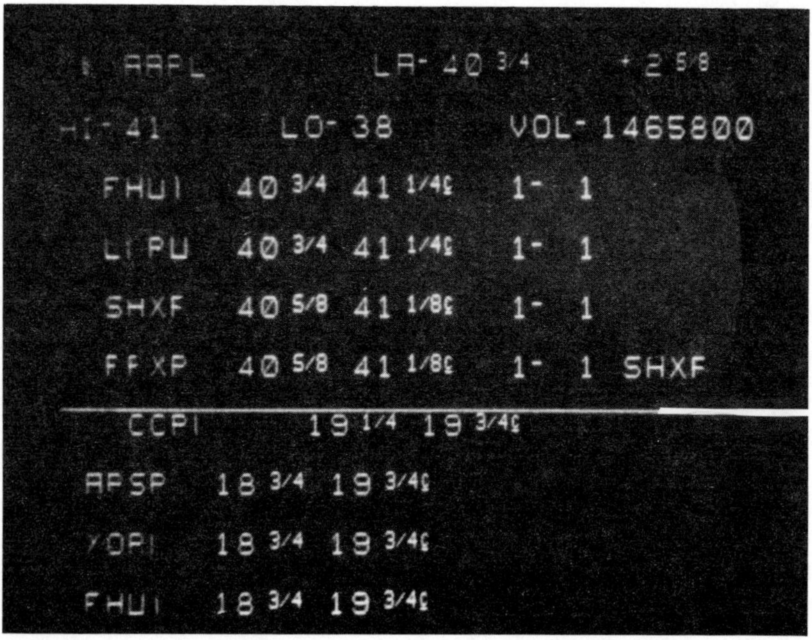

By the time the trader hangs up, only a few seconds later, he is very likely to have executed the order to buy Safeco over the counter for his firm's customer by negotiating the most favorable price available.

This is how an over-the-counter trade is executed.

The OTC market has no trading centers, no geographic boundaries. Instead, it consists of hundreds of brokerage firms located throughout the country and doing business by telephone. These are very often the same brokerage firms that underwrote the issues in the primary offering as the selling syndicate, now acting as "market makers" for the stock in the secondary market. That is, they publish their bids-offer quotations and buy or sell the stock for their own account. In short, they "make a market" for the stock. They are willing to buy or sell the stock at their quoted prices and in round lots. Orders of individual investors to buy or sell the stock are usually filled out of a market maker's inventory.

Firms in the OTC market are generally referred to as "broker/dealers," because they can buy and sell securities either as brokers (agents) or as dealers (principals). As *market maker* (or dealer or principal), the firm can sell the customer stock from its own inventory or buy the security from the customer for its own account. As the customer's *agent* (or broker), the firm can buy the stock from or place the stock with another broker/dealer who is a market maker. Whether acting as agent or principal, broker/dealers must tell their customers in what capacity they acted in filling an order.

When acting as a broker or agent, the firm must disclose to the customer the actual dollar amount of the commission charged.

When trading from the firm's own account, a broker/dealer who fills a customer order directly, as principal, tries to make a profit on either a markup or markdown. A markup is the difference between what the firm pays for a security and what it charges the customer. Conversely, if the customer is a seller, the markdown is the difference between the firm's bid price and what it actually pays the customer.

Sometimes a broker may receive orders from different customers for both the buy and sell sides of a transaction. This is called a *riskless transaction*, because the broker/dealer is not subject to any risk but has only to cross the two orders. In such a case, each customer sees only his or her part of the commission, markup or markdown.

The OTC regulatory agency, the National Association of Securities dealers (NASD), has declared a 5 percent guideline charge applicable to markups and markdowns. Its purpose is to assure that member firms' profits and commissions are fair, equitable, and proportionate to current market prices. The NASD has issued a number of determinations with respect to this guideline:

* The 5 percent is to be used as a guide, not as a rule, in conjunction with the fair and reasonable requirements of the rule.

* An NASD member cannot justify markups on the basis of excessive expenses.

* Current market prices should be used in determining markups.

* Even a markup of 5 percent or less may be considered unfair in some cases.

The key message is that markups and markdowns must not be unfair, regardless of the guideline percentage.

How does a broker/dealer know what is fair? The NASD board believes that, in determining fairness, NASD members and committees should consider the following:

* *Type of security.* Stocks are typically marked up more than bonds.

* *Availability of the security.* An inactive security is harder to buy and sell and therefore might justify a higher markup or markdown.

* *Price of the security.* The lower the price of the security, the higher the percentage of markup or markdown.

* *Size of the transaction.* A relatively small transaction might justify a higher markup or commission.

* *Disclosure.* Merely disclosing an unfair charge to the customer does not make it fair.

* *Pattern of markups.* The percentages of charges should be consistent and justifiable.

* Nature of the member's business. A broker/dealer who provides better service and facilities than competitors might be justified in charging a higher markup or commission.

The 5 percent guideline applies to all securities in the over-the-counter market, including the following:

* Riskless, or simultaneous, transactions in which the NASD member has a buy and sell order for the same security and simply crosses the orders

* Trades from the member's inventory

* Purchases of securities from customers

* Agency trades, in which commissions must be fair in light of all relevant factors

* Proceeds transactions, in which a customer sells securities and uses the proceeds to buy securities

The guideline does not apply to:

* Sales or purchases of new issues

* Transactions that require the delivery of a prospectus or offering circular, such as those for mutual funds

* Sales or purchases of listed securities

With so many securities trading over the counter, broker/ dealers typically make markets in many of them. In their role as market makers, broker/dealers may deal with many kinds of customers, depending on the size of their firm. Some are wholesalers who deal only with other dealers in what is often called the "inside market." Some deal only with large institutions, such as pension funds or insurance companies. Some smaller firms buy from wholesalers and sell to individual investors.

The market makers *are*, for all practical purposes, the OTC market. This is the basic difference between exchange and OTC trading. Whereas listed stock transactions take place amid a trading crowd on the floor of an exchange, OTC trades are negotiated, trader to trader, over the phone. One is considered an "auction" market, in which bids and offers are made in open outcry, and the other is "negotiated," in which securities are traded one-on-one, on the phone.

FOLLOWING AN ORDER BEING EXECUTED OTC

OTC orders enter the firm through the customer's broker, or account executive, who forwards them to the order room. From there, the order in an OTC-traded stock is passed on to the firm's OTC trading desk. There the traders may act in one of two capacities: "as agents" (or brokers) if the firm is not a market maker in the stock, or "as principals" (or dealers) if the stock is in the firm's inventory.

If the firm is a market maker, the trader may simply execute the order "as principal" at the firm's quoted bid or offer. For a buy order from the customer, the trader adds a markup to the price; for a sell order, the firm deducts a markdown from the price. In either case, the size of the markup or markdown is governed by the 5 percent guideline, just explained.

If the firm is not a market maker, the trader has to locate one. On the exchange, the commission house broker would simply walk over to the appropriate trading post. In OTC trading, the trader has two options:

* The National Quotations Bureau (NQB) sheets

* The National Association of Securities Dealers Automated Quotations (NASDAQ) system

The National Quotation Service of the NQB publishes the daily "pink sheets," containing market makers' quotations and phone number on about 11,000 OTC stocks in alphabetical order. (They also publish other sheets, such as yellow for corporate bond offerings.)

Created in 1971, the NASDAQ system is an electronic communication network with hookups for market makers, registered representatives, and regulators. Market makers can enter their quotations for display on terminals throughout the system.

Three levels of service are available on NASDAQ:

* *Level one* is used by registered representatives whose terminal screens reflect the highest bids and the lowest offers available for NASD securities.

* *Level two* is used by retail traders. This service not only provides current quotations, it also identifies market makers and provides for order execution capability within the system.

* *Level three* is used by market makers. For each security, the system provides current quotes and identifies all market makers. Level three also allows users to enter, delete, or update quotations for securities in which they are making a market. To be an authorized subscriber to level three, an NASD member must meet certain net capital and other qualifications.

More and more trades are being executed by means of computer. The NASD uses the Small Order Execution

System (SOES), which executes agency orders for 1,000 shares or less on the current inside market for National Market System stocks. This system frees the Level III NASDAQ machines and brokerage firms' computers to transact orders for customers, with market makers participating through the NASD.

NASDAQ has currently about 4,000 stocks in the system. Some of the larger companies that are traded have as many as 40 market makers, such as MCI and Apple Computers.

If the price from one market maker is not right, it is easy enough for a trader to shop around. If the order is for Dressbarn, for example, the trader keys in the Dressbarn symbol and gets all the quotations—sizes and prices—for this stock. Perhaps Bear Stearns shows a 16⅜ bid and 16⅝ offered, 5 by 5. That means Bear Stearns is ready to buy up to 5 round lots at 16⅜ and/or sell up to 5 round lots at 16⅝. The quotation shows both the "price" and the "size." At the same time, Merrill shows 16⅜ bid, 16½ offered, 10 by 5. Paine Webber shows 16¼ bid, 16¼ bid, 16½ offered, 15 by 15.

This is why NASDAQ is so successful. It is a computerized, real-time, video display screen "trading crowd," in which the market makers publish their bids and offers (their quotes), with, as always, the forces of supply and demand constantly nudging prices up and down. The execution of the trade occurs at the screen by a flick of the hand.

The National Market System consists of a growing list of stocks for which more information is available than is available for other OTC stocks. For most stocks traded over the counter, the newspaper listing shows the name, dividend, volume, bid/asked, and day-to-day price changes. National Market System stocks—approximately 4300 currently—meet guidelines set by the National Association of Securities Dealers (discussed later in this chapter). In addition to the normal information, listings for these stocks also include high and low prices for the previous 52 weeks and high and low prices for the day. Trades in NMS stocks are reported within 90 seconds.

With non-NASDAQ-traded stocks, the trader must call several market makers to obtain the best quote. To know that, he has to make at least two calls. Once he has the best offer, he enters into a quick negotiation with the other trader. This method, called "shopping the street," means that a trader might have to redial a market maker. But what if the quotation has changed in the ten seconds or so that it takes the trader to get back? Shopping the street depends on a number of OTC rules and conventions that provide for this and similar contingencies. Let's look at these before seeing what the trader does next.

While on the phone with the market maker, the trader may obtain one of several types of quotes. *Firm bids* or *firm offers* are prices at which the broker/dealer is committed to buy or sell a stock right away. A firm bid or offer is usually good for the moment that the quote is given, but it may also be firm for a longer period. Also, unless otherwise stated, it is good for one round lot. In other words, the broker/dealer's commitment to buy or sell at the quoted price is limited to 100 shares of stock or 10 bounds at the quoted price.

Broker/dealers can give a firm quote in a number of different ways:

* "The market is 10–10½."

* "It's 10–10½."

* "We can trade it 10–10½."

A firm quote of "10–10½" means that the quoting broker/dealer stands ready either to buy at least 100 shares at $10 a share or to sell at least 100 shares at $10.50 a share.

The prices quoted in the NQB pink sheets are not firm quotes. Firm quotes sometimes referred to as the "actual market," must be obtained verbally from the market maker or through NASDAQ.

If the broker/dealer gives a "subject" quote, the quote is subject to confirmation; it is not firm. Generally, the broker/dealer has to have more information before making the quote firm. Subject quotes should be expressed as follows: "It's 10–10½ subject." Sometimes the broker/dealer gives a quote with a very wide spread and follows it by the word "workout." A workout quote is not firm. Instead, it provides a range in which the dealer believes a price can be worked out. These quotes are typically used for infrequently traded securities.

Occasionally, a broker/dealer wants to buy or sell but receives no bids or offers. In such cases, the market maker hangs something like a "for sale" sign on the security by advertising the would-be transaction in the National Quotation Bureau sheets. The term "bid wanted" (BW) in the sheets tells other broker/dealers that the stock is for sale and that the advertising market maker is looking for bids. "Offering wanted" (OW) means that the market maker wants to buy the security and is soliciting offers.

TYPES OF ORDERS

The most common types of order entered by customers in the over-the-counter market are market orders and limit orders. Like its counterpart in an exchange, a market order must be executed as soon as possible and at the best possible price. A limit order specifies the price at which the security must be bought or sold. Limit orders may be entered for the day or be marked good-till-canceled (GTC).

Regardless of the type of order entered, the broker must always attempt to get the best possible price for the customer. Let's see how the trader negotiates that price. When asked, "What's the market in Safeco?" or "How are you quoting Safeco?," the market maker does not know whether the inquiring trader wants to buy or sell. The market maker responds with a quote, that is, his current bid, offer, and size: "Twenty-four and a quarter bid, twenty-four and three-quarters offered, five by five." This is an abbreviated way of saying "Twenty-four and a quarter bid for five round lots, and twenty-four and three-quarters asked for five lots on the sell side." Note that the quotation handles both the "size" and the "price." This means that the market maker is willing to *buy* up to 5 round lots at 20¼ or *sell* up to 5 round lots at 20¾. The size of the bid and offer will vary.

This quotation is what the trader was listening to on the phone.

If the terms get mixed up, thousands of dollars will be spent in error and a fair amount of time will have to be spent on undoing and minimizing the damages. This type of mistake can be one of the most common trading errors made. Traders have to be clear and alert on the phone.

Usually a negotiated trade will occur within the spread. The quote given to the trader in this transaction is a ½ point, which is "wide." The tighter the spread, the better the market. A tighter spread would be 24¼ bid and 24⅜ offered. (You can't get any tighter than one-eighth.)

Given the ½-point spread, the trader might say to the market maker "Twenty-four and one-half for one." Now, for the first time, the market maker knows that the trader is buying. It's up to the market maker to either come down with a new offer or stand firm.

If the market maker comes back and says, "Sell one at twenty-four and one-half," the market maker has "hit" the broker/dealer's bid. Safeco now has been bought for the customer at 24½.

If the market maker says, "One at twenty-four and five-eighths," a counteroffer has been made. The trader now knows that the market maker will not come down to 24½. Now it's up to the trader either to accept the stock offered at 24⅝ or, if he feels he can get a better price, to call another market maker.

Let's look at another example. An order to sell 1,000 shares of Panhandle Enterprises is transmitted to the order room, where it is sent to the OTC trading room. A trader telephones a market marker for a quote and obtains a market of "22½, 23, 10 by 5." In other words, the market maker is ready to buy 10 round lots at 22½ or sell 5 lots at 23.

The trader executing the sell order has several options. He can execute the order right away and sell at 22½. He can also try to negotiate within the bid and offer (the spread) by saying something like "Offering ten at twenty-two and three-quarters." If the market maker takes the offer, the order is executed. Still another option might be to offer to sell 5 at 22¾, 3 at 22⅞, and 2 at 23. If the market maker accepts the offer, the sale is made at "staggered" sizes and prices.

Obviously there is no magic number or formula. Other traders might have handled each of the preceding orders differently. Much depends on traders' expertise as negotiators and their understanding of not only the stock but what the market will bear.

In addition to orders for individual investors, over-the-counter trades may include certain stocks listed on the New York Stock Exchange (or on any other national stock exchange). Again, such trades are called "third-market transactions," that is, OTC trades of an exchange-listed stock.

"Fourth-market transactions" also take place on the over-the-counter market. These trades are made directly between large institutional investors, such as mutual funds, insurance companies, pension funds, and bank trust departments. Broker/dealers are not involved in these trades and obviously no commissions are involved.

THE NATIONAL ASSOCIATION OF SECURITY DEALERS (NASD)

The National Association of Security Dealers (NASD) was organized under the Maloney Act, an amendment to the Securities Exchange Act of 1934. Although established by Congress and supervised by the SEC, the NASD operates not as a government agency but as an independent membership association sets operating standards to promote commercial honor and integrity. (See Figure 7–2.)

The NASD's power to regulate is based upon its ability to suspend the membership of—or to fine or censure—any

Figure 7–2. Objectives of the NASD.

To promote the investment banking and securities business.
To standardize principles and practices.
To promote high standards of commercial honor.
To promote the observation of federal and state security laws
by members.
To provide a medium through which members may consult
with government and other agencies.
To enable members to cooperate with governmental authority
in the solution of problems affecting the securities of indus-
try and investors.
To adopt and enforce rules of fair practice.
To promote just and equitable principles of trade for protec-
tion of investors.
To promote self-discipline among members
To investigate and adjust grievances between the public and
NASD members, as well as between NASD members.

---

broker/dealer operating in an unethical or improper manner. Because only NASD members have the advantage of
price concessions, discounts, and similar allowances, the
loss of membership privileges all but prevents a firm from
competing in the marketplace. In addition, NASD members
are permitted to do business domestically only with other
members. Nonmembers are therefore severely restricted in
the business they can do.

Membership in the NASD is open to all properly qualified brokers and dealers whose regular course of business
is transacted in any branch of the investment banking or
securities business in the United States. All broker/deal-
ers must be registered with the SEC and the state authorities, as required by law, to be eligible for membership in
the NASD. By definition, banks are not broker/dealers and
are therefore not eligible for NASD membership.

Some broker/dealers may not become members of the
NASD if they:

* Have been suspended or expelled from any regulatory association.

* Have had their SEC registration revoked or denied.

* Employ individuals who have been convicted for securities-related crimes or who otherwise do not qualify for registration.

NASD RULES OF FAIR PRACTICE

The Rules of Fair Practice are a part of the NASD bylaws designed to promote and enforce the highest ethical conduct in the securities business. The most basic of the rules is Section 1, Article III, which states the fundamental

Figure 7–3. Violations of the Suitability Rule.

Members should not recommend low-priced, speculative securities if they do not know the customer's other holdings, financial situation, and other relevant information. For example, a low-priced security may be suitable for a wealthy investor with large holdings who understands the risks. The same investment would not be suitable for a person of modest means on a fixed income with no other investments.

Creating excessive activity in a customer's account to generate commission is a violation known as "churning" or "overriding."

Trading in mutual fund shares is a violation of the Rules of Fair Practice. Mutual fund shares are considered long-term investments, and many of them charge a sales commission (or "load") on purchase. They are therefore clearly not trading vehicles, and trading these shares does not benefit the customer.

Members may not establish fictitious accounts to execute trades that would otherwise be prohibited, such as purchases of hot issues.

Members may not execute transactions that are not authorized by the customer.

Members may not use or borrow customers' securities without authorization from the customer.

Registered reps may not conceal transactions from the member firm that employs them.

---

philosophy of the NASD: "a member, in the conduct of his business, shall observe high standards of commercial honor and just and equitable principles of trade."

Following are several rules that directly affect the relationship of NASD member firms with their customers:

* It is a violation of the rules for a member to publish, circulate, or distribute any advertisement, sales literature, or market letter that it knows to contain untrue, false, or misleading statements. Similarly, no material fact or qualification can be omitted from advertising material if the omission causes the material to be misleading. In short, all advertising, sales, and market literature must be fair and in good faith.

* So that all customers may benefit from a free and open market, NASD members must use "reasonable diligence"—that is, after considering all pertinent factors—to make sure that the customer gets the best possible price under prevailing market conditions. The rules also state that a member's obligation to do the best for customers is not fulfilled by channeling business through another broker/dealer, unless using a third party reduces costs to the customer.

* No member may accept a customer's purchase order for any security without first making sure that the customer agrees to receive those securities against payment. On the sell side, no member may sell securities for a customer without being reasonably sure that the customer possesses the securities and will deliver them within five business days. To satisfy the requirement of "reasonable assurance," the broker/dealer or registered representative should note on the order ticket the present location of the securities to be sold.

* When securities are held for a customer by a brokerage firm, they usually are held in "street name"

(that is, in the name of the broker/dealer). In these cases, the issuer of the security sends all literature, including reports and proxies, to the brokerage firm, not to the customers. If NASD member firms do not promptly forward such material to customers, their conduct can be regarded as inconsistent with high standards of commercial honor.

* All recommendations to customers to purchase, sell, or exchange securities must be based on reasonable grounds and be suitable for the individual customers. In all recommendations, the controlling factor is the best interest of the customer. To determine suitability, the registered representative of the member firm is expected to learn about the specific financial condition and needs of each customer. (See Figure 7–3.)

OTC and exchange trading make up the large, active secondary market that many regard as "the stock market." This market is so visible to so many people—in the daily newspapers and in the TV and radio newscasts—that it is regarded almost as something with a life of its own. "The stock market edged up on heavy trading today." "The stock market recovered from morning losses, making substantial gains before the closing bell." The stock market "did" this or that.

Anyone who stops to think about it, of course, will see that the market really doesn't "do" anything. In fact, it is a very passive thing. If it is anything, it is merely an arena in which two fundamental forces constantly interact: the forces of supply and demand. If someone could analyze how these forces interact so as to predict precisely how they would affect prices in the future, that person could make a great deal of money. That is what stock market analysis and Chapter 11 are all about. Before getting to the subject of analysis, however, we need to see how transactions are "cleared" in the brokerage firm's back office. This is the focus of Chapter 10.

CHAPTER 8

Investment Companies

*Closed-End and Open-End Funds—
the "Package-Plan" Approach*

We have made the case that investing in stocks is considered almost a necessity for many people. Of the many hurdles to overcome before you can begin investing, the most daunting is selecting the stocks to be purchased. Many investors are fully aware that they should not put all their investment funds into just one stock. If you could somehow know what the single "best" stock was, there would be no problem. Clearly, that is an impossibility.

If an investor had a very large amount to invest—say, several million dollars—she could afford to buy a large selection of securities representing many different industries. She might include in her *investment portfolio* the securities of older, fairly stable companies, those of newer companies believed to be in a growth phase, income stocks, defensive stocks, and venture capital shares. She might include in her portfolio common stocks, straight preferreds and convertible preferreds, warrants, investment-grade and speculative bonds ("junk" bonds), and other investment instruments. If you can afford it, that's definitely the way to go—spreading your investments and your risk among many different securities. At work is the principle of *diversification.*

Another consideration is the *maintenance* of the portfolio after it is put together. Even if the investor is interested only in the longer term, the investments must be constantly monitored to ensure that they are still in line with her overall objectives and the degree of risk that she is willing to assume. For example, some poorly performing stocks might have to be weeded out and replaced with others in more progressive industries, or the balance between fixed-income (preferred) and fluctuating-income (common) stocks might have to be altered. Only a small number of investors have the skill, patience, and time to devote to this activity.

Dividends, if they are not being spent as received, should be reinvested. This has a *compounding* effect, over time, similar to leaving interest in a savings account to earn "interest on interest." This presents other problems: how to invest these relatively small amounts as they are received, and what to invest them in. Many hundreds of thousands of investors have chosen an investment medium that relieves them of many of these anxieties and problems—the *investment company.*

CLOSED-END AND OPEN-END FUNDS

Several thousand companies, called *investment companies*, pool the investment funds of many different investors into a single portfolio of securities, with individual investors sharing the risks and returns of the complete "package" of securities, in proportion to their individual holdings. The people managing these investment companies are financial professionals. As such, they are presumably better qualified to choose the specific securities to be invested in, and to constantly monitor these investments, than is the average investor. The general idea is to "leave it to the pros." The professionals will:

* Select the securities to be invested in.

* Buy and sell other securities as they deem appropriate.

* Collect dividends and interest payments.

* Safeguard the securities.

* Arrange for investors either to invest more money in the pool, to cash in some or all of their investment, or to reinvest their dividends and capital gains, if they so choose, in an attempt to compound their investment gains.

These professionals manage many different types of pooled investment funds, with many different investment objectives. The people investing in a given fund will have a similar overall objective—either conservative growth, speculative growth, income, preservation of capital, or a combination of these aims.

PRICING A CLOSED-END FUND

Some investment companies make a one-time offering of shares, invest the money received in a portfolio of securities, and thenceforth monitor the portfolio, making sales and additional purchases as they see fit. Investors who did not buy shares on the original offering can only purchase them, in the secondary market, from current shareholders. The investment company is not involved in this trading of its "used" shares. This type of company is known as a *closed-end fund* or *publicly traded fund.*

The financial press regularly publishes the actual "worth" of a single share of each of these funds. It is called the fund's *net asset value per share.* To determine this value, the fund's total assets are added together (the current maket value of their entire portfolio) and then the fund's liabilities are subtracted to arrive at *net* asset value. The net asset value is divided by the number of outstanding shares (that is, the shares of the fund itself, *not* the number of shares of other companies that they own for investment purposes). The result is the net asset value per share. This is, at least in theory, the *liquidating value* of a share of the fund: what the owner of a single share would receive, in cash, if the investment company were to be liquidated.

Many of the larger closed-end funds are listed on stock exchanges while some trade over-the-counter (OTC). After the initial offering, which is at a set price, the funds' shares trade in the open market at prices set by the investing public (that is, by supply and demand). Sometimes the funds trade at a price that is *higher* than their net asset value per share—*premium* prices. More often than not, however, they trade at a price *lower* than their liquidating value—*discount* prices. Secondary market trades are effected just like trades in other stocks, and a buyer can usually expect to pay "standard" commission rates.

PRICING AN OPEN-END FUND

Open-end funds (*mutual* funds) are *initially* offered in the same manner as closed-ends. But the secondary market for mutual funds is dramatically different in that the funds continually offer new shares to interested investors. Mutual funds are essentially a perennial new issue!

How they are sold is also very different. The mutual fund redeems outstanding shares upon request, effectively permitting fund shareholders to "cash in their chips." A mutual fund can be purchased at its offering price (asked price), which is always at least equal to the actual net asset value per share. Unlike closed-end funds, mutual funds are never available at a discount from net asset value. True "no-load" mutual funds do not charge a commission and are thus both bought and sold (redeemed) at their then-current net asset values. Some funds are "loaded" and their offering prices may include a sales charge (the *load*) of up to 8½ percent of the amount invested.

Reading from left to right in Figure 8–1, the various columns indicate:

Figure 8–1.

Friday, June 4, 1993
Ranges for investment companies, with daily price data supplied by the National Association of Securities Dealers and performance and cost calculations by Lipper Analytical Services Inc. The NASD requires a mutual fund to have at least 1,000 shareholders or net assets of $25 million before being listed. Detailed explanatory notes appear elsewhere on this page.

	Inv. Obj.	NAV	Offer Price	NAV Chg.	%Ret YTD	Max Initl Chrg.	Total Exp Ratio R
AAL Mutual:							
Bond	BND	10.55	11.08	−0.04	+5.0	4.750	1.030 ..
CaGr	GRO	15.06	15.81	−0.08	+3.2	4.750	1.280 ..
MuBd	GLM	10.99	11.54	−0.01	+4.8	4.750	0.950 ..
AARP Invst:							
CaGr	GRO	33.91	NL	−0.22	+5.7	0.000	1.130 ..
GiniM	BND	16.04	NL	−0.03	+3.9	0.000	0.720 ..
GthInc	G&I	31.28	NL	−0.21	+7.0	0.000	0.910 ..
HQ Bd	BND	16.50	NL	−0.07	+5.2	0.000	1.130 ..
TxFBd	ISM	18.28	NL	−0.02	+6.0	0.000	0.740 ..
ABT Funds:							
Emrg	CAP	13.28	13.94	−0.12	+3.8	4.750	1.440 ..
FL HI	MFL	10.38	10.90	−0.02	+6.3k	4.750	NA ..
FL TF	MFL	11.24	11.80	−0.01	+5.8	4.750	0.410 ..
GthIn	G&I	11.01	11.56	−0.06	+3.1	4.750	1.230 ..
UtilIn	SEC	13.79	14.48	−0.05	+9.0	4.750	1.170 ..
Acc Mortg	BND	12.26	NL	−0.02	+4.0	0.000	0.840 ..
Acc Sht Int	BST	12.33	NL	−0.04	+3.1	0.000	0.830 ..
AHA Funds:							
Balan	S&B	12.77	NL	−0.08	+5.8	0.000	0.380 ..
Full	BND	10.60	NL	−0.05	+5.5	0.000	0.420 ..
Lim	BST	10.46	NL	−0.03	+2.4	0.000	0.290 ..
AIM Funds:							
AdiGv p	BST	9.88	10.19	−0.01	+2.1	3.000	0.140 ..
Chart p	G&I	8.88	9.40	−0.03	+4.1	5.500	1.170 ..
Const p	CAP	15.54	16.44	−0.15	+4.2	5.500	1.200 ..
CvYld p	S&B	14.98	15.73	−0.11	+6.0	4.750	2.120 ..
HiYld p	BHI	5.84	6.13	...	+8.0	4.750	1.530 ..
IntlE p	ITL	10.35	10.95	−0.08	+15.5	5.500	1.800 ..
LimM p	BST	10.17	10.27	−0.02	+1.9	1.000	0.480 ..
Sumit	GRO	9.80	NA	−0.06	+1.7	8.500	0.760 ..
TF Int	IDM	10.78	11.11	...	+3.8	3.000	0.020 ..
Weing	GRO	16.56	17.52	−0.11	−4.4	5.500	1.100 ..
Agrsv p	SML	19.88	21.04	−0.16	+7.3	5.500	1.250 ..
GoSc p	BND	10.29	10.80	−0.03	+3.8	4.750	0.980 ..
Grth p	GRO	11.85	12.54	−0.12	−3.5	5.500	1.170 ..
Inco p	BND	8.41	8.83	−0.04	+7.9	4.750	0.990 ..
MuB p	GLM	8.49	8.91	−0.01	+5.2	4.750	0.900 ..
TeCt p	SSM	10.98	11.53	−0.01	+5.6	4.750	0.250 ..
Util p	SEC	14.10	14.92	−0.05	+7.9	5.500	1.170 ..
Valu p	G&I	19.51	20.65	−0.07	+7.0	5.500	1.160 ..
HYldC p	BHI	9.83	10.32	...	+9.3	4.750	1.150 ..

(1) *The name of the fund.* Notice that the first three funds listed are under their "family" name of AAL Mutual. The second and third fund families (AARP Invst and ABT Funds) have five different funds each. But then Acc Mortg appears by itself, without a family name, indicating that there is only one fund under supervision by that particular group of organizers.

(2) *The fund's investment objective* (the newspaper listings currently list 27 different objectives). This indicates whether the fund is investing for conservative growth, aggressive growth, income, or some other objective (or combination of objectives), or whether it is specialized so as to be invested exclusively in bonds or "small capitalization" stocks.

(3) *The fund's net asset value per share.* This is calculated by "netting out" the fund's assets (subtracting liabilities from assets) and dividing by the number of fund shares outstanding. This is the price a shareholder would receive when *redeeming* (selling) shares of the fund. Occasionally a fund will charge a redemption fee, but most such charges are relatively modest, and they are reduced or eliminated for investors who have held the shares for a fair length of time.

(4) *The fund's offer price.* This is the fund's purchase price. When this column reads "NL," it signifies a no-load fund, that is, one that can be both bought and sold at its per-share net asset value.

(5) *The day's change in price (the NAV price) from the previous day* .

(6) *How the fund has performed.* The "% Ret YTD" column assumes that all distributions (dividends and capital gains) have been reinvested.

(7) *The maximum sales charge* (the maximum "load").

(8) *The expense ratio.* This measures how effectively the fund handles its managerial expenses. A low number indicates efficient operations.

The commissions on loaded funds can be reduced through a number of techniques. Most loaded funds offer reduced sales charges for

relatively large orders. For example, a fund might charge 8½ percent for orders under $5,000, but might reduce the sales charge to 7 percent or so for orders between $5,000 and $10,000, with further reductions at $25,000, $50,000, and beyond. These dollar levels are referred to as *breakpoints*.

It is possible, through the use of a *letter of intent*, to be charged one of these reduced commission rates even if you don't purchase the required total dollar amount all at once, but rather in a series of smaller purchases spread over 13 months.

Under *right of accumulation*, once an investor has amassed a given dollar amount, say $25,000, by buying in small lots over a very long period, then *additional* investments may be made at the $25,000 breakpoint level.

Most funds offer a *withdrawal plan*, a popular feature for retirees. After you have achieved a certain dollar amount of the fund, usually $10,000 or more, you can direct the fund to send you a regular monthly or quarterly payment. The fund liquidates just enough of your fund shares to make the requested payment. If you ask for a relatively large amount, and/or if the fund's portfolio does not perform well, you may well exhaust your entire investment. On the other hand, it may be possible to "have your cake and eat it too" if the fund does well with their investment portfolio. Your gains might very well be great enough to replace the amounts of your withdrawals. Withdrawal plans are sometimes described as *self-directed annuities.*

The typical mutual fund holds dozens of different issues. Buying a fund ordinarily provides purchasers with "instant diversification" since they effectively own a great number of different securities wrapped up in a single package. The promoters of the fund will collect all dividends and interest payments and (after deducting expenses) will distribute them or reinvest them in additional fund shares, as the shareowners direct. The fund's managers make all portfolio buy and sell decisions, and they attend to all security-related matters including redemptions and conversions. These are some of the reasons that investing in mutual funds has become so popular: They provide diversification, convenience, and professional management.

Most mutual fund organizations will open an account for those who are making initial investments of as little as $500. Additional investments in any dollar amount of $50 or more may be made at the client's discretion. The fund will hold your shares, freeing you of the responsibility for safeguarding them. There are several thousand different funds to choose from. They are offered with a wide variety of different investment objectives, and different degrees of risk, to suit almost any investment situation. They bring together the assets of many different investors who share a common investment objective.

CHAPTER 9

Stock Options

Multipurpose Instruments

Stock options are little understood by the investing public. They are popularly supposed to be very speculative instruments—and so they are! But they serve a great variety of other purposes including leverage, protecting profits and preventing losses on other investments, and producing income.

PUTS AND CALLS

There are two types of options:

* The *put* option permits its holder to *sell* a stock at a given price.

* The *call* option permits its holder to *buy* a stock at a given price.

The *owner* of an option, whether a put or a call, has the right to do something, but doesn't have to exercise that right.

There may be a great number of puts and calls outstanding on a single stock, all at the same time. Here's how an investor's XYZ put positions might be reported:

(1)	(2)	(3)	(4)	(5)	(6)
5	XYZ	April	60	puts	@2½

The customer is long "5 XYZ April 60 puts" at a per-put price of 2½.

(1) *The number of puts.* The customer has 5 puts, each of which gives the holder the right to sell 100 shares of XYZ common stock. The person owing these puts would thus have the right to sell 500 shares of XYZ. One put would entitle the holder to sell 100 shares, 2 puts control the sale of 200 shares, and so on.

(2) *The "underlying" stock.* The put holder has the right to sell a total of 500 shares of *XYZ common stock*, the underlying stock. He is not *obligated* to do so, but he *may* sell 500 shares of XYZ if he chooses to.

(3) *The month of expiration.* All options have a limited life, with the longest currently offered options expiring about three years after they are first traded. The vast majority of "listed" options expire in less than one year. This option, an *April* option, will expire late in next April.

(4) *The strike price.* Also known as the *exercise* price, this is the price at which the put holder can sell [at 60 ($60) per share].

(5) *The type of option.* In this case, the option is a put.

(6) *The premium.* This is the option's price in the open market, set by supply and demand. The options illustrated were purchased at 2½. Since each option controls the purchase (call) or sale (put) of 100 shares of the underlying stock, the option's price must be multiplied by 100. The premium of 2½ thus translates to a total dollar cost (excluding commissions) of $250 per option (100 × $2.50), or a total of $1,250 for all 5 puts (5 × $250).

That's what this option buyer has purchased. But what is he hoping for? How much can he make? How much can he lose?

Mr. Jones is hoping for XYZ to decline; he is *bearish* on XYZ stock. He thinks it is too highly priced at 61 (the current market price for XYZ common stock) and that it will drop substantially between January (when he bought the puts) and late April when the puts expire. He is betting that XYZ common stock will go down—rooting for the stock to decline.

How much can Mr. Jones make? How far can any stock decline? That's right, to zero. It's improbable, but at least in theory it could happen. If XYZ stock goes bankrupt, Mr. Jones will be a very happy man. He can then buy 500 shares of XYZ in the open market—essentially for close to nothing—and then "put" the stock by exercising his option to sell 500 shares at $60 per share. Some unlucky person has to honor that put (the loser is the one who sold the put), and pay $60 a share for all 500 shares. Mr. Jones will then make the difference between what he bought the shares for—zero— and $30,000, the amount he will receive when he exercises his puts by selling 500 shares at 60. His net profit will be $28,750 [$30,000 – $1,250 (the cost of the puts)].

How much can Mr. Jones lose? The stock might "go the wrong way" (as far as Mr. Jones is concerned) and *rise* substantially in price to, say, 75 per share and stay at that price until the puts expire. Then it will not be to Mr. Jones' advantage to buy stock in the open market at 75 and sell it through exercising his puts at 60. That would give him a large loss. He would certainly be much better off simply *not* exercising the now worthless put options and letting them expire. In that case, all he loses is the premium. It's important to remember that when you buy an option—any option—the most you can lose is what you paid for it, the premium. That's one of the advantages of buying options— the fact that your maximum loss is limited to the price you paid, and never any more.

But what if XYZ did not go all the way down to zero? Suppose it went down to, say, 54? Then Mr. Jones could buy XYZ at 54 and exercise his "60" put, making a profit of 6 points (buying at 54 and selling at 60). The 6 points profit "cost" Mr. Jones 2½ because that's what he paid for each put. His net profit (excluding commissions) will then be 3½ points on each put, for a total of $1,750. That's not bad for an initial investment of only $1,250! It illustrates the tremendous *leverage* that options afford.

Note: If Mr. Jones, being bearish on XYZ, had instead sold 500 shares short, his potential loss would have been unlimited! That's one good reason for buying a put, to profit from a downward movement in the price of a stock: your loss is limited rather than unlimited.

TIME VALUE AND INTRINSIC VALUE

The value of the option depends greatly on its relationship to the market price of the underlying stock. Is the strike price of the options greater than, equal to, or less than the underlying's market price? For example, Mr. Jones was bearish on XYZ, which was then selling at 61. That was the price of the "underlying" when Mr. Jones bought his "60" puts. At that price level (61), it would not, of course be profitable to buy XYZ in the open market and sell at 60 by exercising the put. In situations like this—when exercising an option is not profitable—the option is said to be *out of the money*. Out-of-the-money options have no *intrinsic value*.

Should XYZ decline below the 60 strike price, then it would be advantageous to put the stock. With XYZ at 54 (as in our example), the put holder would make 6 points by exercising the option at 60. With XYZ at 54, the option is *in the money* by 6 points. This 6 points is said to be the option's *intrinsic value*.

Should XYZ trade at 60 (at the same level as the put strike price), then the option would be trading *at the money*, and again it would have no intrinsic value.

Why would Mr. Jones buy an option with no intrinsic value, one that was out of the money? He knew that the option had three more months to run—from the January purchase date to late in April when the puts expire—and he believed that during those three months the stock would go down below 60. When he bought the options, with the underlying 1 point above his put strike price, they were out of the money 1 point. Since the options had no intrinsic value, but were trading in the open market at 2½ (the premium), the entire premium price consisted of *time value*.

The price of an option can thus sometimes consist of two elements: its intrinsic value and/or its time value. The difference between an option's intrinsic value and its premium (if there is any) is its time value. For example, CYA is trading at 48¾ while its 50 puts are selling for 3. The puts are in the money 1¼ points (50 − 48¾) and that is their intrinsic value. The premium is 3, which is 1¾ points above intrinsic value. The option thus has 1¾ points time value. In this instance the premium consists of two elements: 1¼ points intrinsic value and 1¾ points time value. You can check the accuracy of these calculations by adding the time value and the intrinsic value. They should add to the premium: 1¼ + 1¾ = 3. It checks out!

At-the-money and out-of-the-money options have no intrinsic value, and so their premiums consist only of time value. Options are called *wasting assets* because they have termination (expiration) dates. As an option's expiration date approaches, its time value will be reduced since people are naturally unwilling to pay "extra" for an option that only has a short time to run. Time values are higher for options that have a long period of time until expiration, and for those whose underlying stocks are volatile (that is, vary greatly in price over time).

OPTIONS AS A HEDGING TOOL

Ralph Chrico has a profit on his 100 shares of NFW common stock, having purchased them at 32 per share and watched them rise to their present price of 56. He is reluctant to sell, even though he could lock in a capital gain of 24 points, because he believes that NFW will continue to rise in price. Ralph knows he has a "sure" profit of 24 points, but he wants to shoot for an even bigger profit. He is also afraid *not* to sell because he realizes that the stock could also fall from these levels, wiping out part, or even all, of his gain. What to do?

One solution is for Ralph to purchase an NFW 55 put as "protection" for his gain. Assuming that NFW 55 puts were trading at 2, Mr. Chirico would continue to hold his 100 NFW and also own an NFW 55 put, which cost him $200. He is really hoping that his NFW will continue to rise in price and that he will never exercise his put. Buying the put is like buying life insurance; you want to live, but have the policy as protection. In this case Mr. Chirico hopes never to use the put and that it will expire unexercised, even though it cost him $200.

While the put is "alive" Mr. Chirico has guaranteed himself a net profit of 21 points—until the put expires—even if NFW goes bankrupt!

Here's how it works: Ralph is long his 100 NFW and can extend his gain if it goes even higher. That's what he wants—for NFW to continue to increase in price. The put merely acts as "downside insurance." If NFW falls sharply in price to, say, 38 or so, then Mr. Chirico will exercise his put and sell his stock for 55, the strike price of the put. While the put is alive, the worst Ralph can do on the sell side is to sell at 55. Thus, his poorest result will be to exercise at 55, after having bought originally for 32, for a gross profit of 23 points and a net profit of 21 points as the put (his downside insurance policy) cost 2. As long as the put is alive, Mr. Chirico still has the opportunity for further profit, but has protected himself against losing most of his accumulated gain.

Most investors buy put options for one of two reasons: because they are bearish on a stock and hope to profit through a decline in the stock's value; or because they want to protect a profit or guard against a large loss.

CALL OPTIONS

The other major type of stock option is the call, which permits holders to buy at the strike price. Calls provide leverage for a bull because they fix a buy price (the strike price). The call holder hopes that the underlying will go well above the strike price so that she can exercise the call (that is, buy the stock at the strike price) and then sell the underlying at the higher market price. Here's an example of a call position:

(1)	(2)	(3)	(4)	(5)	(6)
1	RFQ	July	35	call	@3½

(1) *The number of options held.* One option entitles the holder to buy 100 shares.

(2) *The underlying stock.* In this case, the underlying is RFQ common stock.

(3) *The expiration month.* The option will expire late next July.

(4) *The strike price.* The option can be exercised at $35 per share.

(5) *The type of option.* This is a call option.

(6) *The premium.* This is the cost of the option. A 3½ premium means the option costs $350.

The holder of this option has, at least in theory, an unlimited profit potential since there is no limit to how high in price RFQ might sell before the buy option expires. The option holder is bullish and wants the underlying to go up in price. As with a put, the holder's maximum loss is the cost of the option, in this case, $350. There's the leverage: unlimited profit potential and a limited exposure to loss. If RFQ goes up sharply in price, the holder of an RFQ call option will gain substantially more, percentagewise, than a holder of the stock itself.

Of course, keep in mind that the option will only last until the expiration date, and that the stock must go up before the option expires. So timing is more important than it is with outright stock purchases. Another negative feature of call options is that they don't generate income in the form of dividends as do long stock positions.

OPTIONS TO INCREASE PORTFOLIO INCOME

Many institutions and substantial investors sell (*write*) *covered calls*, that is, they receive premiums for selling calls on the stocks that they own. These premiums are paid by call buyers. If the institution's long positions don't rise above the strike prices, the calls expire and they keep the premiums. These premiums from expired calls provide income in addition to any dividends received. The downside is that, if the underlying stocks sell above the strike prices, the institution will be "called" and will have to surrender their stocks at the strike prices. Writers of covered calls are in the odd position in that they don't want their stocks to go up until *after* the call options expire! If the calls they write (sell) expire unexercised, they will keep the premiums and will probably then sell another call.

Options are a fascinating subject. For further information, see another book in this series, *How the Options Markets Work.*

CHAPTER 10

The Back Offices:

Following the Long Paper Trail

Whether on an exchange or in the OTC market, a trade can take place in seconds. Yet because the stock market is so highly regulated, and because money and stock are to be transferred, every aspect of a sale has to be documented and checked. As a result, behind every transaction is a long paper trail that winds through many departments in the brokerage firm. Collectively, these departments are known as "operations" or, more colloquially, "the back office." (See Figure 10–1.) Here is where trades are "processed" or "cleared."

On any given trading day, the typical back office processes a huge volume of transactions, day in and day out, with astonishing accuracy. This is particularly remarkable given

Figure 10–1. A Typical Back Office Setup.

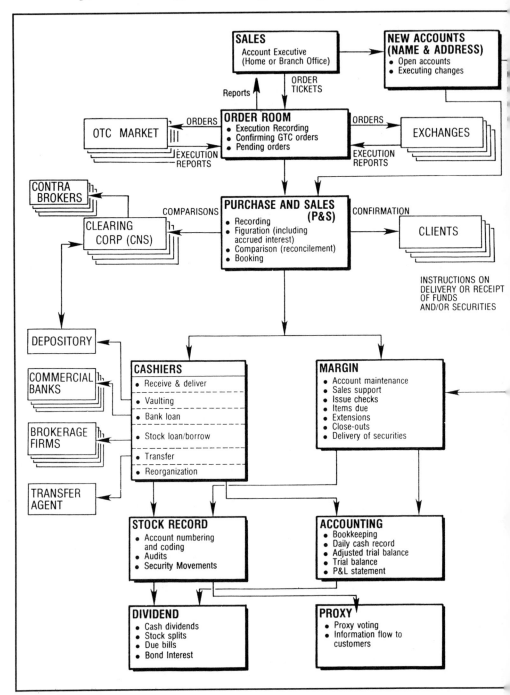

the detailed nature of regulatory requirements of the stock market.

While the back office has always striven for great accuracy, the volume it could handle took a quantum jump in the late 1960s. Up to that time, stock trades were handled on a "cash-and-carry" basis. Before 11:30 A.M. on the settlement date, usually the fifth business day following the trade (T+5), a messenger, sent by the selling firm, carried the stock certificates to the offices of the purchasing firm. The messenger was given a receipt for the securities and then moved on to the next delivery.

The receiving firm then checked the certificates to make sure that they were the same ones that were purchased and that all of the other paper work was complete. Once it was determined that everything was in order, the purchasing firm "cut a check" to the selling firm and arranged for the securities to be reregistered in the new owner's name.

Around 2:30 P.M. the same day, the delivering firm's messenger came back, presented the receipt, picked up the check, and returned it to the selling firm. That firm then verified that the check was for the correct sum and deposited it in the bank.

This system left very little time for trades to be verified in detail for accuracy and for errors to be corrected. Also, for every trade, it required separate paper work, messenger pickups, check cutting, and stock reregistrations (or transfers). No matter how hard the brokerage firms' employees worked, there was a limit to how many transactions they could correctly process in a day. This became abundantly clear in the late 1960s when the New York Stock Exchange had to shorten its trading hours and finally take every Wednesday off in an attempt to reduce the number of transactions occurring in a day—to permit the firms to keep up with the paper work. During this time, many firms went out of business due to the financial strain of keeping up with the mountains of paper work created by the cash-and-carry system of settlement.

Clearly, a new system was needed, and one evolved that is still used today.

THE DEPOSITORY AND CLEARING HOUSE

The cornerstone of the system is a *securities deposi-*
tory that acts as a central depot for most firm's securities.
In the depository's vaults are most of the actual stock
certificates owned by the firms that use the depository's
services, and by those firm's clients. Most brokerage houses
also maintain a cash balance at their depository. A second
key player in the system is SIAC, the Securities Industry
Automation Corporation, which is a processing facility
jointly owned by the NYSE and ASE that provides a match-
ing comparison service for all trades. For example, brokerage firm A buys 200 XYZ stock at 43½ from firm B. At the
end of the trading day, firm A reports to SIAC that it bought
200 XYZ at 43½ from B. Firm B reports that it sold 200
XYZ at 43½ to firm A. SIAC "pairs off," or compares, the
trade as reported. If there is no disagreement between the
two reports, there is no problem; the trades compare with
each side knowing the other.

However, after most of the trades are paired off, usually some trades are left over with no identical countertrade. For example, if firm B reports a purchase of 200
shares of XYZ at 43⅜, there is no reported countertrade.
Most likely, one firm or the other made a price error. In this
case, both firms are notified that their trades do not match
up, that is, there is a "break." It is left to them to resolve
the error. Perhaps one firm can prove to the other that it
is right by comparing the price at which the transaction
occurred to the price at which the stock was trading in the
market at the time the order was executed. Or maybe one
firm finds that it made a paperwork error and corrects the
report it sent back to SIAC. If neither firm can prove it is
right, then the two traders of the firms involved may
negotiate a settlement between themselves.

It's important to note that the firm, not the client,
suffers the loss resulting from an error. To take an example, a firm reports a purchase to a client at 43⅜ when it
actually bought the stock for 43½. The client pays only
43⅜. The extra eighth of a point is absorbed by the firm.

SIAC therefore verifies that the details of the transaction, as reported by the two parties to it, agree in all respects. SIAC does this for the millions of trades that take place every day in the stock market—and does it with amazing reliability. Each exchange, as well as the OTC market, has its own clearing agency, and compared trades are forwarded to the clearing corporation for settlement. That is, payment and delivery.

With the physical stock certificates in one place, all a selling firm has to do is to electronically instruct the clearing house to transfer the securities from its account at the depository to the purchasing firm's account there. The purchasing firm notifies the clearing house to pay the selling firm from the cash reserve in its account. When the clearing house has instructions from both firms, it verifies that they are correct and then transfers the securities and the money. With this system, no messengers need to be sent and no checks need pass between firms. Let's see how this works in an illustration. For their respective clients, firm A sells 100 shares of XYZ, Inc. to firm B, and firm B sells 100 shares of XYZ to firm C has 100 shares more. The total for firm B does not change because it has both bought and sold 100 shares of XYZ. Because firm B has both bought and sold 100 shares of XYZ, these trades can be paired off internally by journal entry at the cashier department. The clearing house simply instructs firm A to deliver 100 shares to firm C to settle all three transactions, thus reducing the number of transfers from three to one. Any price differentials are subtracted from, and/or added to, the firms' cash accounts, and each firm has the securities reregistered in the new owners' names.

Thus the time-consuming, labor-intensive tasks of delivering securities, transferring ownership, and issuing checks for payment can now all be done by means of telecommunicated instructions instantaneously. Only because of the automated depository/clearing house arrangement can brokerage firms process today's incredible daily volumes of transactions.

But these tasks are only part of the paper trail. Many other steps have to be taken before the trade is legally "cleared."

THE ORDER DEPARTMENT

The trail begins as soon as a sales representative opens a new account for a client. To do that, the rep has to have a number of forms filled out and sent to the new accounts (or name and address) department. The chief form is the *new account agreement,* which contains information on where the client's statements are to be sent, the client's investment objectives, and financial net worth, usually some information about the client's employer, and/or some credit references. The client who wishes to open a margin account has to sign a *margin account agreement.* To authorize the broker to make the decisions on what to buy and sell, and/or when to buy or sell, without first having to check with the client, the client also has to sign a *discretionary account agreement.* If the client is a corporation, partnership, charity, or any entity other than an individual, still more forms need to be completed.

When all these forms are sent to the new accounts department, the people there check to be sure the forms are completed properly, store the paper work, and open an electronic file for the client on the firm's computer system. They also make sure that the information is kept up-to-date, changing the file information whenever the client moves, gets a new phone number, changes employer, and so on.

With the account opened, the client is now ready to have the brokerage firm execute trades. Any orders that the client sends or calls in to the account executive are passed on to the order department, often called the order room or wire room, which acts as a "go-between" for the firm's salespeople and its traders. In a small firm, the orders may simply be carried to the order department as they are received.

In a large firm, with offices all over the country, the brokers forward their orders via an electronic mail system, or wire. If a branch office sends an order to the order room via this system, the order quickly prints out in the order room on a teletyper. The order department staff checks the order for obvious errors (missing account numbers, missing office numbers, and the like). Then, since speed is of the essence, it immediately forwards the order (either electronically or via a phone) to the exchange or to the OTC trading department for execution. In the meantime, the order department keeps a copy of the order in its file. When the trade is executed (which may take seconds or months depending on the type of order), the floor clerk or trader then sends back an execution report to the order department.

The people in the order department then record the price on the execution report on the order copy and notify the broker (via the wire system) of the execution and the execution price. The broker, in turn, notifies the client. All this activity, however, serves only to get the trade executed. It is only the beginning of the paper trail.

P&S DEPARTMENT

After the order has been filled, the order department personnel notify another department, known as the purchase and sales (P&S) department, whose staff do basically three things.

1. They "record" the trade, that is, they book it on the firm's master records. Since these records are the basis for later notifying SIAC of which securities have been bought and sold by the firm, accuracy is a must.

2. They do the "figuration," that is, the calculation of all other charges related to the trade. For a purchase order, the initial step in this process is, of course, to detemine how much the client owes the firm for buying the stock. For a sell order, the computation is for how much the firm owes the client selling the stock. In addition, however, they compute commissions (added to a buying client's bill and subtracted from a client's sales proceeds), "ticket charges" (processing fees that some firms charge), and any applicable state or federal transfer taxes.

The P&S department clerks then, *usually on the same day as the trade,* mail the confirmation statement to the client. This statement contains the details of the trade and shows what the client owes the firm or what the firm owes the client.

3. The P&S staff compares the details of the trade, from its firm's point of view, with the P&S department of the contra firm, to be sure that both firms agree on the details of the trade. Because of the sheer speed at which orders are executed and the number of trades performed each day, some misunderstandings are inevitable. For example, firm A may think it sold firm B 200 shares of a stock, whereas firm B thinks it bought only 100 shares of the stock from firm A. It's important that these disagreements be discovered, resolved, and corrected prior to settlement day. Otherwise the trade will not settle and a costly error could occur.

Given the average daily volume in today's stock market, confirming each trade with every other firm would be an overwhelming task for any P&S department. So catching most of these disagreements prior to the settlement date is an important responsibility.

When P&S sends the confirmation notice to the client, it also sends a copy of the statement to the cashier department. This area of the back office is sometimes referred to as "the cage" because it is frequently enclosed in a floor-to-ceiling protective enclosure. The reason for the security is that here is where the firm's vault (or "box") is located.

In the cage are personnel with a number of duties:

1. The receive and/or deliver section of the cashiering department takes or makes delivery of stock certificates

from customers, other firms, or depositories. The actual deliveries take place at a counterlike window in the cage. When receiving or delivering the certificates, the firm must make sure that they are in negotiable form. That is, the back of the certificate has to be signed by the owner. If a stock has more than one owner (such as a husband and wife), both must sign the certificate just as their names appear on the front of the certificate. Without the appropriate signatures, the securities cannot be delivered to the new owner. If the stock actual physical certificates registered in the customers name, are being held by the broker, clients must sign a separate form (called a "stock power"), which the firm attaches to the certificate.

2. Every time a stock changes hands, it has to undergo "transfer." That is, the existing certificate, which carries the name of the former owner, must be canceled and a new certificate, which reflects the name of the new owner, must be issued. This is the job of the *transfer agent,* usually a commercial bank or other organization outside the brokerage firm. Another outside agency, often a trust company or bank, acts as registrar. Its duty is to keep track of the number of shares or bonds an issuer has in circulation and maintain the record owner list. It verifies that no more shares are issued than are destroyed, so that the total number of outstanding shares remains constant. (Often, the transfer and register duties are handled by the same bank or agency.) When a firm receives securities that have been sold, it passes them on to the transfer agent so that they can be reregistered in the name of the new owner. If the firm has the old certificates at a depository, the depository sends them to the transfer agent to be reregistered.

3. When the cashier department gets back the reregistered certificates, it forwards them to the new owner if the client wishes to hold the securities. If not, then the firm holds the stock for the client in the firm's name (or "street" name). In this case, the certificates are placed either in the company's vault or in the depository.

Whether held at the depository or in the vault, the certificates must be divided into the two groups: (1) securities that are owned outright by the firm's clients and (2) securities that the firm itself owns or that the firm's clients have borrowed against (that is, margined). By law, securities that are owned outright by the firm's clients must be segregated from the other securities, regardless of whether the certificate is registered in the client's name or in the broker's name. For that reason, these securities are said to be "in seg" (short for segregation).

4. The securities that the firm owns, as well as the margined securities owned by clients, can be lent out by the firm to short sellers to enable them to complete delivery. The short sellers can be clients either of the same brokerage firm or of other firms. The stock loan clerk arranges to lend surplus securities and to borrow, from other firms and sources, the securities that the firm's clients want to sell short.

5. The bank loan section of the cashiering department arranges to borrow money from the firm's commercial banks, either to finance the purchase of securities for the firm's own account and/or to provide funds for margin loans to customers.

Investor Jane Jones has analyzed XYZ stock, selling at $25 per share, and concluded that its market price will go down over the next few weeks. Given her expectations, she reverses the time-honored dictum to, "Buy low, sell high." Instead, she sells high and then hopes to buy low. She does that by selling short.

Jane calls her broker to place an order to sell 100 shares of XYZ short at $25. Again this can only be done in a margin account. The brokerage firm executes the order, selling 100 XYZ to another firm at $25. The difference between a long sale and a short sale, however, is that Jane does not own any shares of XYZ, which she has sold short.

The buyer's brokerage firm delivers $2,500 ($25 × 100 shares), but how does Jane deliver securities to her

How Cashiering Handles a Short Sale

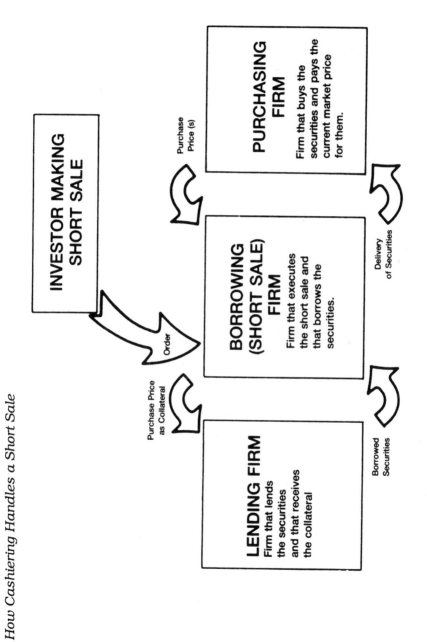

INVESTOR MAKING SHORT SALE

Purchase Price as Collateral

Order

LENDING FIRM
Firm that lends the securities and that receives the collateral

BORROWING (SHORT SALE) FIRM
Firm that executes the short sale and that borrows the securities.

Purchase Price (s)

PURCHASING FIRM
Firm that buys the securities and pays the current market price for them.

Borrowed Securities

Delivery of Securities

brokerage firm for delivery to the buyer's firm? The answer is that, since Jane entered an order for a short sale, she indicated to the broker that she does not intend to furnish the certificates. (The reason may be that she does not own them, but it might also be that she owns them and does not want to surrender them as a tax hedge.

For a short sale, therefore, the cashier department in the seller's brokerage firm borrows 100 shares of XYZ, either from another firm or from one of its other customers, and delivers the borrowed securities to the buyer (in return for the $2,500 purchase price). The lender of the stock is paid for the "use" of the stock, and the short seller pays interest on the "margin" loan.

Several weeks later, XYZ stocks drops to $18 per share—this is as low as Jane thinks the stock will go. She calls her broker again, this time to buy the 100 XYZ at 18, referred to as a short cover. This stock is then used to close out her short position: The 100 shares are paid for by deducting $1,800 ($18 × 100 shares) from the $2,500 proceeds of the short sale, and the certificates are "paid back" to the lender.

Jane's gross profit is $700 (ignoring commissions and other expenses)—$2,500 less $1,800. As you can see, a short sale eventually has to be offset by a purchase.

The reorganization (reorg) department handles a number of duties relating to changes in the status or structure of an issuing corporation.

A *redemption call* is the exercise by the issuer of a call privilege on a bond or callable preferred stock. An absolute, or full, call requires all holders to submit their bonds or shares for redemption. In a partial call, only the holders of specific certificate numbers must respond; these certificate numbers are chosen at random by the company, often by electronic means. If the called securities are held in safekeeping and segregated by owner through individual identification methods, reorg simply submits the appropriate certificates to the company and credits the customer with the cash received. But if the securities are segregated in bulk form, the firm must either (1) record the specific certificate numbers for each customer account, or (2) adopt an impartial lottery system.

In conversions, the reorganization department processes requests to convert convertible bonds into the underlying common stock, which sometimes results from a full or partial call in a convertible issue. The issuing company forces the holders to exchange their securities for the common stock or accept the call price, which is typically lower than the market value of the comparable common shares.

In such a typical bond call, the bondholder is advised that, unless some personal action is initiated before the close of business on a given day, (1) the conversion privilege is revoked, (2) accrued interest on the bond ceases, and (3) the holder must accept the redemption price. In the meantime, the reorganization department must contact the beneficial bond owners and solicit instructions from them.

Reorg also handles *exchanges,* of which there are a couple of types. When one class of security is exchanged for another of the same issuer, it is called reorganization. Sometimes, if a corporation is in dire financial straits, its bondholders may accept stocks in exchange for their bonds to avoid prolonged and expensive bankruptcy proceedings. Or such an exchange may result from a decision in bankruptcy court. Either way, the reorg department submits the old certificates on behalf of the owners and accepts the new ones in satisfaction. If the exchange is voluntary, reorg needs a voluntary exchange request, that is, written instructions from the beneficial owner. In an involuntary exchange, no instructions are needed. Another type of exchange results from a merger, which is when one company's stock is exchanged for that of another. In a merger, reorg submits its customers' shares for shares in the surviving company or for shares of a newly organized third company. When the exchange is complete, reorg adjusts the records of the holdings of the firm and its customers. If the merger is an outright acquisition for cash, the customers' accounts are credited with the funds received after the reorganization department submits the old shares and obtains payment.

In a *preemptive rights (subscription privilege) offering,* a corporation offers its existing stockholders the right to purchase additional stock from an upcoming primary offering at a favorable price prior to the offering's effective date. The right to "subscribe" to the offering permits the owner to purchase the new stock at a "discount" price. As such, the right itself has a dollar value and can be bought or sold until its expiration date, after which it is worthless.

The reorg department handles the disposition of the rights for the firm's clients. If the beneficial owner of the rights wants to purchase stock (that is, "exercise" the rights), the reorg staff uses funds from the customer's account and the rights to subscribe to the new offering. If additional rights are needed to satisfy the customer's written instructions, reorg purchases them, either from the issuing company's agent or in the open market. Conversely, if certain customers decide not to subscribe or if they own rights in excess of the amount needed to subscribe for the number of shares they want to buy, the reorganization department disposes of the extra rights before they expire. It may either sell them to the company's agent bank or standby underwriter, or accept someone else's bid in the open market. Either way, the appropriate customer accounts are credited with the net proceeds of that sale.

Reorg provides a similar service for *warrants,* which are also subscription securities to buy the corporation's stock, but whose expiration dates are often years in the future. A few have no expiration dates. When the warrant holder exercises the purchase option, reorg handles the procedure but needs written instructions from the beneficial owner before taking action.

Reorg staff handles all the paper work in a *tender offer,* which is a formal solicitation to induce shareholders to sell their shares. A tender offer can be a successful method for acquiring large amounts of stock. It is often used by corporations or large institutions to effect a merger with, or to gain control of, another "target" company. If not enough shares are submitted for sale, the offering company is denied its objective. Under these circumstances, the offerer usually reserves the right to refuse the purchase of any shares tendered—a valuable privilege not available in open-market transactions. Similarly, if a tender offer produces more than enough shares to satisfy the offerer, the offerer can accept all the shares, any portion of them, or only the amount specified in the proxy statement. If only some of the shares are to be purchased, they can be bought either on a first-come/first-served basis or on a pro-rated basis.

MARGIN DEPARTMENT

At the same time that P&S sends a copy of the confirmation to the cashier department, it sends a copy to the margin department. The name of this department, however, is a bit of a misnomer. Staff members do handle all the calculations relating to margin transactions, but they also do a whole lot more. In fact, they are responsible for ensuring that *all* the firm's accounts—margin or other types—meet all the financial requirements of the various regulatory bodies.

Before listing their other duties, however, let's see how a margin account works. Customers may buy stocks in two types of accounts. In a *cash* account, they pay for the securities in full no later than the settlement date. For example, a client buys 100 shares of ZAP at 42. The market value of the securities is therefore $4,200 (100 shares of ZAP × $42). (Ignore commission and other expenses.) The client pays for the purchase in full, and the equity in the account is therefore $4,200. If ZAP rises to $60 per share, the market value becomes $6,000 (100 ZAP × $60), and the client's equity becomes $6,000.

In a *margin* account, the customer puts up a percentage of the sale price, and the brokerage firm puts up the rest. The cash that the client places into the account is the "equity," and the brokerage's part is called the "margin" or "debit balance," which is just another name for loan. The firm borrows the margin amount from a commercial bank at one rate and lends it to the client at a higher rate. (The customer pays an interest charge.) The firm keeps the purchased stock in its vault as collateral for both loans: the one to the customer and the one from the bank.

How much cash does the client have to pay to buy stock on margin? The percentage is determined by the Federal Reserve Board in its Regulation T. (Although Fed writes the regulation, the NYSE and NASD enforce it.) "Reg T" currently requires customers to initially put up at least 50 percent of the purchase price. The Fed has the authority to change the requirement. For example, a customer who wants to purchase $10,000 worth of stock on margin must put $5,000 (50 percent of $10,000) into the account. The brokerage firm lends the customer the other $5,000. Disregarding, for the sake of simplicity, commissions and other charges, this account now looks like this:

Current market value	$10,000 (100 shares × $10)
Less: Debit balance	$ 5,000
Equity	$ 5,000

As we know, however, stock prices generally do not remain the same for very long. Let's assume that the market price of ZAP rises to $12 per share. In that case, the account looks like this:

Current market value	$12,000 (100 shares × $12)
Less: Debit balance	$ 5,000
Equity	$ 7000

Because the market value of the stock rose, the client's equity increased. There is no question that the client's account meets the 50 percent requirement: $7,000 is greater than the initial $5,000 equity (50 percent of $10,000). The account is said to have "excess equity" of $2,000 ($7,000 less the initial requirement of $5,000).

But suppose the market value of ZAP declined to $8 per share. Now the account looks like this:

Current market value	$8,000	(100 shares × $8)
Less: Debit balance	$5,000	
Equity	$3,000	

Now the equity ($3,000) is considerably less than the 50 percent requirement of $5,000 (50 percent of $10,000). As you can see, equity decreases with market value. But that's all right because the 50 percent requirement no longer applies; it is only an *initial requirement.*

The current market value of a margined stock may drop somewhat without the firm having to "call" the client for additional money. In fact, the market value may decline without a "margin call" until the equity is less than one-third of the debit balance as established by the brokerage firm. This is called the "maintenance" requirement. In the example, the equity is $3,000 and the debit balance, $5,000. This account is still adequately margined. If the market value drops to, say, $6.50, then the account is in need of more money:

Current market value	$6,500	(100 shares × $6.50)
Less: Debit balance	$5,000	
Equity	$1,500	

Equity is only $1,500—less than one-third of the $5,000 debit balance. When this happens, the brokerage firm issues a "maintenance" or "margin" call. The call would be for at least another $167, enough to bring the equity up to $1,667, which is one-third of $5,000. If the market value drops again, another call would go out.

The minimum maintenance requirement established by the NYSE is 25 percent. If an account of position equity is less than one quarter of the debit balance, the firm must issue a mandatory call to bring the account into compliance.

Note: While the Fed sets the initial requirement of 50 percent (which is subject to change), the exchanges and other regulatory bodies are allowed to—and do so—set higher requirements, both for initial and maintenance margin. The brokerage firms themselves often set even higher requirements for the sake of self-protection. Just as customers have to deposit "call" money if the stock's market price goes down, they are entitled to use any excess equity in the account if the price goes up. For example, when the price of ZAP rose to $12, the account had excess equity of $2,000. The customer may withdraw that money or apply it toward the purchase of more stock.

Let's say the customer wants to buy ABC stock, on margin, with that $2,000. How much stock can the customer buy? That is, what is the "buying power" of the excess equity? To answer that question, you need a simple formula:

Buying power = Excess equity ÷ Margin rate
= $2,000 ÷ 0.50
= $4,000

This customer can buy up to $4,000 worth of ABC, currently at $40 per share, with the excess equity ($2,000) and a loan from the brokerage firm ($2,000). If both ZAP and ABC increase enough in value, whatever excess equity develops can be used to purchase still more stock. As you can see, buying on margin is an excellent leverage technique—a way of controlling as much stock as possible with the dollars available for investment. As long as stock prices keep rising, as in a bull market, the leveraging of excess equity can go on forever. The opposite is true when prices decline. As the current market value of the stocks drops, so does equity. As price declines continue, more and more margin calls go out, and stock owners have to decide whether to keep meeting those calls or just to sell off the stock and take their losses. In a bear market, therefore, two things happen: margin calls and sell-offs increase in frequency. The sharper the drop in price, the faster the calls and sell-offs.

In addition to supervising cash and margin accounts, the margin staff:

* Instructs the cage to issue checks or to deliver securities

* Notifies account executives of "items due," such as cash or securities due from clients

* Files for extensions on payment of margin calls

* Closes out positions when necessary

STOCK RECORD DEPARTMENT

During the course of trading each day, the status of the securities under the firm's care changes constantly. Certificates arrive from and go out to customers and other brokers. Others go to the transfer agent, and still others come back. Book-entry changes of ownership occur, even though the certificates do not change hands. Separate logs of activity are maintained in the dividend, proxy, and reorg departments, but some kind of central control and reference source is needed.

The stock record department keeps track of all the securities for which the firm is responsible (bonds too, despite the department's name). For financial and regulatory reasons, the individual record of each issue must be unquestionably current and accurate.

The position lists used by the dividend, proxy, and reorganization departments are a part of the records that are prepared and maintained by the stock record depart-ment. This part of operations serves as a control and reference source for monitoring securities under the bro-kerage firm's jurisdiction. An individual record is main-tained for each issue. The stock record ledger shows the following:

* Name of the security

* Owner of the security

* Location of the certificate

In terms of location, the stock record also has to identify whether that security is in one of the following:

* Safekeeping (the "box")

* Segregation

* Pledged in a loan arrangement at a bank

* Pledged in a loan to another broker/dealer

* In reregistration proceedings at the transfer agent

* In transit to the customer's agent bank or broker versus payment

* In fail-to-receive status from a contrabroker/dealer or customer

Throughout all the changes within a given day, the stock record has to remain balanced. A *break* in the record indicates that a mistake has been made. Given the amount of activity surrounding this document, errors must be corrected immediately—or they might never be corrected at all.

To ensure that record books are kept to a minimum size and corrected as soon as possible, the stock record department issues a daily report and a weekly report. The *daily stock record* reports the movement of all securities involved in any kind of movement: sale, purchase, transfer into or out of the vault, received from a customer, and so on. The *weekly stock record* is a balance sheet of all securities under the supervision of the firm, whether or not they were involved in a transaction the preceding week. Both of these reports must balance—like a balance sheet. Stock may not be removed from a part of the record without being accounted for in some way or another.

ACCOUNTING DEPARTMENT

The accounting department in a brokerage firm performs all the tasks that it would in any other type of company. However, in addition to its quarterly and annual reports to stockholders, the accounting department also issues special reports for regulatory bodies such as the SEC or NASD. Sometimes the regulatory authority calls for a report as the result of a special audit.

Other reports are generated periodically, such as the Financial and Operational Combined Uniform Single (FOCUS) Report. This statement gives regulators vital information about the financial health of the brokerage firm, because it demonstrates the firm's financial ability to carry on its business. The report discounts all nonliquid assets by 100 percent (that is, ignores their value completely). Then it reduces the value of other assets according to the amount of "prudent risk" they represent. Liabilities are carried at full exposure; only those that are 100 percent covered are excluded. Total liabilities are then divided by total assets. The ratio resulting from this test dramatizes the firm's strength in the face of adversity. Under this rigid test, liabilities usually exceed assets. Ratios of 4 to 1, to 8 to 1 are normal. The various self-regulatory organizations monitor firms and grow suspicious of those whose ratios reach 10 to 1 or 12 to 1. The rule is that a firm's ratio may not exceed 15 to 1. At this point, a firm usually goes out of business anyway.

The *15c3–3 report* is another responsibility of the accounting department. Under this SEC rule, the brokerage firm has to maintain a free credit balance in a "special reserve bank account for the exclusive benefit of customers." The 15c3–3 report compares this cash credit balance with the total of all customers' debit balances. If the total customers' credit balances exceed their debit balances, the firm has to deposit cash in a bank account. If total customer debit exceeds credit, the deposit is not necessary.

This rule denies the brokerage firm the right to use these funds in the speculative conduct of its own business. The accounting department, employing a formula approved by the stock exchange or the NASD, supervises the firm's compliance with this rule and ensures that customer money is used only for customer purposes.

The accounting department is also involved in the very last step in customer operations activity—the preparation of the statements of account. Under federal law, if there has been any transaction activity, security position, or money balance in an account within the preceding calendar quarter, the customer must receive a statement of account. Many firms comply by sending their customers (particularly margin account customers) monthly statements instead of the mandatory quarterly report.

Whether monthly or quarterly, the statement summarizes all that has occurred in the customer's account during the period. All purchase expenses are debited to the account, and sales proceeds are credited. However, each purchase and/or sales transaction is posted on the contract settlement date, whereas all other activities are posted on the day they occur. For example, a check received from a customer is credited to the account on the day it is received, and money delivered out of the account is debited on the actual day of reimbursement. But a regular-way sale of a corporate security on June 26 is not posted until July 3, five business days later. This difference is often a point of confusion for customers, especially when they receive their monthly statements of account without certain month-end trades posted on it.

Despite the best efforts and intentions of the accounting department, mistakes occur. Perhaps an issue is not carried forward to the following month's position listing, or duplicate entries are processed accidentally and both items are posted in the account. A typical customer statement, therefore, carries a self-protective legend, "E&OE," which means, "errors and omissions excepted." This statement allows the brokerage firm an opportunity to correct the mistake without legal liability.

DIVIDEND DEPARTMENT

Many people have their stocks registered not in their own name but instead in the name of their brokerage firms (or "street" name). By so doing, they do not have to worry about signing the securities or a stock power when they want to sell. Instead, all they have to do is call their broker and say "sell," and an officer of the firm endorses the certificate. The issuing corporation, however, may not know who those clients are. As a result, it sends the firm anything that it would normally send to the stockholder, such as annual statements and other company-related information. One of the things that the corporation sends the brokerage firm is a check for any dividends due on preferred and common stock held in street name. But those dividends rightfully belong to the "beneficial" owner of the stock, the client. For example, if 100 clients, each of whom owns 100 shares of a given stock, should decide to register their stock in their broker's name, then the company's books show that the firm "owns" 10,000 shares. When it's time to pay a dividend, the company makes one check payable to the firm, since the company has no way of knowing the actual beneficial owners. The firm, when it receives the check, then distributes the proceeds on a proportional basis to all of the actual owners.

This task falls to the dividend department employees, who are responsible for checking every security in every account to make sure that all clients receive the dividends to which they are entitled (and to make sure clients do not keep any dividend to which they are not entitled). Their work, however, is complicated by the dividend-paying process.

For cash dividends, the process hinges on four dates. First, on the *declaration date*, the company's board of directors announces that the company will pay a dividend of a certain size. On the second date, the *record date*, the company asks its registrar to provide a list of its current shareholders so that it knows who is entitled to the dividend checks. *To receive the dividend, the stockholder has to be on the company's books as a shareholder as of this date.* Third, on the *payment date*, the company actually cuts the dividend checks, usually about two weeks after the record date.

Many investors don't understand this cycle, and they angrily call their stockbrokers to demand dividend checks to which they are *not* entitled. Generally, the reason is that they were not the holders of record on the record date, but they don't understand why.

Hence, the fourth date, known as the *ex-dividend date*. Most stock trades take five business days to be cleared, that is, they settle "regular way." Someone who buys the stock five days before the record date will be the holder of record on that date. But a regular-way (that is, five-day settlement) trade made four or fewer days before the record date will not be settled when the corporate registrar takes the list of stockholders. Therefore the purchaser receives no dividend. Ex means without. Buy on an 'ex date and you will receive no dividend. Why? Because the regular way trade will settle after the record date. You are a record holder on the date the trade settles. The dividend will therefore be mailed (rightfully) to the seller of the stock.

Something else happens on the ex-dividend date. Would-be purchasers of the stock know that they are not going to get the dividend as of this day. As a result, the market value of the stock generally drops by the value of the dividend when it opens for trading on the ex-dividend date.

Let's look at an example which involves the following calendar:

			May			
S	M	T	W	T	F	S
	1	2	3	4	5	6
7	8	9	10	**11**	12	13
14	15	16	**17**	**18**	19	20
21	22	23	24	25	26	27
28	29	31				

The board of directors puts out a press release on May 2 saying that it will pay a $0.50 dividend to the owners of record as of May 17,. with checks to be mailed as of May 26. May 2 is the declaration date, May 17 is the record date, and May 26 is the payment date. The ex-dividend date is therefore May 11. If an investor buys the stock on May 11 for regular-way settlement, the trade does not settle until May 18. The investor is not recorded as the owner of the stock on the company's books until May 18. Thus, the seller is still entitled to receive the dividend. May 12, 15, and 16 are also declared to be ex dates.

Sometimes the dividend check is mailed to the wrong person. Either the firm does not get the information about the new owner to the registrar in time, or the registrar does not process the information in time, or someone commits an error somewhere along the line. If the dividend check is inadvertently mailed to the wrong party, that party must return it so it can be correctly routed.

Stock dividends work a little differently. "Small" stock dividends (less than 25 percent) are handled like cash dividends. For large stock dividends (25 percent or larger) and all stock splits, the sequence of the dates is different. The ex-dividend date, now called the ex-distribution date, comes after the payment date instead of after the declaration date. Thus the sequence for a stock distribution is as follows:

* Declaration date

* Record date

* Payment date

* Ex-distribution date

The ex-distribution date is usually the business day following payment by the corporation. For example, using the same calendar:

			May			
S	*M*	*T*	*W*	*T*	*F*	*S*
	1	**2**	3	4	5	6
7	8	9	10	11	12	13
14	15	16	17	18	19	20
21	22	23	**24**	**25**	26	27
28	29	31				

If the company declares a 25 percent stock dividend on May 2, for payment on May 24, then the stock starts to trade ex-distribution on May 25. Anyone who buys the stock so as to receive delivery before May 25 is entitled to receive the stock dividend.

If someone buys the stock between the record and payment dates, it is possible that the stock could be delivered without the stock dividend. So, from the fourth business day before the record date until (and including) the payable date, all trades in a stock-dividend-paying security carry *due bills*, which are IOUs for the stock to be issued on the payable date.

For example, RIP is undergoing a two-for-one split. A client buys 100 shares of RIP at 50, so that the purchase settles before the record date. But delivery of the stock to the brokerage firm occurs after the record date. The receiving firm pays $5,000 to the delivering firm (100 shares × $50) and demands a due bill for the additional 100 shares that will result from the split. On the day following the payable date for RIP's two-for-one split, the shares are worth only $25 each. Now the dividend department has to claim the second 100 shares with the due bill. In return for the due bill, the dividend department receives the second hundred:

• Client buys	100 RIP @ 50 = $5,000
• Client receives	100 RIP @ 50 = $5,000
• Value of stock after split	100 RIP @ 25 = $2,500
• Client's account after due bill is satisfied	200 RIP @ 25 = $5,000

PROXY DEPARTMENT

In addition to dividend checks, firms receive proxy statements for any stocks they hold for their clients. Proxies, or "advisory and voting solicitations," give shareholders the right to elect members of the corporate board of directors and to decide on other important matters brought before an annual or special meeting of the stockholders.

Handling these proxies is the job of the proxy department. To allow the beneficial owners of the shares to vote, the proxy department sends a request form, called a proxy, to each of the beneficial owners. As the owners return their proxies, the firm tallies the votes and reflects the owners' wishes when it votes its shares at the annual meeting.

As an example, two owners leave their stock in street name. The first owner has 200 shares, and the second has 100 shares. The firm receives the right to cast 300 votes at the annual meeting. The firm sends proxies to the owners, collects their responses, and votes as they would have voted if they had actually attended the annual meeting and voted for themselves. If investor A votes yes and investor B votes no on a certain proposal, then the firm casts 200 yes votes and 100 no votes at the annual meeting.

Sometimes the beneficial owners do not bother to advise the proxy department about their preferences. Exchange regulations prevent a firm from voting on crucial issues unless it receives instructions from its clients. (However, firms can vote unreturned proxies on routine matters.)

The proxy department also acts as agent for any person or group wishing to communicate with the beneficial owners whose shares are in the firm's custody. The group, however, must have registered its proxy statement or solicitation with the SEC, per Section 14 of the Securities Exchange Act of 1934, and must agree to reimburse the brokerage firm for postage and other out-of-pocket expenses connected with a mailing.

A stockholder solicitation may be a simple plea for a vote to effect a reform or to change the company's present management. Or it may be a request for the beneficial owners to tender their shares in response to a purchase proposition. The latter, in larger firms, is often assigned to the reorganization department. Finally, the proxy department distributes corporate publications (including financial reports), notices of meetings, and voting information to the beneficial owners who have their securities in street name.

When they think of the securities industry, many people call to mind the busy floor of the stock exchange, the electronic trading screens, and the Wall Street area. Not many can picture the sometimes feverish back office work that is necessary to keep the records and books straight, to comply with regulations, to protect the interests of customer and firm alike, and through it all, to make a profit.

Never, however, were modern stock market mechanisms tested more than on Monday, October 19, 1987. On this day, the volume of trading reached unprecedented levels, while prices dropped out of control. What happened that day on the exchange floors, at the trading desks, and elsewhere is the subject of Chapter 14. Before getting to the events of so called "Black Monday," however, the next chapter covers market theories—how analysts try to predict market movement.

CHAPTER 11

Stock Market Theories:

Can Prices Really Be Predicted?

Like so many simple-sounding maxims, "Buy low, sell high" is far more easily said than done. Living and profiting by this dictum means predicting the highs and lows of stock prices. It entails knowing when and for how long buyers will outnumber sellers and vice versa. Anyone who could accurately foresee bull and bear markets would never have to work another day and could live like a monarch. So the search for highs and lows goes on and on.

According to some market observers, however, that search is just about futile. Their reasoning is based on the assumption that any influence on supply or demand is already reflected in stock prices. For example, if a company is rumored to be going bankrupt, if an arms manufacturer is about to be awarded a fat defense contract, or if a corporation is a takeover target—these and other influences must have been considered by reasonably well-informed investors before they place their buy or sell orders. The market is regarded as "efficient," that is, it takes into account—or "discounts"—all the conditions affecting supply and demand.

A corollary of this theory is that the conditions resulting in stock prices are so complex and, for the most part, patternless that predicting them is all but impossible. No one can say with any great certainty where prices will be tomorrow, next week, or next year. That is, stock prices are said to take a "random walk." That's the "efficient market" or "random walk" theory.

Many professional traders make a great deal of money on "inefficiencies" in the market. For one thing, not all investors are equally well informed, nor are they all informed at the same time. This transmission of secret "insider" information is by law prohibited. Most brokerage firms have securities systems and procedures, collectively known as a "Chinese Wall," to keep such information secret. So its delay is guaranteed. Further, each investor may react differently to the same information. For example, some risk-aversive investors might regard a downswing of prices as a good reason to sell off stocks and get out of the market. More speculative market participants might look upon the same downturn as an opportunity to sell short and reap profits. Long-term buy-and-hold investors might dismiss the drop as a temporary setback in a trend that will not fail to turn upward again presenting them with an opportunity to buy low. These individuals would buy. Different investors, different investment objectives, different reactions.

Inefficiencies resulting from either varied investor reactions or the delayed diffusion of information are opportunities for profit for those who watch the stock market closely. Arbitrageurs are market watchers who are more quick to capitalize on such inefficiencies. Suppose a stock is, for the moment, selling at a significantly lower price on one exchange than it is on another. Arbitrageurs may buy the stock at the lower price and simultaneously sell it at the higher price. To make money from such fleeting aberrations, arbitrageurs must have on-line access to information from many exchanges, a large amount of capital to work with, and the ability to get orders executed on a moment's notice. Inefficiencies do exist, and some market participants make money on them. Nevertheless, the efficient market—or random walk—theory does not sit well with most analysts. It implies that prices cannot really be predicted other than to say that, for as long as prices have been charted, they have worked their way generally upward. (Also by implication, the only viable strategy is to "buy and hold.") Yet to make real money, which is what brokerage firms are in business to do, you have to be able to predict prices more precisely and on a shorter-term basis.

THE FIRST AMERICAN ANALYST

The theoretical futility of analysis did not prevent a 31-year-old man from co-founding a financial information service company in 1882. The co-founders were Charles Dow and Edward Jones, and the company was the Dow Jones Company. The purpose of the company was to provide information and news that affected the stock market. Over 100 years later, the name "Dow Jones" has become associated with the financial newspaper (*Wall Street Journal*), a major publishing firm (*Dow-Jones Irwin*), and the most widely quoted and followed stock market averages in the world.

Only two years after founding the company, Charles Dow devised a method by which the prices of 11 railroad company stocks were averaged out and used as an indicator of prices in the railroad industry. By 1897, 20 railroad stocks were included in the average. In the same year, he created an industrial stock average, comprised of 12 such stocks.

Figure 11-1. The Dow Jones Average

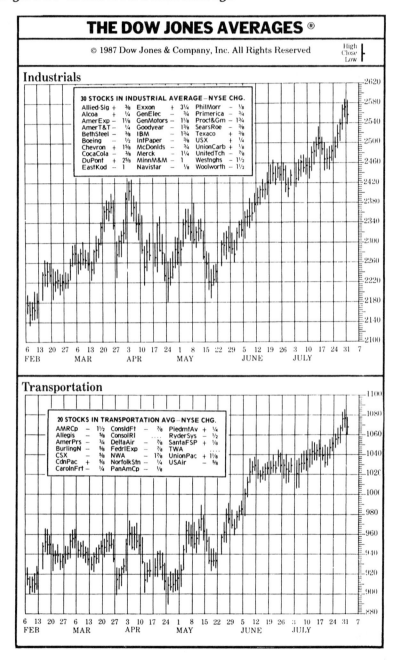

Figure 11–1. The Dow Jones Averages (cont.).

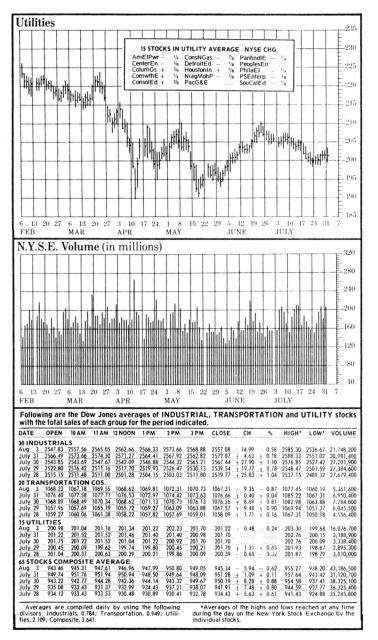

Utilities

15 STOCKS IN UTILITY AVERAGE –NYSE CHG.

AmElPwr — ¼	ConsNGas — ⅞	PanhndlE — ¼
CenterEn — ⅛	DetroitEd — ⅛	PeoplesEn —
ColumGs + ¾	HoustonIn + ⅛	PhilaEl — ⅛
ComwthE + ¼	NiagMohP — ⅛	PSEnterp — ⅛
ConsolEd + ⅜	PacG&E	SouCalEd — ⅛

N.Y.S.E. Volume (in millions)

Following are the Dow Jones averages of INDUSTRIAL, TRANSPORTATION and UTILITY stocks with the total sales of each group for the period indicated.

DATE	OPEN	10 AM	11 AM	12 NOON	1 PM	2 PM	3 PM	CLOSE	CH	%	HIGH*	LOW*	VOLUME
30 INDUSTRIALS													
Aug 3	2547.83	2557.56	2565.05	2562.66	2566.33	2573.66	2568.88	2557.08	− 14.99	− 0.58	2585.30	2536.67	21,748,200
July 31	2566.49	2573.66	2574.30	2571.27	2564.41	2567.92	2562.82	2572.07	+ 4.63	+ 0.18	2588.33	2551.02	20,981,400
July 30	2543.85	2543.69	2547.67	2542.09	2546.88	2544.32	2565.21	2567.44	+ 27.90	+ 1.10	2576.85	2527.42	27,201,900
July 29	2522.80	2516.42	2511.16	2517.70	2519.93	2526.47	2530.13	2519.77	+ 19.77	+ 0.78	2548.47	2501.59	27,384,600
July 28	2515.15	2511.48	2511.00	2501.28	2504.15	2503.03	2511.80	2519.77	+ 25.83	+ 1.04	2537.15	2489.32	27,679,400
20 TRANSPORTATION COS.													
Aug 3	1068.23	1067.18	1069.55	1068.62	1069.81	1072.31	1070.73	1067.31	− 9.35	− 0.87	1077.45	1060.19	5,361,600
July 31	1076.40	1077.58	1077.71	1076.53	1072.97	1074.42	1073.63	1076.66	+ 0.40	+ 0.04	1085.22	1067.31	6,950,400
July 30	1068.89	1068.49	1070.34	1068.62	1071.13	1070.73	1076.13	1076.26	+ 8.69	+ 0.81	1082.98	1063.88	7,784,800
July 29	1057.96	1057.69	1055.19	1055.72	1059.27	1063.09	1063.88	1067.57	+ 9.48	+ 0.90	1069.94	1051.37	6,045,500
July 28	1059.27	1060.06	1061.38	1058.22	1057.82	1057.69	1059.01	1058.09	+ 1.71	+ 0.16	1067.31	1050.18	4,556,400
15 UTILITIES													
Aug 3	200.98	201.04	201.16	201.34	201.22	202.23	201.70	201.22	− 0.48	− 0.24	203.30	199.68	16,076,700
July 31	201.22	201.52	201.52	201.46	201.40	201.40	200.98	201.70	....	....	202.76	200.15	3,188,900
July 30	201.75	201.22	201.52	201.04	201.22	200.92	201.70	201.70	....	....	202.76	200.09	3,338,400
July 29	200.45	200.09	199.62	199.74	199.80	200.45	200.21	201.70	+ 1.31	+ 0.65	201.93	198.67	2,895,300
July 28	201.04	200.37	200.63	200.39	200.21	199.86	200.09	200.39	− 0.65	− 0.32	201.87	198.79	3,010,000
65 STOCKS COMPOSITE AVERAGE													
Aug 3	943.46	945.31	947.61	946.96	947.99	950.80	949.05	949.05	− 5.94	− 0.62	955.27	938.20	43,186,500
July 31	949.74	951.76	951.94	950.94	948.50	949.64	948.09	951.28	+ 1.09	+ 0.11	957.64	943.42	31,120,700
July 30	943.22	942.77	944.28	942.36	944.14	943.32	949.67	950.19	+ 8.28	+ 0.88	954.58	937.41	38,325,100
July 29	935.08	933.43	931.37	932.99	934.43	937.21	938.07	941.91	+ 7.48	+ 0.80	944.59	927.77	36,325,400
July 28	934.12	933.43	933.53	930.48	930.89	930.41	932.78	934.43	+ 5.63	+ 0.61	941.43	924.84	35,245,800

Averages are compiled daily by using the following divisors: Industrials, 0.784; Transportation, 0.949; Utilities, 2.109; Composite, 3.641.

*Averages of the highs and lows reached at any time during the day on the New York Stock Exchange by the individual stocks.

Today, the financial news is not complete without a report on the three Dow Jones averages: 30 industrials, 20 transportation, and 15 utilities. Millions of newspaper readers and newscast viewers and listeners know about "the Dow."

Yet some critics say the Dow Jones average does not represent American industry today because the issuing corporations represented in the averages are "big cap." Their research and development projects are big-budgeted and long-term, unlike those of younger, more responsive corporations, such as "hi-tech" computer systems or software companies. As a result, their successes or failures are "lag indicators," that is, they occur long after the rest of the market has moved.

Other averages are available, and they serve as indicators along with the Dow. The Barron's average includes 50 leading stocks. The Value Line Composite Average includes over 1,600 of both NYSE and OTC issues. The Indicators Digest includes some 2,500 stocks, both exchange, and OTC traded. Yet the Dow persists as the first, the oldest, and the most widely recognized of averages. The Dow averages are *the* key indicators used to interpret the so-called *Dow theory*. Charles Dow never formulated a theory in a single writing, but his successors attempted to organize his work into a coherent system, which today is normally called the Dow theory.

According to this theory, these types of price movements are at work in the stock market at the same time:

* The "narrow movement" consists of day-to-day fluctuations.

* The "short swing" is made up of trends that last from two weeks to a month or a little more.

* The "main movement" is the long-term trend—bull or bear—that lasts four years or more.

Perhaps the greatest criticism of this three-part theory, however, is that it is not intended to predict the duration of a trend. Rather it is intended only to *mark* trend reversals. The theory is therefore a market-following system (or lag indicator), not a market-predicting system (or lead indicator). It tells, supposedly through the Dow averages, only where the market's been, not where it's going.

Indexes, on the other hand, are also constructed to reflect American industry and the stock market. They are generally composed of many more stocks than are averages, and those stocks make up a more representative array of American business.

Indexes are usually weighted according to float, so that each stock is represented proportionately in the resultant figure. Let's look at how Stocks A-D might be used in an oversimplified index:

	Market Price	Number of Shares Outstanding (Float)
1. Stock A	$50.00	10,000,000
2. Stock B	$45.00	2,000,000
3. Stock C	$55.00	3,000,000
4. Stock D	$60.00	1,000,000

To prepare a weighted index, multiply each stock price by the number of shares outstanding and add up all the totals:

	Market Price		Float		
1. Stock A	$50.00	×	10,000,,00	=	500,000,000
2. Stock B	$45.00	×	2,000,000	=	90,000,000
3. Stock C	$55.00	×	3,000,000	=	165,000,000
4. Stock D	$60.00	×	1,000,000	=	60,000,000
Total					815,000,000

To this total is applied a divisor, which might be the total weighted value of the stocks in the index at the time the index was created. For example, suppose the baseline value, or divisor, is 125,000,000). This index value would be 6.52

(815,000,000 divided by 125,000,000). Naturally, actual indexes are much more complicated than this. Our illustration is a grossly oversimplified view of both averages and indexes. In truth, some averages are weighted and some indexes are not. In addition, both averages and indexes undergo adjustments for stock splits, companies that "disappear" due to mergers or other reasons, and other changes.

Indexes are a relatively new development in the securities industry, and they have become very popular as indicators. Some of the widely used indexes are

* The New York Stock Exchange Composite Index of the 1750 or so common stocks listed on that exchange, grouped as industrials, transportation, and financial/utility.

* The American Stock Exchange Market Value Index of all 800 or so common stocks listed on that exchange.

* NASDAQ Composite Index, comprised of some common stocks organized as industry, bank, insurance, other financial companies, transportation, and utilities.

* Standard & Poor's OTC 250 uses 250 of the OTC market's largest industrial stocks. Price-weighted, it is disseminated by the minute.

* The Value Line Composite, made up of about 1,700 stocks, includes both "big cap" and smaller companies.

* The Wilshire 5,000 Equity Index is perhaps the broadest index available, comprising all stocks for which daily quotations are available.

Another popular index is the Standard & Poor's 500, which includes 400 industrials, 20 transportation, and 40 public utility. (Standard & Poor's also publishes an index of 100 stocks.)

In addition to acting as market indicators, indexes have been widely adopted as underlying instruments for futures. The seller of a futures contract agrees to sell an underlying commodity or instrument at a specified price and time. The "underlying" interest can be anything from pork bellies to precious metals or Treasury bonds. The buyer of the futures contract, of course, agrees to buy the underlying commodity or financial instrument on the same terms.

Historically, the futures contract grew out of the agricultural economy of the past. Farmers needed to lock in a profitable price for their crops, that is, they needed to "hedge" their risk of losing money if the crop did not command a profitable price at the market. To assure a profit, they agreed to sell their crops, when harvested at some specific future date, at a profitable price. Speculators entered into these contracts with the expectation of reselling the crops at even higher prices, thereby making a profit for themselves. In addition to speculators, processors bought such contracts to lock in the cost of raw materials. For example, a baked goods company might buy wheat contracts to lock in future costs at a level that enables it to make a profit on the end products—bread, cakes, rolls, and the like.

What has all this to do with indexes? Over the years, the futures contract has become a trading vehicle on its own. Futures contracts are traded not only on the traditional agricultural commodities (soybeans, sugar, and the like), but also on precious metals, U.S. government securities, currencies, and a host of other underlying interests, including stock indexes.

Indexes, however, present a wrinkle. Implied in a futures contract is the actual delivery of the underlying commodity or instrument the seller decides to "exercise" the contract. In practice only a few percent of futures are exercised, so delivery is not likely. Nevertheless, when a contract is exercised, the seller's duty is to delivery soybeans, wheat, orange juice, or whatever. What does the seller deliver when an index futures contract is exercised? The answer is cash.

Here's how a futures contract on an index works. Let's say that you own—that is, if you are "long"—one December S&P 500 Stock Index futures contract. Assume that the current market price for the contract is 129, which is the "index number." If you exercise the contract—that is, demand delivery—you will be paid $64,500, which is the index number (market price) times $500, the contractual value of each point in the index number. If you paid less than 129 ($64,500) for the contract, then you make a profit. If you paid more, you lose money.

Who trades index futures? Among others, anyone who needs to protect a large position in stocks—pension funds, insurance companies, banks, brokerage firms, and other institutional investors. The portfolios for these investors typically include large positions in many different stocks. By diversifying their stock holdings, they hedge the risk of loss if one or another stock drops in value. The gains on other stocks in the portfolio generally more than offset such a loss in value. This type of risk is referred to as "specific," "nonsystematic," or "diversifiable" risk.

Harder to hedge is the risk of an across-the-board loss, in which all or most of the securities in a portfolio take a nose dive due to a downturn in the market itself. This is called "market," "systematic," or "nondiversifiable" risk. Very little can be done to protect against losses due to this kind of risk other than to watch the market very carefully.

This is where index futures come in. By buying futures contracts on an index whose composition resembles the mix of stocks in their holdings, portfolio managers can limit their losses due to market downturns. For example, a mutual fund portfolio manager controls $500 million in stock values, and foresees a sharp near-term drop in the market. Trying to sell $500 million quickly at reasonable prices would be technically very difficult, and probably an undesirable course of action anyway, if the long-term prognosis is bullish. The stock market futures contract offers downside protection without exposing the portfolio manager becomes a farmer with a silo jammed full of stock certificates rather than with ears of corn. A short futures position may be used by each as a hedge against the loss of inventory value. Speculators and others may likewise attempt to profit by taking outright long or short positions, thus providing the same type of risk transfer mechanism that has worked so well previously with farm products, industrial goods, and other financial instruments.

Here's an example. An investor holds a diversified portfolio of blue-chip stocks worth $250,000. The investor fears a sharp setback could occur prior to the resumption of a long-term bull market. Because of its greater concentration of blue-chip issues, the S&P 500 is the best hedge vehicle for this portfolio and the investor sells short three contracts at an assumed current price of $168. With each contract worth $500 × $168, the short position's dollar value is $252,000 ($500 × $168 × 3), hedging the entire portfolio value and then some.

If the value of the portfolio declines by 10 percent, the shares will be worth $225,000. However, if the portfolio's actual decline is 10 percent, the S&P futures position would have had a similar decline, possibly 9 percent, to 152.90. If the three futures positions are closed out at this price, the profit is $22,650, largely offsetting the loss in value on the portfolio. The futures profit is computed as follows:

	$	Points/Contract
Sold 3 contracts @ 168	$252,000	168.00
Loss: Covered short @ 152.90	$229,350	152.90
Profit .	$ 22,650	15.10

As you can see, this is basically the same type of arrangement as that between the farmer and the speculator or processor. The manager needs to hedge the future value of the portfolio, and other stock market participants are willing to "speculate" that the market will not decline. Options are also traded on indexes. An option is the right to buy or sell an underlying instrument at a specified price (the strike price) by a certain time (the expiration date). An option to buy is a "call"; an option to sell is a "put."

While the first options were based on stocks, today options are traded, like futures, on a number of instruments, such as U.S. government securities, currencies, and, of course, indexes. Like futures, options imply the "delivery" of the underlying interest, whether it is IBM stock or deutsche marks, except in the case of indexes, where exercising the option results in a cash payment. While options are very different from futures in many ways, they are also used by portfolio managers to hedge market risk.

To further complicate things, options are also traded on futures, including index futures. When an option on a futures contract is exercised, the option holder takes delivery of the futures contract. To take delivery of the cash, the manager then has to exercise the futures contract. Many institutional investors maintain huge positions in index futures and in options in index futures, for the sole purpose of protecting their holdings against market risk.

Needless to say, these positions can become extremely complicated, very often far too complex for any one person to control without the aid of computerized trading programs. The manager of such a program calculates the size of the futures and/or options position necessary, specifies the stock price levels at which the contracts should be exercised, and then leaves it to the computers to enter the orders necessary to exercise the option and, if necessary, the futures. Such trading programs are therefore set like mousetraps, to go off when the market declines to a certain level.

These programs also have created a stock market phenomenon known as the "witching hour." Both options and futures have expiration dates, at which time the contracts must be exercised or be allowed to expire. At these expiration dates, the volume of exercised contracts has increased drastically. This sudden surge of volume can, and often does, upset the market values of the underlying stocks and indexes. The result is a brief period of high volume and volatility, which runs counter to the essential principle of maintaining a "fair and orderly" market.

Of even greater concern is the "triple witching hours," when the expiration dates of futures, options contracts, and index contracts coincide. When this happens, the resultant volatility is synergized, playing havoc with the stock market. This represents such a threat to the market that stabilizing regulatory requirements have been implemented. The modern stock market is therefore much more complicated than in years past. It is an arena in which many institutional investors, both domestic and foreign, participate by means of sophisticated program trading systems.

THE ANALYSTS

Into this crowded and fast-paced trading stage, enter the analysts, of whom there are two basic types. Some analyze the stock itself in terms of the issuing company, the industry, the stock market, and relevant economic conditions. On the basis of their analyses, they attempt to predict whether there will be enough interest among investors—both individual and institutional—to drive the price of the stock upward. These areas of analysis are known as "fundamentals," and these analysts are called "fundamentalists." Fundamentalists look for "what" to buy or sell based on economics and economic principles. Generally at odds with fundamentalists are "technical analysts." Although their aim is to predict stock prices, they dismiss the likelihood that accurate forecasts can be made by analyzing fundamentals. Instead, their approach is to closely follow price movements, the assumption being that *any* influences on prices are already reflected in these movements. Therefore, you do not need to gauge investor motivations and market conditions—just follow the prices themselves. To follow price movements, technicians use two types of charts: bar charts and point-and-figure charts. (See Figure 11–2.) For this reason, these analysts are also known as "chartists." In following price movements on their charts, technicians look for patterns. They are primarily concerned with "when" to buy or sell based on market timing. (See Figure 11–3.) Once they can identify a

Figure 11–2.

Charting

The technician uses two types of charts: the bar chart and the point (P&F) chart.

Point and Figure (P&F) Chart

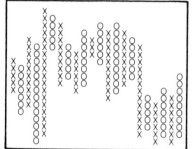

The Bar Chart

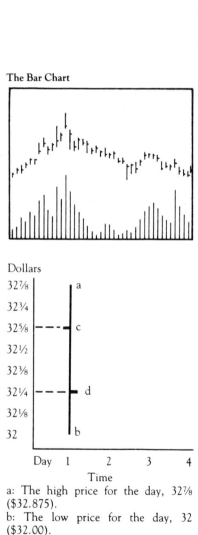

Constructing a bar chart is simple. At the top of the chart, enter the name of the stock (industry, index, market, or whatever you are charting). To the vertical axis assign a price scale, such as points or ⅛-points. On the horizontal axis, mark off the calendar time scale— days, weeks, or months. On a daily bar chart, every five-day period (a trading week) may be marked by a vertical line that is heavier than the others. For each day, the high, low, and closing prices are plotted. Vertical line, or *bar*, connnects the high and low prices. A horizontal tick to the right of the bar indicates the closing price. A tick mark on the left side of the bar marks the opening price for the day. With so many chart services available, however, plotting one's own charts is often an unnecessary and unprofitable way to spend time.

a: The high price for the day, 32⅞ ($32.875).
b: The low price for the day, 32 ($32.00).
c: The opening price (not always on the bar chart), 32⅝ ($32.625).
d: The closing price, 32¼ ($32.25).

Figure 11–3.

Point and Figure (P&F) Chart

Unlike bar charts, point and figure charts record only price movements; if no price change occurs, the chart remains the same. Time is not reflected on a P&F chart, although time reference points, such as "Mon," are sometimes used. Volume is indicated only by the number of recorded price changes, not as a separate entity.

Box Size. In a P&F chart, a rising price change is represented by an X, a declining price movement by an O. Each X or O occupies a box on the chart. One of the first decisions in constructing a P&F chart is therefore how great a price change each box should represent. For example, a chart might have a box size of a $\frac{1}{4}$-point ($0.25). On a less sensitive chart, a box might equal a point ($1); price movements of less than $1 would not be registered. On a more sensitive scale of, say, $\frac{1}{8}$-point per box, more detailed price action would be visible. Obviously, the smaller the value assigned to the box, the movement the chart will reflect—and the more tedious it is to construct.

Reversal Criterion. On a P&F chart, the analyst moves one row of boxes to the right every time prices change direction. The question is what constitutes a reversal? If prices move $\frac{1}{8}$-point against the trend, is that a significant enough reversal to warrant recording? Or is a 1-point reversal sufficient? Whatever the chartists decides to use as the occasion to move to the next row becomes the *reversal criterion* for the chart.

Example: A stock trades at the following prices:

25⅛	25⅜	25⅛	24¼
25⅛	25	25	
25¼	25½	24⅞	
25⅜	25⅛	25⅛	

If we want to chart these movements, the box size should probably be equal to $\frac{1}{8}$-point. A box size that is only slightly larger—$\frac{1}{4}$-point—would not include most of these movements. The reversal criterion should probably be $\frac{1}{8}$-point also; otherwise, again, most of the reversals would not be reflected on the chart. The movements, as charted, would look like this (the dot represents the first transaction):

25½	X O
25⅜	X O X O
25¼	X O X O
25⅛	● O X O X O
25	O X O X O
24⅞	O X O
24¾	O
24⅝	O
24½	O
24⅜	O
24¼	O

As you might suspect, box size and reversal criterion play a great role in how sensitive the chart is to price movements and in how the price movement data is represented. A "1x1" chart, for example, presents data so that every box is equal to a point and every point reversal is recorded. This would be a much more sensitive—and very different-looking chart—than a "2x3" chart, in which only two-point price changes and three-box reversals are reflected.

pattern, they will try to predict the direction of prices for a stock or for the market as a whole.

At any given time, many influences are at work on stock market prices: budget and trade deficits, fear of inflation or recession, rumors of war, good news or bad news about a company, and so on. The fundamentalist's task is to assess the effect of each of these factors and then, in light of those assessments, predict what the price of a stock or the market itself will do. To simplify things, the analyst categorizes influences into two groups. One group consists of business fundamentals which have to do with the issuing company. The other is made up of economic fundamentals which relate to the economy and the market.

One type of business fundamental consists of a company's earnings. The assumption is that if management is capable of producing high earnings in the future, the company is likely to grow considerably. When all that happens, the stock generally appreciates in value because it draws increasing numbers of buy orders, thereby "bidding up" the price in the marketplace, "Growth stock," as this kind of investment is called, offers an opportunity for significant increases in value over the original investment.

To measure earnings objectively, fundamentalists apply something known as a price-earnings (P/E) ratio. This ratio, as its name implies, compares a stock's price with the company's earnings per share. For example, suppose a company earns a profit of $500,000 and it has 1 million shares issued and outstanding. Its earnings are 50¢ per share ($500,000 divided by 1 million shares). Suppose further that the stock is selling for $10. To calculate the P/E ratio, simply divide the market price by the earnings per share: $10 divided by 50¢ equals 20 to 1. What does that number tell the analyst? For one thing, this ratio is on the "high" side, indicating that this might be considered a growth stock. The rationale is that earnings heavily outweigh the current market price of the stock (by 20 to 1) and that the price is likely to rise dramatically as the company's earning power is recognized.

It also might be that the market is generally in an uptrend and that this stock is simply being swept along with the market. For example, in the bull markets of early 1929, 1938, and 1946, the Dow Jones Industrial companies had P/E ratios of 19 to 1, 25 to 1, and 20 to 1, respectively. In the bear markets of 1942 and 1953, P/E ratios were closer to 10 to 1. As a rule, P/E ratios are "bid up" during bull markets and "sold down" in bear markets. Investors evaluating a stock for its growth potential must distinguish how much of the ratio is due to the stock's potential and how much is due to the market.

The P/E ratios of large, established companies tend to be lower. The reason is that their growth phase is largely over, and so the market value of their stock reflects their actual current earnings rather than potential future earnings. There is therefore a close correlation between price and earnings. Usually, in this category of low P/E ratios, for example, are the "big cap" (that is, large, well capitalized) companies of the Dow Jones averages.

In addition to growth, investors also buy stocks for yield, or income, in the form of dividends. To some, if earnings are the "two birds in the bush," then dividends are the "bird in the hand."

Expressed in terms of dollars, however, a dividend is not a very good indicator. If the holder of preferred stock is paid, say, $5 per share, how good a return is that on the original investment? How can it be compared fairly with yields on other investments? To make such evaluations and comparisons, a share of pressed in terms of a percentage. For example, if preferred stock with a par value (the original price at issuance) of $100 is paying $5 in dividends, the yield is 5 percent ($5 divided by $100). But 5 percent can be an unappealing yield when other instruments, such as bonds, are currently paying 8 percent, 9 percent, or 10 percent. In such a case, with the numbers of preferred stock buyers dropping below that of sellers, the market price of the preferred drops and the yield increases. Suppose the price of the preferred drops to $52. (Par value stays at $100; just the market price drops.) At that price, the stock is said to be selling at a "discount" (that is, below it original par value), and the yield increases. If you pay $52 for the stock and still get a dividend check for $5, the yield is 9.6 percent ($5 divided by $52). Given that yield, called the "current" yield, the preferred is now competitive with other instruments yielding 8 to 10 percent.

The instruments that compete chiefly with preferred stocks for investors' dollars are bonds, which, like preferreds, pay a fixed income. For example, a bond with a $1,000 face value and an 8 percent yield pays an annual yield of $80 ($1,000 × 0.08).

The traditional assumption is that, when stock yields are lower than bond yields, investors' money "migrates" to the bond market. Yet history repeatedly has gainsayed this dictum. In early 1929, during the stock market's heyday, and again from 1959 to the crash in October of 1987, stock yields were lower than bond yields. Conceivably the lure of large gains during a bull market outweighs the "wisdom" of opting for the higher, fixed yields of the bond market.

In evaluating the investment-worthiness of a stock, a fundamentalist employs many more analytical tools than the P/E ratio and percentage of yield. Using information in a company's financial statements, security analysts (as fundamentalists are known in this role) make many financial comparisons or ratios: debt to equity, earnings to sales, book value per share or net asset value per share as it is sometimes called. This is calculated by subtracting liabilities from assets and dividing the difference by shares outstanding

$$\left(B.V. = \frac{A - L}{\text{shares outstanding}} \right)$$

If a stock is trading below book, it is fundamentally said to be "cheap," meaning its a bargain. They also compare the company's ratios with accepted industry standards: is the company doing better or worse than the industry norms? They further try to establish trends in the company's progress from year to year. Are earnings up from last year?

Has management put the company deeper in debt? Have increased sales yielded higher profits, or have increased selling expenses offset the gains? These are the types of questions asked by the fundamentalist when analyzing a particular stock.

Beyond evaluating the merits of a single stock as an investment, fundamentalists face a broad array of market fundamentals, including prevailing interest rates, trade and budget deficits, the value of the dollar, and program trading. Chief among market fundamental factors, interest rates are thought to affect the stock market in several ways. First, when interest rates rise, they represent an increase in the "cost" of money borrowed by corporations. As such, they act as a damper on expansion and on stock market prices. On the other hand, "cheap" money (low interest rates) is typically expected to be anti-recessionary because it encourages corporations to undertake large, capital-intensive projects. Low rates therefore are thought to create jobs, increase the demand for raw materials, and generally stimulate the stock market. Second, fluctuations in prevailing interest rates alter the relationship between stock and bond yields. As interest rates rise, investors can get better yields on short-term instruments like certificates of deposit. Two things then happen: The prices of bonds and preferred stock with lower yields begin to drop, so as to increase their current yields, and new issues of bonds start to carry higher coupon, or nominal, yields. The net effect is that money tends to flow out of the market for common stock and into the bond market. As we've seen, however, this is not always the case when a bull market is in motion.

Finally, higher interest rates mean that investors have to pay more for margin, that is, for the funds they borrowed from their brokerage firms to buy stock. Escalated interest expenses eat into earnings, thereby cutting down on the number of would-be stock buyers. Demand is thus decreased, with a deflating effect on prices.

Compared to interest rates, the effect of budget and trade deficits on the stock market is not as clear. There certainly seems to be a negative psychological impact of the word "deficit." Beyond that, however, budget deficits mean that our government owes money, and in fact the amount owed is measured in the trillions of dollars. That debt is represented by the bonds, notes, and bills—the IOUs—issued by the Treasury. Much of those securities are being bought by foreign institutions, notably Japanese brokerage houses and banks. Every time the U.S. government issues more Treasury debt securities, the Japanese and other foreign investors are there to buy. To many observers, this arrangement represents fearful dependence on the affluence of other countries. Should foreign holders opt to stop buying U.S. debt, the overall economic effect could be catastrophic. Although this situation remains basically the same on a day-to-day basis, most market participants do not include it in their considerations, except in times of market crisis, when the sensitivity to this precarious arrangement rises dramatically.

The trade deficit is more of an ongoing and immediate consideration, because it means that American industry, as a whole, is paying more money to overseas companies than those companies are paying to their U.S. counterparts. Thus, capital is leaking out of the country, capital that could be fueling growth in stateside firms, with concomitant activity in the stock market.

Yet, neither type of deficit seemed to hamper the raging five-year bull market that preceded the crash of 1987. Although these deficits should have starved the bull market of 1982–1987 of capital, their "predictable," "Logical" effects simply did not happen. Only in the aftermath of Black Monday (October 19, 1987) did analysts become wary of these presumably negative influences. In fact, the deficits commanded newspapers' headlines for weeks thereafter.

Also in the headlines, with suddenly stepped-up emphasis, was the falling value of the dollar. The fears were threefold. First, foreign investors would be discouraged from buying U.S. stock because stock prices are generally expected to fall with the value of the dollar. Second, inflation would start up again, the norm being that 1 percent of inflation can be expected for every 10 percent drop in the value of the dollar. Finally, the prices of foreign goods would increase, in terms of dollars, thereby drawing capital out of the stateside market.

As it turned out, the Fed eventually let the dollar float according to the push and pull of supply and demand. The thinking is that two things should happen. One, buying of American goods by both domestic and foreign companies should pick up. Second, given a floating U.S. dollar, the Fed can allow a decline in interest rates, thereby forestalling the recession that many analysts expected. By the end of 1987, the dollar had indeed lost some value, but the United States was getting the cooperation of other governments in stabilizing the trend. Interest rates were holding steady, and economic analysts were becoming slightly more optimistic in their forecasts. Again, the expected effects of the loss in value did not come to pass.

As you can see, the fundamentalist approach is fraught with complicated and perhaps ambiguous cause-and-effect relationships, as well as with complex interrelationships among the many influences on the market. One wonders whether, beyond selecting a suitable growth or income stock, anyone can foresee the effect of these many causes in any accurate, coherent way. In fact, some critics maintain that one solution to the complexity of modern analysis—automation—is in itself a self-defeating approach. If the market is for the most part efficient, then the automated trading programs of institutional investors, both in the United States and abroad, may be considered just one more factor in a market that discounts all factors. From this point of view, automation only makes the market *more* efficient and therefore the task of predicting future price movements all the *more* difficult, perhaps impossible.

THE TECHNICAL APPROACH

Technical analysis referred to as chartists, sidestep the whole question of "beating" an efficient market. They do not attempt to relate economic causes to effects. In-

stead, they study the effects of all the many, often inscru-
table influencing factors and follow price movements.

How do present price movements indicate future levels? The primary approach of technical analysis is that
certain patterns of price movements repeat themselves. If
you can correctly identify the pattern early in its development, you can then foretell future prices. Their belief is
that history will always repeat itself in their search for
continuing patterns.

Let's take an example. After a fairly steady rise in
prices, the market turns sharply downward. The chart
looks like this:

Where is the market going? Will it continue to decline?
Or will it turn upward again?

The chartist watches and charts prices, following a
principle of "retracement": the closer prices get to retracing
two-thirds of the preceding price rise, the more likely they
are to go back the full 100 percent—and perhaps below
that level. A bear market may be in the making.

On the other hand, if prices begin to rise again after
retracing only a third of the previous rise, perhaps another
pattern is developing, which eventually will look like this:

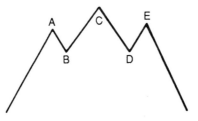

It is called a "head and shoulders top" pattern, and it
signals a downward trend in the market. It is consistently
repetitive enough for chartists to predict the drop. Chart-

ists who correctly identify this pattern can buy at points B-D and sell at points A-C-E. That is buying low and selling high in its most efficient form. Like the maxim itself, however, it is often easier said than done. (See Figure 11–3 for some of the many other price patterns in charting.)

In addition to price patterns, technical analysts also keep an eye on a number of indicators, such as trading volume, breadth of the market, and new highs/lows. With respect to trading volume, the working assumption is that light volume means that the accompanying pattern will not gather a lot of momentum; on heavy volume, it will. A lot of trading means that many investors are involved in the price movement and that the movement is not likely to peter out easily.

The "breadth" of the market also counts. This represents the number of issues advancing or declining. If more issues are being bought than sold, the market is said to be "technically strong." If more stocks are being sold than bought, it is "technically weak." This makes sense. Whereas volume does not indicate which or how many issues are trading, breadth does. If a handful of "big cap," high-priced stocks have an active day and pull the Dow Jones averages upward slightly, a technically weak report on breadth would indicate technically a very weak market, despite volume.

Another indicator for technical analysts is the number of new highs or new lows. This is not to be confused with stocks that advance or decline. A "new high" or a "new low" is a price level not achieved by a stock in the prior 12 months. A series of new highs or lows is taken to indicate an up-or-down trend. So, if many more stocks are reaching new highs than are dropping to new lows, this is considered a bullish sign. Many more new lows than new highs are looked upon as a bearish indicator.

Volume, breadth, and new highs or lows are all grouped under the heading "technical indicators." Another group consists of "sentiment indicators." Short interest—or the amount of short selling in the market—is one type of sentiment indicator. By going short, people in the market are saying that they expect prices to go down.

Built into short sales, however, is their own undoing. "He who sells what isn't his'n, gives it back or goes to prison." Sooner or later, short sale positions have to be closed out. The only way to do that is for the short sellers to deliver the stock to the lending brokerage firm—and so they must buy it back in order to return the stock to the lender. Once the buying starts, the buy orders infuse demand—upward pressure—into the market. Prices stop dropping and may even start to climb a bit. The point at which prices start turning upward again is called a "support level." This is a level below which prices should not drop because of purchase interest at that price. The reason could be that short sellers are covering their positions, but there are other reasons as well, most of them having to do with investor psychology.

Let's look at an example. Suppose the market is "overvalued" (that is, people are paying more for stocks than they really should because of a generally bullish air in the market). Sooner or later, holders of stock will start selling off, expecting a downturn. Those who do not own stock, with the same expectation, will start to sell short. Before long, the market has indeed turned downward. As prices drop off, more "longs" sell off and more "shorts" are created. Selling always seems to cause more selling. When that happens, other longs, hoping perhaps to salvage some portion of their losses, sell off, driving the prices down again. At a certain point, the remaining longs start to sell to the shorts who are covering their positions. Perhaps others are buying the stock simply because its price is low. At this point, the buy orders are starting to offset sell orders, and prices edge upward again. Those who've been waiting for the turn, start to buy, thus accelerating the move upward.

If support is a price floor, resistance is a ceiling. Perhaps a stock is attracting a lot of investors, demand is high, and the price is being bid up. At some point, the market runs out of buyers, the buy orders dry up, and the price rise slows. Some stockholders will begin to wonder whether the stock is about to drop in price, and some will sell off. Now there are more sellers than buyers. The price backs off and there are more sellers than buyers. The price backs off and may rise again to the same level, only to back off once more. Thus a resistance level—a price ceiling—has been established.

What are the reasons for it? There is no formula that tells you exactly what a stock is worth. The market price is certainly the result of the issuing company's performance and profitability. But that's not all. A price can be driven up just because the corporation is in a "popular" industry among investors, because the market "looks strong," or because of any number of other reasons. The answer to the question why is largely psychological.

While fundamentalists might try to analyze why prices move as they do, technicians simply accept such movements and chart them. Baron Meyer Rothschild did not seek such answers. Instead, he simply determined what the market was doing—buying or selling—and did the opposite. His assumption was that most market participants were doing the opposite of what they should be doing. If he acted contrary to the market, he'd generally profit. His thinking, still followed by many today, came to be known as the "contrarian opinion" theory. Indeed, the theory might have merit. Most individual investors, acting on old information, wind up buying when they should be selling and vice versa. It's the old "What's dummy doing?" theory.

Another theory that takes a pessimistic view of the individual investor's ability is the "odd-lot theory." Small investors often deal in odd lots (trades involving 1 to 99 shares), and odd-lot activity can therefore be taken as a gauge of what the small investor is doing. According to this theory, you should always take positions opposing those and contrary to the odd-lot trend. In other words, if odd lotters are on balance buying, "sell," if odd-lotters are selling, "buy."

While testing the contrarian theory is difficult, the odd-lot theory can be compared to total stock market volume. That is, you can put the odd-lot buy-sell volumes next to the market's total buy-sell volume. When you do, you note two things.

First, you wonder whether such a small group can act as a reliable indicator of the whole market. For instance, throughout 1986, odd-lot volume—buy and sell—added up to 329.1 million shares, averaging a little over 1.3 million shares per day. This is less than 1 percent of the average daily total volume of 141 million shares on the NYSE, and has continued right to today.

Second, even if such a small group is representative as a sample from a statistical point of view, it doesn't seem to be very consistent. For example, on the last trading day before the October 19 crash, odd lotters bought 729,000 and sold 2.1 million. According to the odd-lot theory, you should buy! On October 19 itself, they bought 1.9 million shares (mostly blue chip) and sold only 620,000.

If odd lotters are inconsistent, it might be because they are "outsiders," that is, they get information about stocks much later than most others. But there is a way for "outsiders" to know what "insiders" (corporate officers) are doing.

The illegal insider trading scandals that centered around Levine and Ivan Boesky struck right at the heart of the securities industry because they short-circuited its whole structure. All the regulations, all the requirements, all the procedures, and all the people in the industry are supposed to strive for a *fair* and orderly market. As soon as someone enters the market with the unfair advantage of having highly valuable secret inside information, all other participants are being cheated. All of the mechanisms become meaningless. What's worse, given enough of such scandals, with the related loss of faith in the market, such abuses could lead to a severe drain of capital. Investors, both private and institutional, would eventually feel safer with their money invested elsewhere. Whether fundamentalist or technician, today's stock market analyst faces a far larger job than any analysts in the past.

Today's market is tied to, and in many way, dependent on what goes on in Washington and, for that matter, in financial centers and governments throughout the world. In Chapter 14, we will see what happened in the U.S. stock market when it crashed in October of 1987.

Analyzing Stocks

The Corporation's "Report Card"

Most people measure their personal financial success by the amount of their earnings and by the amount of their accumulated assets. Everyone wants to earn a decent salary and hopes to get an increase each year. We also strive to provide for a better life style, with a graceful retirement, by putting our "extra" earnings aside. We hope that our "nest egg" increases over time. It is a fairly simple matter to estimate our income each year. In fact, we *have* to, because we owe part of this income to the federal government, and possibly another portion to our home state and/or city, in the form of taxes. Not too many people keep track of their accumulated assets on a continuing basis, although it is a very good idea to do so.

Corporations *do* track their income and assets on a regular basis. Their income is reported at least annually in the company's income statement, also known as its *P&L (profit and loss statement)*. The corporation's assets (and liabilities) are also carefully tracked and reported, at least annually, in its *balance sheet.* A corporation's balance sheet and income statement show its earnings and its assets. The publication of these statements is looked forward to eagerly by security analysts and the investing public. These reports are the company's "report card." They show its progress, with respect to how much they are earning for their shareholders—how much the company is actually worth, at least with respect to assets.

Every publicly held corporation strives for growth in earnings, dividends, and assets. While a single balance sheet or income statement might not be all that informative, the *trend* of earnings and asset growth is important. Analysts and individual investors attempt to spot companies that are in a growth phase, and they pore over corporate reports looking for such "buys." Serious investors should be able to read and interpret these statements. They may not have the same thoroughness and degree of professionalism as an accountant or securities analyst, but they should at least know how to apply some of the more common "tests" of corporate well-being. We'll just do a few simple applications in this chapter, but a number of excellent tests develop these issues further, such as *The NYIF Vest-Pocket Guide to Stock Brokerage Math.*

CURRENT ASSETS AND CURRENT LIABILITIES

A corporation's *current assets* include its cash, as well as other items that will become cash within the next year. These "soon-to-become-cash items might include, in addition to the company's current cash position, its marketable securities, accounts receivable, and inventory. These are *assets*, things of value that a company owns or has owed to it. It owns its marketable securities and inventory, and is owed its accounts receivable. Most of these assets are quite liquid and may easily be converted to cash. The one current asset that isn't readily convertible into cash is its inventory. A company's *quick assets* include all of its current assets *except* inventory.

The company's *current liabilities* include those items that the company expects to pay out during the next year, its "budget." These would include, among other items, the company's accounts payable, salaries and wages, taxes and interest. Whereas current assets reflect where the cash is coming from, current liabilities show where the money is going. Here is only the "top" half of a balance sheet. It shows the company's current assets and current liabilities and, as shown, is far from being a complete balance sheet:

Cash	$1,100	Accounts payable	$700
Marketable securities	300	Salaries payable	400
Account receivable	800	Interest payable	25
Inventory	1,100	Accrued taxes	75
	$3,200		$1,200

It is obvious that a company should have more money coming in than it expects to pay out. Our "sample" company has $3,200 in current assets and $1,200 in current liabilities. It has $2,000 more than it needs to meet its current obligations ($3,200 – $1,200), and this amount, $2,000, is called the company's *working capital.* If we divide the current assets by the current liabilities ($3,200 ÷ $1,200), we get the company's *current ratio*: 2.7 to 1. This indicates that the company has $2.70 in current assets for every dollar of current liabilities; it has its short-term debts "covered" 2.7 times over. A vey general rule of thumb is that a manufacturing company should have a current ratio of at least 2 to 1. So our illustrative company seems to be in good shape.

CAN THE CORPORATION PAY ITS WAY ?

The most severe test of a company's ability to meet its short-term obligations is known as its *quick asset ratio,* also known as the *liquidity ratio.* This ratio measures the relationship between a company's *quick* assets and its current liabilities. We can easily calculate our company's quick assets by simply subtracting inventory (a nonliquid asset) from total current assets: $3,200 – $1,000 = 1.8 to 1. This is a respectable ratio, as 1 to 1 is the usual standard. At least for the near term, the company we have "analyzed" seems okay.

DOES THE CORPORATION HAVE A SPECULATIVE CAPITAL STRUCTURE?

A company's *capital structure,* also known as its *capitalization,* shows its financial framework. It includes the company's sources of long-term funds, including:

* The par value of its bonds and preferred stocks.

* The par value of its common stock.

* Any excess over par value that the company may have received through the sale of common stock (paid-in capital).

* Accumulated earnings (retained earnings) that the company has reinvested in additional assets rather than paying such earnings out to shareholders in the form of dividends.

Collectively, its capitalization consists of its long-term debt and its shareholders' equity.

Interest on the company's outstanding bonds *must* be paid; if not, the trustee for the bonds may force the company to liquidate. It is extremely important, therefore, that the company earn enough money to meet any interest and principal payments due on its bonds (its *debt service*). If the company is able to properly utilize its debt, by making more money on the borrowed funds than it is paying out to service the debt, things are fine. But when earnings are insufficient to pay debt service, it can be catastrophic. The "leveraged buyout" craze of the 1980s and early 1990s saw many companies fail because they were too heavily laden with debt. The "junk" bonds that were issued proved, in many cases, to be too great a burden. Companies that have a capital structure with a disproportionate amount of debt are considered speculative and, as such, should be avoided by the conservative investor.

The balance sheet shows what a company owns (its assets), what a company owes (its liabilities), and the difference between the two, its *net worth*. In theory, the sum of the balance sheet's last three items (the common stock account, paid-in-capital, retained earnings), show what total amount would be due the common stockholders if the company were to be liquidated. This liquidation value, per share of common stock, is known as *book value*. You are encouraged to examine a corporate balance sheet to become familiar with these items, which are beyond the scope of this text.

THE INCOME STATEMENT

The "books" of a corporation are known as its P&L, or income statement. The income statement shows how much the company took in (sales) and what it laid out in expenses. The famous *bottom line* is the company's *net earnings*. From the income statement we can derive, among other things, the company's margin of profit, its expense ratio, its cash flow, and its earnings per share. Here's a simplified income statement:

Figure 12–1. Digest of Earnings Reports.

DIGEST OF EARNINGS REPORTS

AOI COAL CO. (A)

Quar Mar 31:	1993	1992
Sales	$3,988,000	$10,982,000
Net income	(2,008,000)	(666,000)
Shr earns:		
Net income .	(.13)	(.04)

Figures in parentheses are losses.

BAY MEADOWS OPERATING (A)

Quar Mar 31:	a1993	1992
Revenues	$9,132,000	$11,032,000
Net income	b(1,204,000)	911,000
Shr earns:		
Net income .	(.21)	.16

a-Revised by co. b-Includes a $1,400,-000 charge related to the settlement of litigation.
Figures in parentheses are losses.

BEVERLY HILLS FAN CO. (O)

Quar Apr 30:	1993	1992
Revenues	$2,532,000	$2,906,000
Net income	207,000	140,000
Avg shares	4,330,603	4,655,603
Shr earns:		
Net income .	.05	.03
6 months:		
Revenues	3,315,000	4,806,000
Net income	44,000	303,000
Avg shares	4,330,603	4,655,603
Shr earns:		
Net income .	.01	.07

ESTERLINE TECHNOLOGIES (N)

Quar Apr 30:	1993	1992
Sales	$71,588,000	$77,003,000
Net income	483,000	1,025,000
Shr earns:		
Net income .	.07	.15
6 months:		
Sales	138,912,000	149,087,000
Net income	814,000	1,215,000
Shr earns:		
Net income .	.12	.18

EVERGREEN RESOURCES (O)

Year Mar 31:	1993	1992
Revenues	$4,500,000	a$3,500,000
Net income	725,738	(272,352)
Shr earns:		
Net income .	.15	(.08)

a-Restated.
Figures in parentheses are losses.

GANDALF TECHNOLOGIES (O)

Quar Mar 31:	1993	a1992
Revenues ..	$38,485,000	....
Net inco	(975,000)	....
Avg shares	15,762,000	....
Shr earns:		
Net inco	(.06)	....
Year:		
Revenues ..	160,900,000	....
Net inco .	b(19,507,000)	....
Avg shares	15,702,000	....
Shr earns:		
Net inco	(1.24)	....

a-Comparative results not shown; company has changed its fiscal year-end from July 31, to March 31. b-Includes a nonrecurring pre-tax charge of $5,547,-000.
Figures in parentheses are losses.

ABBREVIATIONS

A partial list of frequently used abbreviations: Acctg adj (Accounting adjustment); Extrd chg (Extraordinary charge); Extrd cred (Extraordinary credit); Inco cnt op (Income from continuing operations); Inco dis op (Income from discontinued operations).

HACH CO. (O)

Quar Apr 30:	1993	1992
Sales	$25,672,000	$22,868,000
Net income	2,520,000	2,350,000
Shr earns:		
Net income .	.28	.26
Year:		
Sales	94,001,000	84,739,000
Net income	8,620,000	7,750,000
Shr earns:		
Net income .	.95	.85

NATIONAL SECURITY GRP (O)

Quar Mar 31:	1993	1992
Income	$949,000	$1,105,000
Acctg adj	a263,000	....
Net income	1,212,000	1,105,000
Shr earns:		
Income	.61	.71
Net income .	.78	.71

a-Cumulative effect on prior periods of an accounting change.

OSHMAN'S SPORTING GOODS (O)

13 wk May 1:	1993	1992
Sales	$64,166,000	$62,186,000
Net income	(2,404,000)	(986,000)
Avg shares	5,805,000	5,804,000
Shr earns:		
Net income .	(.41)	(.17)

Figures in parentheses are losses.

POLYDEX PHARMACEUT (O)

Quar Apr 30:	1993	1992
Sales	$2,042,994	$1,011,350
Income	37,256	113,068
aExtrd cred ..	47,417	30,340
Net income	84,673	143,408
Shr earns:		
Income	....	.01
Net income .	....	.01

a-Tax benefit from tax-loss carry-forwards.

SAND TECHNOLOGY SYS (O)

Quar Apr 30:	1993	1992
Sales	4,643,001	7,822,973
Net income	(155,178)	858,983
Avg shares	4,432,103	4,432,103
Shr earns:		
Net income .	(.04)	.19
9 months:		
Sales	14,978,801	29,074,124
Net income	17,013	2,365,022
Avg shares	4,432,103	4,431,659
Shr earns:		
Net income .	....	.53

Amounts in Canadian dollars.
Figures in parentheses are losses.

SOFTIMAGE INC. (O)

Quar Apr 30:	1993	1992
Revenues	$5,970,000	$3,190,000
Net income	834,000	586,000
Avg shares	5,266,494	3,789,320
Shr earns:		
Net income .	.16	.15
6 months:		
Revenues	10,722,000	5,815,000
Net income	1,624,000	1,074,000
Avg shares	5,058,992	3,789,320
Shr earns:		
Net income .	.32	.28

TARO VIT INDUSTRIES (O)

Quar Mar 31:	1993	1992
Sales	$6,578,000	$5,722,000
Income	(235,000)	294,000
Extrd cred	....	a223,000
Net income	(235,000)	517,000
Avg shares	9,240,845	9,089,363
Shr earns (com & com equiv):		
Income	(.03)	.03
Net income .	(.03)	.06

a-Tax benefit from tax-loss carry-forwards.
Figures in parentheses are losses.

U.S. INTEC INC. (A)

Quar Mar 31:	1993	1992
Sales	$16,362,021	$15,133,195
Income	217,603	(410,838)
Acctg adj	....	a500,000
Net income	217,603	89,162
Shr earns:		
Income	.07	(.14)
Net income .	.07	.03

a-Cumulative effect on prior periods of an accounting change.
Figures in parentheses are losses.

VALUE CITY DEPT STORES (N)

13 wk Apr 25:	1993	a1992
Sales	$166,500,000	$174,800,000
Net income	600,000	4,400,000
Shr earns:		
Net income .	.02	.14
39 weeks:		
Sales	643,800,000	616,300,000
Net income	27,700,000	27,200,000
Shr earns:		
Net income .	.86	.85

a-Restated.

VILLAGE SUPER MARKET (O)

13 wk Apr 17:	1993	1992
Sales	$169,431,000	$179,022,000
Net income	182,000	395,000
Shr earns:		
Net income .	.06	.14
38 weeks:		
Sales	510,056,000	518,229,000
Net income	1,563,000	(455,000)
Shr earns:		
Net income .	.54	(.16)

Figures in parentheses are losses.

(N) New York Stock Exchange (A) American Exchange (O) Over-the-Counter (Pa) Pacific (M) Midwest (P) Philadelphia (B) Boston (T) Toronto (Mo) Montreal (F) Foreign.

Sales	$100,000
Less:	
Cost of good sold	– 55,000
Selling, general, and administrative	– 20,000
Depreciation	– 7,000
Operating income	18,000
Plus: Other income	+ 2,000
Total income	20,000
Less:	
Interest	– 1,000
Taxes	– 6,500
Net income	12,500
Less: Preferred stock dividends	– 500
Net earnings	$ 12,000

The company's *expense ratio* is calculated by dividing the first three expenses listed by the sales: $55,000 + $20,000 + $7,000 = $82,000 ÷ $100,000 = 82 percent.

The *margin of profit* is simply the difference between the expense ratio and 100 percent: 100 percent - 82 percent = 18 percent.

Cash flow is the sum of net income and depreciation: $12,500 + $7,000 = $19,500 cash flow.

Earnings per share, probably the most important measure of a company's success, is calculated by dividing its net earnings by the number of common shares outstanding. Assuming that this company has 6,000 common shares outstanding, its earnings would be $2.00 per share ($12,000 ÷ 6,000 shares).

Figure 12–1 shows the "Digest of Earnings Report," which is printed daily in the *Wall Street Journal*. It shows how well, or how poorly, a company fared during the quarter (or year) covered. Note that the first listing shows deficit earnings, a *loss* for the quarter ended March 31. Look at Evergreen Resources; it recovered from a loss of $0.08 a share in fiscal 1992 to a profit of $0.15 a share in 1993. This figure shows the "bottom line" for the companies listed— which companies *made* money (and how much) and which companies *lost money (and how much). It's the bottom line!*

Investors are understandably eager to purchase stocks that have ever-increasing earnings. They also look for "special situations" in which the company's earnings might be dramatically affected by a nonrecurring event such as a merger or a new discovery. Knowing how per-share earnings are derived, as well as how they are influenced by different cicumstances, is part of being a well-informed investor in the stock market.

CHAPTER 13

Taxation

How Dividends and Capital Gains Are Taxed

Investors are subject to taxation, both federal and state, on some or all of their income from existing securities. It is important to understand, at least in general, which of these distributions are taxable and by whom. Taxes can eat into an apparent "profit" and turn it into an "after-tax" loss. Tax loss carryforwards (described in this chapter) can ease the tax burden in years ahead. The broad rules relate to:

* The taxation of interest.
* The taxation of dividends.
* The taxation of capital gains.

* Tax loss carryforwards.

* Multiple positions.

* Stock gifts to minors.

* Stocks received as gifts or inheritances.

THE TAXATION OF INTEREST

Most interest on municipal bonds (MUNIs) is federally tax exempt, and generally also free from state taxation, especially if investors own municipal securities issued in the state where they live.

The interest earned on corporate bonds is subject to both federal and state tax.

Interest earned on United States government bonds is subject to federal tax, but not state tax.

The tax rates on these interest payments, if they are taxable, is about the same as the taxes levied on "regular" income such as your salary. The interest rate on tax-exempt municipal bonds is actually higher than it appears when you take the tax-free nature of the distributions into consideration.

THE TAXATION OF DIVIDENDS

Cash dividends are taxable, by both the federal government and state government, as received. Some dividends are optional, and the shareholder is given the choice as to whether to receive the dividend in cash or in additional shares. Even though the shareholder elects to receive shares instead of cash, the dividend *is* taxable! Optional dividends are taxable, whether cash or shares are received.

Nonoptional stock dividends, where the shareowner receives additional shares, are not taxable at the time they are received.

Stock splits are also not taxable when received. The receipt of such additional shares changes the "tax cost" basis of your original holdings. The corporation distributing these stock dividends and splits will ordinarily explain their tax ramifications in a fair amount of detail.

Reinvested dividends, even though no cash is received, are still taxable. Most not-yet-retired investors in mutual funds elect to reinvest their dividend and capital gains distributions in additional fund shares, thus hoping to pyramid (compound) their overall profits. Although they do not receive any cash, these distributions are taxable at the time they are reinvested. All is not lost, however, since the "cost basis" of the shareowners' total fund holdings is increased, and the capital gain taxes payable when the shares are eventually sold and reduced proportionately.

THE TAXATION OF CAPITAL GAINS

When security positions are "closed out," a taxable event has taken place. A *close out* occurs when a long position is sold or a short position is covered. The difference between the purchase price and the sale price is the capital gain (or loss) on the transaction. Gains and losses can either be long-term or short-term, depending on the length of time elapsed between the date of purchase and the date of sale. The *trade dates* are used for both the buy and sell, not the settlement dates. When a stock has been held more than one year, the gain or loss is long-term. When a stock has been held for one year (exactly) or less, the gain or loss is short-term. A stock purchased on November 8, 1993 will result in a short-term situation if sold on or before November 8, 1994, and will be long-term if sold on or after November 9, 1994. This section of the tax law has been very flexible in the past, and the short-term/long-term period has varied from six to eighteen months. As of this writing it is one year.

Also very changeable is the tax treatment of capital gains. During most of the past 50 years (but not for the last few years), long-term capital gains have been afforded favorable tax treatment. This practice was abandoned, and currently there is no special tax treatment applied to capital gains: They are taxed in essentially the same manner as is other income. Whether such favorable treatment will be reinstated is a political consideration.

TAX LOSS CARRYFORWARDS

Investors should keep track of their capital gains and losses each year, and at year-end they will have either a *net* gain or loss. If they have a net gain, it is taxable. If they have a net loss, it is deductible for tax purposes. This doesn't recoup the investor's entire loss, but it does reduce his taxes, thus lessening the financial blow. There's a limit to how much an investor can deduct for tax losses in a given year, and that is $3,000. If the losses exceed this limit—for, say, a total of $5,000—then only the $3,000 is deducted in the current year, and the balance of the loss ($2,000) can be deducted in the subsequent tax year. The $2,000 "extra" loss becomes a *tax loss carryforward*.

MULTIPLE POSITIONS

If an investor owns several lots of stock, bought at different times and prices (multiple positions), and she elects to sell one of those lots, a question arises: Which of those lots is being sold as far as the taxing authorities are concerned? Unless the investor otherwise specifies, the oldest (first purchased) lot is considered to be the one sold. This is the *FIFO method*, first-in/first-out.

Here's an interesting example. Lucy Deida has purchased two different 100-share lots of JKL: 100 shares at 92½ in 1992 and 100 shares at 85 in 1993. It is now 1994 and JKL is trading at 89¾. If Lucy instructs her broker to sell 100 shares, then (for tax purposes) she is considered to have sold the first lot she bought, the shares that cost 92½. Miss

Deida will have a capital loss of $275 as a result of the sale (bought 100 shares for $9,250 and sold them for $8,975), she will be left with a remaining position of 100 shares at a cost of $8,500 (the shares she purchased in 1993).

But what if Lucy would rather profit on the sale? If she does, she merely instructs her broker to sell 100 shares of JKL "versus purchase 1993." The tax authorities now consider the 1993 purchase to be the shares sold, and Lucy will now show a capital gain of $475 (bought 100 shares for $8,500 and sold them for $8,975). She will be left with a remaining position of 100 shares at a cost of $9,250 (the shares she purchased in 1992).

STOCK GIFTS TO MINORS

Stocks cannot be registered directly in the name of a minor. They can be registered in a *custodian account,* however, but they must be reregistered in the child's name when he comes of age. When someone wishes to give a gift of securities to a minor, a custodian account is set up. The new account form shows information about the custodian, with the single exception of the social security number used to identify the account. It's the *minor's* taxpayer number, not the custodian's number! This reflects the fact that the taxable consequences arising from the dividends, interest, and capital gains generated by the account are the responsibility of the minor, not of the custodian. The securities actually belong to the minor. A gift of securities to a minor cannot be "recalled," because the gift is irrevocable. No margin transactions are permitted in a custodian account.

STOCKS RECEIVED AS GIFTS AND INHERITANCES

The receipt of securities as a gift or inheritance is not ordinarily a taxable event. Gift and estate taxes, if any, are the responsibility of the donor (for a gift) or of the estate of the deceased (for an inheritance).

Inherited stocks have a tax cost equal to their value at the time of the decedent's death, or six months later, whichever of those dates the estate's executor had chosen when the estate was settled. The holding period, for the inheritor, begins on the decedent's date of death. Most estates with a value of $600,000 or less are not subject to federal tax. A surviving spouse can inherit any amount of securities or property without paying tax.

Your tax cost basis for stocks received as a gift depends on whether the donor had a "paper" loss or profit at the time she made the gift. If you receive a gift of stocks when the price is higher than the donor's cost, then you take over the stock's original cost. If the gifted stock is lower in value than the donor's cost, your cost basis will be the value at the time of the gift was made. Individuals can give away up to $10,000 in securities (or other things of value), each year, to as many different individuals as they choose, without incurring a gift tax! These gifts to individuals are not deductible for the donor (as gifts to charitable institutions would be), but such gifts will lower the donor's taxable estate so that the ultimate tax bill (at the death of the donor) will be lower.

There are many other tax considerations having to do with securities transactions. Mutual funds, options, and futures all have their special tax rules. There are little-known practices that affect taxes, including short-against-the-box sales and wash sales, and special rules for short selling. Certain items on your "confirms" are considered part of your cost basis or proceeds of sale; some are not. It is prudent always to consult competent tax counsel. These few paragraphs have only scratched the surface of this very complex area.

CHAPTER 14

Crash!

How the Stock Market Works
Under Pressure

At about 7:00 A.M. on October 19, 1987, the usual Monday morning strategy conference at Merrill Lynch Pierce Fenner & Smith was attended by William A. Schreyer, the chairman, and Daniel P. Tully, the president. Their attendance was unusual, prompted by the pessimistic pall over the stock market in the past week or so. Robert J. Farrell, the chief stock market analyst at Merrill, warned that the market might be down by as much as 200 points. Scenes like this one had been played out in most firms if not that same morning, then within the past week or so. Most analysts and traders knew that a "market correction" was due. The October 15th *Wall Street Journal,* in an article entitled "Stocks

May Face More Than a Correction," stated: "Recent declines in stock prices, widely regarded as a mere correction in an underlying bull market, may not be reversed so readily."

For various reasons, everyone seemed to understand that the market had gone up for too long for a significant downturn not to happen. Many issues were overvalued in the headiness of the prolonged bull market. There was some gloom about inflation and interest rates. Investors were concerned about the U.S. trade deficit and the falling value of the dollar.

Takeovers did not have the appeal they did prior to the Tax Reform Act of 1986, which eliminated many of the tax benefits of borrowing to pay for takeovers. In fact, Carl C. Icahn, the renowned takeover speculator, said "That was the match that ignited the dynamite." The market had to turn soon.

The morning trading session of October 19 seemed to prove all expectations correct. Even before the opening bell, sell orders flooded the order-handling system at the New York Stock Exchange. By 9:45 A.M., the Dow was down 13 points and continuing to slide. The supply side was dominating the market.

A little after 10:00 A.M., John J. Phelan, Jr., chairman of the NYSE, had spoken with David S. Ruder, SEC chairman, and held a meeting with representatives of leading brokerage firms. The decision was to keep the exchange open. A Reuters report on the decision had the opposite effect: Traders assumed there was a possibility that the exchange would close. Rumors of a trading halt dashed cold water on the small rally that program trading *buy* orders had sparked. The market resumed its slide.

At about that time, the stocks of takeover target companies were dropping fast in value. Arbitrageurs, who seek to profit on price rises of such stocks, could not stay in the market. They bowed out of the trading. with them went over $10 billion in operating capital, at least some of which would have been put to use in buying stock.

By noon, the market had been down 200 points but had rallied over 70 points. The morning trading had been a roller coaster ride, all of it on heavy volume. Just about everyone in the market was shaken. One trader, whose firm normally handles 150,000 shares a day, had done a half-million shares by midday. "Everything is out of control," he commented, "Clerks and teletypists will be here till 7 o'clock."

But the worst was yet to come. By 12:30 P.M., the Dow was down again by 165 points. From that point, it steadily lost 25 to 50 points every half-hour. The news at about 2:00 P.M. that corporations were buying back stock—with National Distillers being the first—had no visible effect on the slide. Volume tipped over 400 million shares just before the market went into an uncontrollable free-fall. By 3:00 P.M., the ticker was almost two hours late, and no one knew where the market was. By 3:30 P.M., the Dow was down another 104 points. By closing, one half-hour later, another 108 were lost.

As the peals of the closing bell died away, no one knew how bad things were. Traders stood quietly staring at others about them. A bear had rampaged through their market, which had become almost completely supply-driven. Only the specialists and market makers held the ground on the buy side—barely. During that unprecedented afternoon, nothing was normal. In the sales offices, phones were perpetually tied up, and clients could not get through on the phones to their AEs. Wire house order systems jammed, with unexecuted sell orders piling up. On the exchange floor, even the orders that made it to trading posts were filled only with difficulty. Floor traders peered helplessly at the electronic tickers and quotation screens. Specialist units were running out of money. In the OTC market, phones rang at trading desks without being answered. There were just too many orders to handle.

At the end of that fateful session, one floor trader remarked: "I thought there would be a correction in the market. But this is shocking. There's hysteria and fear. It's absolute fear."

Another said: "I've lost a sizable amount of money, and others have had losses that have left them speechless. This is the most staggering thing I've seen."

Others compared the afternoon's session to a free-fall drop in an elevator or to plummeting downhill in a car with no brakes.

At one trading desk, a magic-markered sign read, "To the lifeboats!"

By the end of trading, the Dow was off 508.32 points—22.6 percent of the whole market—on record volume of over 6 hundred million shares. In one day, the stock market on the NYSE floor alone lost some $750 million. (It had lost $1 trillion in the month preceding October 19th.) Prices had retreated so far that Peter Eliades, a technical chartist of some 18 years, had to tape five pieces of graph paper top to bottom to follow the whole day. Ordinarily, he gets up to six months' worth of activity on one piece.

That evening, stockbrokers, traders, analysts, and many others went home not to sleep, but to wonder what Tuesday would bring. In the meantime, the lights were on in the back offices well into the night.

The next morning, the newspapers headlined one of the most newsworthy events of the century, each in its own way:

* "CRASH!" (*New York Post*)

* "PANIC!" (*New York Daily News*)

* "STOCKS PLUNGE 508.32 AMID PANICKY SELL-ING" (*Wall Street Journal*)

From that point forward, October 19, 1987 became Black Monday...Monster Monday ... Meltdown Monday.

Perhaps the key question was highlighted in a sub-headline in the *New York Times:* "Does 1987 Equal 1929?" The answer to that question remains to be seen. The prevailing view, however, seems to be that, while the crash has certainly dampened economic and securities activity, there are too many regulatory mechanisms in place for it to has caused the type of depression that we had in the 1930s. Black Monday, however, served at least several worthwhile purposes. For one thing, it was a crucible, in which the industry market structures and support systems were put to the test of fire. By and large, they passed the test. Second, the events of the day demonstrated the interdependence of stock markets, both nationally and globally. Third, it put the acid test to many of the assumptions on which program trading is based. Finally, it raised the significant question as to how much of an economic indicator the stock market is.

Let's look at these points one at a time.

THE FAIR AND ORDERLY MARKET

There's no doubt that the legal requirements put into place in the aftermath of the 1929 Crash prevented a national calamity in 1987.

For example, the Securities Exchange Act of 1933 and the Securities Exchange Act of 1933 and the Securities Exchange Act of 1934 have such rigid disclosure requirements that "bogus" corporations are few and far between. In the 1920s, a corporation could issue stock without disclosing anything about its financial status—whether it owned so much as a desk or had a dollar to its name. When the market plunged in 1929, these companies were blown away. Worse, it became clear that they did not have the financial resources to get through times of adversity. Their collapse helped to escalate the panic and, later, personal bankruptcies of stockholders.

Such shams are almost impossible today. As a result, when prices took a nose dive, most issuers were able to ride out the storm. Some of the "big cap" companies even started creating additional treasury stock for themselves by buying. In one stroke, they retrieved their stock at bargain prices, acted as buyers in a supply-driven market, and cast a vote of confidence in the market and in their companies.

Because of regulatory requirements in a primary offering, the capital was there, backing the issues, to pull the market through. Investors were not left bankrupt because they had bought stock in "paper" corporations.

Brokerage firms are also required to keep certain levels of capital in reserve. Periodically, they must submit a report that reflects their net capital position. The report requires a firm to add up all the money that it has on loan to customers and all the money it has on hand in cash. The ratio of the loan amount divided by the cash amount represents how extended the firm is in terms of credit to its clients. Ratios of 2 to 1 or 3 to 1 are perfectly acceptable; 4 to 1 or more is questionable. Ratios approaching 10 to 1 often result in a firm's being audited and even in its being forbidden to extend further credit until the ratio comes down.

Since brokerage firms, which generally own large inventories of securities, are "net holders" of stocks, they operate on billions of dollars of capital, but much of it is on loan from commercial banks. If the value of a firm's inventory is deflated across the board due to an overall market decline and it does not have money to operate, it has to sell some inventory to raise capital. The last thing the market needs in a panic is more selling by the brokerage firms themselves!

As a result, the net operating capital of a brokerage firm is monitored very closely. The underlying logic of the SEC's Rule 15c3—3, which is the rule that requires frequent reporting of a firm's net capital status, is that a broker/dealer should have enough cash on hand to wind down its operations, while protecting its customers, within a month. A firm must have enough capital, after making a series of deductions from its total capital, to compare well with safety margins established by the SEC. Although the purpose of this rule is to protect investors in the event of one firm's failure, its across-the-board effect is that all firms are obliged by law to have a minimum amount of operating capital in reserve. This capital (not generally available in 1929) no doubt moderated the effect of the 1987 crash.

Perhaps the most conspicuous safeguard against calamity in a down market is Regulation T. With this regulation, the Federal Reserve—the arbiter of credit in this country—requires that, to buy stock on margin, you have to deposit at least 50 percent of the market value of the stock with your broker. Exchange, NASAD, and firm requirements are invariably higher. Margin and maintenance requirements strike a balance by preventing investors from becoming overextended. With this provision, some investors may not have been able to honor monster margin calls. But at least the margin departments were able to sell the margined securities, and minimize losses.

In this environment, investors who were hurt the worst violated prudent guidelines. For instance, the story goes around the street that an AE advised one or more clients to take out equity loans on their homes and use the money to buy stock on margin. That's not only illegal—for the stockbroker to suggest and for the clients to do—but it is also downright stupid. These clients, unable to meet the margin calls, saw their positions sold out and zero balances in their accounts. All they were left with were equity loans to pay off.

Although these cases were by far the exceptions in 1987, they were the norm in 1929. There was no Reg T, no margin regulation. You could buy stock with just a few dollars down. You didn't worry about making a margin call, because everyone knew that calls happen only in down markets. And the market in the late 1920s was going up, up, up. When the crash occurred, people were not only broke; they were in deep debt because the firms had loaned them most of the purchase price. There's no doubt that limiting the use of margin put a brake on the downhill careening of the market in 1987. The margin calls were big, and people lost money—especially those who used their buying power to increase their positions. But it could have been much, much worse.

It could have been worse still, many think, if commercial banks had been invested in the market, as they had been in the 1920s. Back then, banks were allowed to buy and sell stock with depositors' funds, as well as to underwrite primary offerings. As a result, much of the money that investors might have used to meet their margin calls or otherwise to deal with huge losses in the market was unavailable to them. The banks were losing the investors' deposited funds just as fast as investors were losing their investment funds. The Crash was draining both individuals and institutions dry of capital.

In 1933, the Glass-Steagall Act prohibited financial institutions from engaging in investment and commercial banking at the same time. That is, if a bank wanted to take deposits and make loans, it was legally a "commercial" bank. If it wanted to act as a corporate underwriter and carry an inventory of securities, it was an "investment" bank. By law, it could not be both. That is essentially the law today, but it is under siege and yielding rapidly.

Commercial banks for years have been lobbying for a repeal of the Act. Their primary argument is that the market would be *more* stable if investment banks were large, well-capitalized financial service firms.

At the same time, commercial banks have tested the law. In 1986, for example, a bank that was bailed out by the U.S. government in 1984, Continental Illinois Corporation, bought First Option of Chicago, a clearing service firm. Continental Illinois received government permission to become a "broker's broker," on the basis of the argument that First Option derived revenue not from trading profits, but rather from clearing fees. Hence its involvement in the securities industry was regarded as all but risk-free. On Black Monday, however, with capital running scarce, First Option customers found it harder and harder to meet their obligations. The charges for clearing, which, given the volumes involved, were going through the ceiling, were just going unpaid in many instances. Continental Illinois had to funnel some $90 million into First Option to keep it afloat. Without Continental's infusion, First Option might have gone out of business. Being owned by a bank did serve as a stabilizing factor, but where does the capital commitment end?

In another case, First Chicago Corporation (a bank) planned to buy Wood Gundy, a major Canadian underwriting firm. The purchase would be legal because the Glass-

Steagall restriction does not apply to foreign underwriters. Wood Gundy, however, was one of the underwriters in a huge stock issue being offered by British Petroleum, the government-owned oil company of Britain. The value of the stock, offered internationally, took a beating in late October. Wood Gundy lost $45 million on the offering. Although First Chicago walked away from the purchase, the question remains as to how much capital a bank can safely commit to underwriting and other securities-related transactions.

Another question is whether the business of commercial banking is compatible with that of investment banking, "Mega" banks, with enormous loans out to developing nations, make decisions and generally operate in a very different time frame from brokerage houses. A brokerage firm usually needs money in a matter of hours, sometimes minutes. Occasionally decisions involving large sums must be made instantaneously. It is questionable whether the two decision-making environments can mesh, so that the parent bank can act prudently, yet within the time constraints often imposed by the market.

Certainly, the legally mandated separation between commercial and investment banking undoubtedly helped to stabilize the runaway market in 1987. Yet these two examples illustrate the beartraps in allowing commercial banks to participate in securities trading and underwriting. If any changes are to be made, they should be made carefully and wisely.

Of all the systems aimed at maintaining a fair and orderly market, however, the ones put to the severest tests were the exchange specialists and the OTC market makers. "The dealer (specialist and market maker) system," said an officer of a specialist unit, "was very close to the limits of what it could stand. There's no question that by the 20th it had exhausted most of its resources."

The specialists, in their attempts to head off the worst market downturn in over half a century, suffered enormous financial losses. While their holdings normally totaled a maximum of $400 million, their accumulated holdings were between $11.5 and $2 billion by the end of trading on Meltdown Monday—almost all of it purchased in a sliding market. Indeed, a few specialists were put out of business, having had to sell their seats to meet their commitments. On October 22, to enable capital to move into the dealer system, the NYSE lifted its long-standing ban on the ownership of specialist units by brokerage houses. Merrill Lynch bought one right away.

So battered was the specialist and market-maker system that the Fed had to assure commercial banks that there was enough "credit" in the system to go around. The banks needed the reassurance. They had many more times the amount of loans out to firms than they normally did, and many were ready to cut off short-term loans to brokers. Citicorp, for example, had some $1.4 billion on loan to brokerage houses, compared to its normal level of $200 million. Citicorp Chairman John S. Reed went along with the additional amounts only after a call from the New York Federal Reserve President, E. Gerald Corrigan.

The money was needed not only on the exchange floors but also in the OTC market. Most market makers were coping with volumes averaging more than 60 percent higher than usual. As usual, most of these orders had to be handled on the phone—and they were all sell, sell, sell. As dealers, they were obliged to make market by buying, but their capital was dwindling quickly. Many market makers stopped answering phones or giving quotes. Prices that others quoted were often way out of line with the market. "It's clear," said Edward J. Mathias, president of T. Rowe Price New Horizons Fund, "a number of market makers saw their capital impaired and ran for cover. I don't think anybody was willing to stand in front of a speeding train." The members of the dealer system held to their credit but just barely. Like a defensive line after a furious assault, there were the shellshocked and the casualties among their numbers. On the night of October 19, the unanswered question was whether they could stand another assault. Yet, despite the losses and the thinly spread capital, the system withstood the pressure.

This was despite the possibility that not all specialist units acted forthrightly, in as much as price swings in a few stocks seemed unjustified. In January 1988, a specialist firm voluntarily withdrew as specialists for J. P. Morgan & Company because of such an allegation.

Other questions persisted. Clearly, should another crash occur at any time in the future, the dealers needed an emergency reservoir of capital. David S. Ruder, SEC chairman of only a few months, applauded the firms that came to the aid of specialists but called for a formal system to assure the presence of such capital in the future.

In the OTC sector of the stock market, the concern of officials was equally high. On the evening of October 22, an NASD official called a meeting of the managers of the top firms' OTC trading desks at Harry's Bar at Hanover Square. The purpose of the meeting was to come up with proposals on improving access to, and liquidity in, the over-the-counter market. The memo that emerged from that meeting, called "Where Were You When I Needed You?," addressed the criticism that phones were unanswered. Numerous improvements were implemented. One thing is certain. The general lack of capital in the dealer system was compounded in the OTC market by its lack of automated order handling. If the specialists could console themselves with anything, it was the fact that their order-handling systems held up under the deluge. The NYSE's order-relay computers are so redundant with backup systems, and their fault tolerance so high, that the enormous volumes of orders were getting through to the floor.

The only breakdowns that did occur were in the Intermarket Trading System, a computerized network that links regional exchanges and the NYSE. This system did slow down to the point that specialists on the regionals' floors could not get orders executed on the New York Stock Exchange.

Over-the-counter order handling was a different story. Not only were some dealers unable to get orders executed, but many orders (most of them phoned in by clients) were not getting to the trading desks because the phones were jammed. Those market makers who were still accepting orders and doing their best to execute them could only take so many calls. After that, the phones went unanswered. Before long, the overwhelming supply pressure and lack of market-maker response created huge "unnatural" spreads. Despite the cracks in the wall that the exchange and OTC dealers quickly erected between a tidal wave of sell orders and total panic, the wall held, but it was close. Perhaps there should be an emergency capital pool for dealers to draw on. Perhaps greater automation is necessary. Perhaps some broke ranks and ran before the wave. The fact remains that, without the dealer system, the capital markets and the economy as a whole would have been in a very different state after October 19.

PROGRAM TRADING MYTHS

Computerized programs are used basically for three investment goals. When employed to hedge large stock positions, this type of trading is called "portfolio insurance" (as described in Chapter 7). When aimed at conducting arbitrages (that is, taking profits on market price differences), program trading is referred to as "stock index arbitrage." Finally, there is "speculative" program trading. (None of these should be confused with "package traders," which are largely institutional accounts buying quantities of stock on a daily, weekly, or monthly basis, as they receive infusions of capital.)

Computerized trading systems originated in the early 1980s, when personal computers and their related miniaturized circuitry made possible the nearly immediate use of trading information. Clearly, this technology has made the market more efficient; that is, current trading includes, more than ever, the very latest information. Such systems also promised to enable hedgers, arbitrageurs, and speculators alike to act instantaneously on the most up-to-date of information. That was the theory. The actuality was very different.

THE GLOBAL CRASH

Given the high-tech linkages of markets all around the world, it is not surprising that the U.S. market was not alone when it crashed. In fact, the momentous event that fills our perspective from horizon to horizon is only one aspect of a global phenomenon.

For the week preceding October 19, every major stock market in the world was feeling the weight of the decline in American stock prices, as well as their own. Many exchanges resisted the tug to decline, but on that next Monday, they caved in. During the week of October 12, the Nikkei index on the Tokyo exchange plunged 12 percent. In London, the Financial Times-Stock Exchange index dropped 20.36 percent. West German shares were down 11.19 percent, the Swiss 16.56 percent, and so on. Again, technology turned from benefactor to demon. Under normal conditions, global networks enable traders to execute huge transactions by pressing several buttons at a terminal and watching the computer's screen flicker with the execution. Some $750 billion worth of stocks are traded this way, internationally, 24 hours a day, every year. That's the potential upside of global trading. The demon emerges during down markets. At such times, a bear market can be handed around the world, from exchange to exchange, without intermission. A bad trading session at any one major center affects them all. This synchrony is what happened in early October, and what continues to happen, as long as the markets are so closely linked. In the words of Carl F. Adams, managing director of Carl Marks & Company, "It (the worldwide bear market) certainly shows you the downside of globalization of markets."

The bleak Monday in October spotlighted one or two basic flaws in the program trading approach. Traditionally, computerized portfolios were supposed to be almost "self-adjusting," that is, buy or sell orders would be activated automatically as the market dictated. All the planning and thinking was supposed to have been done long before the orders were put into position. The assumption was that no

Figure 14–1. Other U.S. and Foreign Stock Exchanges.

Other U.S. and Foreign Stock Exchanges

WEDNESDAY, NOV. 4, 1987

MIDWEST

Sales	Stock	High	Low	Close	Chg.
5100	GreifBr	31¾	30	31¾	....

BOSTON

Sales	Stock	High	Low	Close	Chg.
100	CapProp	26	26	26	+1
41800	Csll Carib	2⅝	1¾	2 5-16	+5-16
600	CommGrp	3¾	3¾	3¾	....
12600	Digicon	⅛	3-32	3-32	—1-32
11000	Dimis	1¼	1	1	....
1000	ICO Inc	13-16	13-16	13-16	— ⅛
26200	LoJack	2⅝	1⅞	2½	+ ¾
1000	Pantepec	9-32	9-32	9-32	....
200	PremrR	¼	¼	¼	+1-16

Total sales 3,300,000 shares.

PHILADELPHIA

Sales	Stock	High	Low	Close	Chg.
400	AContl pfA	18¼	18¼	18¼	—1¾
z250	BIIGE 4pf	42	42	42	+6
100	FstExec pfA	19⅜	19⅜	19⅜	— ⅜
4700	HlthCpAm	15-32	15-32	15-32	—1-16
20	Homasote	25½	25½	25½	— ½
100	Penguin	5-16	5-16	5-16	—1-16
1500	Ronson	⅞	⅞	⅞	+1-16
2100	Wash Co	4¼	4¼	4¼	....

Total sales 2,249,000 shares.

PACIFIC

Sales	Stock	High	Low	Close	Chg.
300	AlaskGld	⅞	⅞	⅞	— ⅛
5500	AFinl pfH	30½	30½	30½	+ ½
1700	AFin Ent	17	16¾	16¾	— ½
2000	AMdAirl	¾	¾	¾	....
400	AmPac	3¾	3¾	3¾	....
500	AmPace s	9	9	9	— ¾
600	AmShrd	4½	4½	4½	....
4000	CanSoPt g	1¾	1⅝	1¾	+1-16
4200	CapCit ws	93	85	87¼	—4¾
400	CheyR s	4½	4½	4½	....
12300	ChiefCnMin	7	6⅝	7	....
1000	ClaryCp	⅞	⅞	⅞	....
100	ClaySlv	1⅜	1⅜	1⅜	....
1200	CliniTh	1⅛	1⅛	1⅛	— ¼
11500	ColuNth	1-16	3-64	3-64	—1-64
1000	viCwthO	1-16	1-16	1-16	....
100	ConOG wt	½	½	½	+ ⅛
328800	CrystO	3-64	1-32	3-64	....
2000	CrysO pf	7-32	7-32	7-32	+1-32
900	CryO pfA	7-32	7-32	7-32	....
2500	viGnExp	5-16	5-16	5-16	....
15800	GldStd	2 15-16	2 13-16	2 13-16	+1-16
2100	Imreg	6¼	6	6¼	+ ¼
2000	viKaiS pfA	¼	¼	¼	+1-16
30700	viKaiS pfB	7-16	⅜	⅜	....
6300	MagelPt	2	1⅞	2	+1-16
5000	MiniCptr	⅜	⅜	⅜	....
7400	MisnIns	⅞	⅞	⅞	....
600	NEOAX	6⅝	6⅝	6⅝	— ¼
7400	NVF	3-16	5-32	5-32	....
7100	OKC LP un	4¼	4¼	4¼	+ ⅛
300	PalmBb pf	5	5	5	+ ¼
300	Pengo	7-16	7-16	7-16	—1-32
7300	PE Cp	1-16	1-16	1-16	+1-64
199800	PSNH wt	1¼	1⅛	1⅛	....
2200	SharnSt	½	½	½	—1-16
300	SoelPS	2 15-16	2 15-16	2 15-16	—1-16
400	SwstRlt	2	2	2	— ½
31400	TxAir pfG	13¼	12½	13⅛	+ ⅜
2800	TxAir pfH	3⅛	3	3	....
900	TxAr pfI	5⅜	5¼	5¼	— ⅛
38000	TexInt	1 7-16	1⅜	1 7-16	+1-16
16500	Tigrl wt	1⅝	1⅜	1½	— ⅛
7100	WldAr wt	3¼	3⅛	3⅛	+ ⅛
7000	Yuba A	2¼	2 1-16	2⅛	....

BONDS

Sales	Stock	High	Low	Close	Chg.
74000	AFinl 10s99	81	80½	80¾	....
20000	AFinl 12s99	88	87	88	+2
25000	Rastn 12s97	60	59	60	+1
10000	Empir 12s02	60	60	60	....
2000	McGreg 15½94	98	98	98	+7
19000	RapAm 10s06	59⅜	57	57	—1
25000	SesIPS 11⅞98	65	65	65	+2
10000	UnMM 15s04	92	92	92	+4
15000	WAirl 14¼88	120	120	120	....

Foreign

CONSOLIDATED TRADING

TORONTO

(in Canadian dollars and cents)

24176	Abti Prce	$23½	22¾	23¼	
3100	Acklands	$16¾	16⅜	16⅜	— ⅜
19900	Agnico E	$24	23½	23½	— ⅞
3800	Agra Ind A	$12	11½	12	+ ½
60679	Alt Energy	$17⅜	17	17	— ½
400	Alta Nat	$11¼	11¼	11¼	— ¼
3450	Algoma St	$15⅛	15⅛	15⅛	— ⅛
42230	A Barick	$23¾	23	23½	— ½
8100	Alco I f	$9¼	8⅝	8⅝	— ¾
17410	BCED	270	255	260	— 5
54889	BP Canada	$17⅝	17	17⅜	+ ⅛
48750	B C Bancor	61	57	61	+ 2
118600	Bank N S	$12⅝	12⅜	12⅝	— ⅛
2000	Baton	$11¾	11⅜	11⅜	— ⅜
200	Bramalea	$19	19	19	
5700	Brenda M	$12¼	11½	12¼	+ ¾
7891	BCFP	$16⅜	16	16⅜	+ ¼

TORONTO

(in Canadian dollars and cents)

13265	BC Res	87	83	85	— 3
37840	BC Phone	$25⅜	25⅜	25⅜	
350	Brunswk	$11¼	11¼	11¼	
500	Budd Can	$32	32	32	
117051	CAE	$8⅛	7¼	7¼	— ⅞
18500	CCL B f	$8⅛	7⅝	8	
127870	Cambior	$17½	16½	17¼	— ⅜
65025	Campeau f	$14½	14	14¼	— ½
38385	CDC	$9¼	8⅞	9⅛	— ⅛
16535	C Nor West	$18	17½	17½	— 1
9800	C Packrs	$13¼	13¼	13¼	— ¼
700	Can Trust	$60	59	60	+ 1
132	C Tung	$5½	5½	5½	
94865	CI Bk Com	$17¾	17½	17¾	— ⅛
36860	CTire A f	$12⅛	11⅜	11¾	— ¼
300	C Util B	$18¼	18¼	18¼	— ⅜
4000	Cara	$9⅞	9½	9⅞	— ⅛
875	Celanese	$17¼	16¾	17¼	— ¼
1500	Cntrl Cap	$11½	11¼	11½	— ¼
700	CHUM	$16	16	16	—1½
13250	Cineplex	$14¼	13¾	14⅛	— ⅜
12330	CDistb B f	$5⅜	5⅜	5⅜	
9000	Coseka R	64	60	64	+ 2
1000	Canron A	$11	11	11	
4575	Crownx	$11½	11¼	11¼	— ¼
7200	Czar Res	139	136	136	— 2
11002	Denison A p	$5¼	5⅛	5⅛	— ⅛
10800	Denison B f	490	480	490	—10
19900	Derlan	$9⅛	8⅜	8½	— ¾
500	Develcon	290	275	275	—15
14937	Dicknsn A f	$8¾	8⅛	8⅛	— ⅜
134390	Dofasco	$22	21	21	—1⅛
500	Donohue	$28½	28½	28½	— 1
1500	Du Pont A	$26	25⅛	26	+ ½
202150	Dylex A	$8½	8	8½	+ ⅜
330	Emco	$12½	12⅜	12½	
37117	Encor	$6⅛	5⅞	6⅛	+ ⅛
17900	Equty Svr A	$6¼	5⅝	5⅝	— ⅛
1400	FCA Intl	$11	10¼	10¼	— ¾
432125	Ficnbrdge	$19	18⅜	19	— ¼
36485	Fed Ind A	$13	12⅝	12¾	— ¼
28000	Fed Pion	$9	9	9	— ¼
200	F City Fin	$14¼	14⅛	14⅛	
200	Gendis A	$13½	13½	13½	
150	GE Canada	$15½	15½	15½	— ½
1600	Gibraltar	$9	8¾	9	+ ¼
10200	Goldcorp f	$7⅞	7½	7⅝	— ⅛
4500	Graft G	$11	11	11	
9875	GL Forest	$41	39¾	39¾	—1¼
700	Greyhnd	$19¼	19¼	19¼	— ½
3200	Hawker	$20	19	20	
6000	Hayes D	$10½	10¼	10½	+ ¼
38037	Hees Intl	$18¼	17⅝	18¼	+ ¼
89497	Hemlo Gld	$18	17¾	17⅞	— ¾
11100	Hollingr I	$8	7½	7½	— ¾
7506	H Bay Co	$19	19	19	
49424	Imasco L	$26⅞	26½	26¾	— ⅜
3000	Indal	$9½	9¼	9½	+ ¼
2500	Inglis	$17¼	17¼	17¼	
600	Inland Gas	$11¾	11½	11½	
10700	I Corona o	$49⅜	48½	49⅜	— ½
16585	Intl Thom	$10½	10⅛	10½	
8975	Intpr Pipe	$41½	41½	41½	— ¼
1122	Ipsco	$10⅜	10	10⅜	
4400	Ivaco A f	$11¼	11⅛	11¼	
100	Ivaco B	$11	11	11	— ½
20714	Jannock	$15¾	15¼	15½	— ¾
2500	Kelsey H	$15	14¾	15	+1⅛
5400	Kerr Add	$18⅝	18½	18½	
16212	Labatt	$24	23½	24	+ ⅛
34350	Lacana	$12⅜	12	12	— ⅜
2800	Loblaw Co	$11⅞	11¾	11⅞	— ⅛
2900	Lumonics	$6⅞	6½	6⅞	+ ⅛
51611	Magna A f	$11⅝	11¼	11½	— ⅜
100	MDS H A	$21½	21½	21½	+ ⅜
701	MICC	$10	9½	9½	— ½
9829	Mclan H X	$18¼	17¾	17¾	— ⅝
901	Maritime f	$14¾	14½	14¾	+ ⅜
6899	Mark Res	$9⅝	9⅝	9⅝	— ¼
3500	Minnova	$19⅛	19	19	— ⅛
10408	Molson A f	$20½	20⅛	20⅜	+ ¼
401	Nabisco L	$30½	30½	30½	+ ⅜
90988	Noranda I	$21⅝	20¾	21¼	— ⅜
32545	Norcen	$19	18⅜	18⅜	— ½
128461	Nova Cor f	$8⅜	8¼	8⅜	— ⅛
5451	Nowsco W	$14¾	14⅝	14¾	— ¼
85706	NuWst sp A	25	22	25	+ 2
7000	Oakwood	260	250	255	—45
10161	Oshawa A f	$20	19½	19¾	+ ¼
79776	Pac W Airln	$17¾	16¾	17⅜	+ ⅛
5400	Pamour	$9¾	9⅛	9⅜	— ⅜
1901	PanCan P	$24¾	24¼	24¾	+ ⅛
200	Pembina	$15½	15½	15½	— ½
570	Pine Point	$12½	12⅛	12⅛	— ⅜
347531	Placer Dm	$16⅞	16½	16⅜	— ⅜
12500	Que Sturg o	380	375	375	—20
6200	Rayrock f	$8⅞	8⅜	8⅜	— ¼
3429	Redpath	$8⅝	8⅜	8½	+ ⅛
1	ReedSt I Sp	$26⅝	26⅝	26⅝	+1¾
10501	Rogers B f	$18¾	18⅜	18⅜	— ⅛
1040	Roman	$9¾	9½	9½	— ¼
501	Rothman	$41	41	41	
29037	RyTrco A	$14¼	14	14⅛	
107678	Royex	$5⅞	5⅝	5¾	— ⅛
11061	Sceptre R	365	350	350	— 5
23851	Scotts f	$9¾	9½	9⅝	— ⅛
7436	Sears Can	$8⅝	8¼	8⅜	— ¼
20001	SHL Systm	$18½	17¾	18	
201	Selkirk A f	$21	21	21	— ¾
13040	Shell Can	$35½	35	35½	+ ¼
23150	Sherritt	$5⅜	5¼	5¼	— ¼
500	Slater B f	$5¾	5¾	5¾	
142150	Southam	$17⅛	16½	16¾	— ¾
6950	Spar Aero f	$14⅜	14¼	14⅜	+ ⅛
30642	Stelco A	$19⅝	18¾	19¼	+ ¼
100	Teck Cor A	$31¾	31¾	31¾	+ ¼
18611	Teck B f	$33	32⅝	33	+ ¼
15264	Tex Can	$26⅞	25¾	25¾	—1½

TORONTO

(in Canadian dollars and cents)

28125	Thom N A	$25½	24½	25½	
89305	Tor Dm Bk	$24	23⅝	24	— ⅛
1550	Torstar B f	$24½	24¼	24½	+ ¼
550	Trns Mt	$13	12⅞	12⅞	— ⅛
84419	TrnAlta UA	$27⅞	27	27⅞	+1¼
14330	TrCan PL	$16	15¾	15¾	— ¼
12000	Trimac	370	360	370	
55550	Trilon A	$15⅝	15⅛	15½	
6200	Trizec A f	$23	22½	23	
80000	Turbo	68	65	65	— 2
4500	Unicorp A f	$6	5⅞	6	
100	Un Carbid	$14	14	14	
2950	U Entprise	$8⅞	8¾	8⅞	
5600	U Keno	$8¾	8⅜	8⅜	— ⅜
1000	VGM Cap	370	300	300	—65
1218	Weldwod	$13½	13¼	13½	+ ¼
1300	Westmin	$9⅜	9⅜	9⅜	
10775	Weston	$31¼	30¼	30⅞	— ⅜
412	Woodwd A	$5¼	5¼	5¼	— ¼

Total sales 18,748,575 shares

MONTREAL

(in Canadian dollars and cents)

Sales	Stock	High	Low	Close	Chg.
21684	Bank Mont	$26	25⅝	25⅞	— ¼
52700	BmbrdrA	$8½	8⅛	8½	+ ⅛
78540	BombrdrB	$14⅜	14⅛	14⅛	— ⅛
3500	CB Pak	$13	13	13	
44387	Cascades	$7½	7¼	7¼	— ¼
500	CIL	$26⅜	26⅜	26⅜	— ¼
153475	ConBath	$15¾	15½	15½	— ⅛
732	DomTxtA	$16⅜	15¼	15½	
5349	MntTrst	$12½	12	12	— ¼
32957	NatBk Cda	$10½	10¼	10⅜	— ⅛
422114	Noverco	$11½	10½	11	+ ¼
129840	Power Corp	$12⅛	11¾	11¾	— ½
13000	Provigo	$8¾	8⅝	8¾	
6000	Repap Entr	$10¾	9⅞	10¼	+ ⅛
52732	Royal Bank	$27⅝	27⅜	27½	— ¼
1800	SteinbrgA	$33	33	33	
6150	Videotron	$10⅝	10¼	10⅝	+ ¼

Total Sales 6,640,801 shares.

TOYKO (in Japanese yen)

Asahi Chem	1,070	Mitsu Chem	990
Bank of Toky	1,300	Mitsui	672
Banyu	1,340	NEC	1,820
Canon Cam	922	Nippon Oil	1,230
C. Itoh	675	Nippon St	435
Dai-Ichi Kan	2,870	Nissan	696
Fuji Photo	3,530	Pioneer	2,120
Fujitsu	1,100	Sharp	932
Hitachi	1,110	Sony	3,880
Isuzu	413	Sumitomo C	780
Kajima	1,770	Takeda	2,930
Kansai	3,320	Teijin	787
Kawasaki Steel	347	Tokio Mar	1,920
Komatsu	645	Toray	731
Kubota	539	Toshiba El	667
Matsushita	1,980	Toyota	1,790
Mazda	418		

ZURICH (in Swiss francs)

Brown Bov	2,100	Swiss Alum	475
CIBA Geigy	2,875	Swiss Reins	12,000
Cred Suisse	2,590	Swiss BankCp	403
Fischer	870	Sulzer nv	410
a-Hoff LaR	100,000	Swissair	910
Jelmoli	2,600	Union Bk Sw	3,760
Nestle	8,150	Winthur Assr	4,850
Sandoz	11,000	Zurich Ins	5,250
a-Pirelli Int	346	a-Basel.	

HONG KONG

(in Hong Kong dollars and cents)

Bk EastAsia	18.50	HongK Tel	11.50
Cheung Kong	6.75	Hutchn Whmp	6.95
China Light	17.40	Jardine Math	9.10
HangSeng Bk	27.30	SunHung Kai	7.80
HonkK Elec	7.20	Swire Pacif	13.10
HongK Land	6.55	World Intl	2.10
Hongkg ShBk	7.05	n.t.-not traded.	

Foreign Stock Index

WEDNESDAY, NOV. 4, 1987

	Today	Prev. day	1987 High	1987 Low
Ams'dam (a)	213.2	221.5	354.4	213.2
Brussels	3844.69	3947.33	5447.88	3739.24
Frkfrt (b)	1427.9	1485.3	2061.1	1427.1
Frkfrt (c)	466.93	483.93	671.71	466.93
Hong Kong	2077.11	2180.74	3944.24	2077.11
London (d)	1255.6	1386.1	1942.6	1255.6
London (e)	897.63	930.29	1369.88	897.63
Milan	725	736	1057	721
Paris (f)	265.27	273.67	393.13	229.04
Sydney	1972.9	2079.3	3407.3	1972.9
Tokyo (g)	23060.53	23358.60	26643.43	18544.05
Toronto	2968.35	3005.91	4118.94	2837.79
Zurich (h)	458.8	473.0	644.9	458.8

a-ANP-CBS ; b- Commerzbank; c- fu,5.7:7.5,7.5:9.3Allegemeine Zeitung;d- FinancialTimes 30; e-Financial Times 500; f-Agefi; g-Nikkei Average; h- Credit Suisse; r- Revised; n.a. Not Available; x- Holiday.

LONDON (in British pence unless otherwise specified)

AA Corp	$16.50	ICI	1,018
Allied Lyons	320.00	Jaguar	288.00
Amstrad	119.00	JCI	n.q.
Babcock	n.q.	Kloof Gld	$10.00
Barclays	423	Leg & Gen	251.00
B.A.T.	425.00	Leslie	$6.50
Beechams	397	Lloyds	225
BICC	290.00	Libanon	$16.00
Boc Group	309.00	Lon Rho	214.00
Boots	224.00	Lucas	494
Bowater	352	Marks	191.00
Bracken	$1.70	Metal Box	179
Brit Arrow	103.00	Midland	325
Brit Pet	246.00	Nt West Bk	525
Brit Telecm	216.00	P & O	497.00
BTR	239	Plessey	143.00
Burmah Oil	369.00	Prudentl	785
Caddy Schw	203.00	Racal El	202.00
Chartr Cons	270	Rank	484
Comm Unin	291.00	Reed Intl	342
Cons Gold	788	Royal Ins	375
Courtaulds	310.00	RTZ	278
DeBeers	$9.50	Shell	980
Doorns	$9.00	Std & Ch Bk	415
Fisons	242.00	Stilfontn	$5.25
GEC	184.00	Tate & Lyle	569
Gen Accid	750	Thorn EMI	448
Glaxo	10.20	Trafalgar	283.00
GKN	245.00	Ultramar	176
Gold Fields	$15.75	Unilever	455
Grand Met	365.00	Vaal Reefs	$8.75
Gus A	1,129	Vickers	143
Hanson	127.00	Welkom	$7.75
Harmony	$11.25	Wellcome	312
Harties	$6.25	Winkels	$15.00
Hawker	404		

BONDS

Consol 2½ pc	28.53	Tres 15½-98	139.50
Tres 11¾-91	107.28	War Loan	40.03
Tres 14½-94	124.56	s-2 for 1 split.	

SYDNEY

(in Australian dollars and cents)

Amatil	6.40	Nat Bank	4.30
ANZ Bk	3.75	Pan Cont	2.00
ACI	3.50	Pac Dunlop	3.78
BHP	7.50	So Pac Pet	0.47
Cen Pac Min	1.20	Westpac	4.40
Coles	5.60	WMC	4.95
Crusader Oil	1.45	Woodside	1.20
CSR	3.20	Woolworths	2.45
MIM	1.60		

AMSTERDAM

(in Netherlands guilders)

ABN bank	36.70	KLM	31.90
Ahold	60.50	Nat Ned	46.50
Akzo	93.00	Ned Lloyd	117.00
Amro Bank	61.30	Philips	30.50
Buhrmn-Tetr	38.00	Royal Dutch	201.00
Fokker	24.80	Unilever	101.50
Heineken	121.50	Van Omren	21.50
Hoogovens	28.80	Wessanen	59.00

BRUSSELS (in Belgian francs)

Arbed	1,160	Petrofina	9,500
Cockerill	127	Soc Generale	2,400
GB-Inno-BM	808	Sofina	9,900
Gevaert	6,040	Solvay	10,150
Hoboken	6,000		

JOHANNESBURG

(in South African rands)

Anglo Amer	59.00	Rust Plat	31.00
De Beers	33.00	Samanco	8.00
Kloof	35.00	St Helena	39.00
Messina	7.50		

MILAN (in Italian lire)

Fiat Common	9,000	Pirelli Spa	3,750
Generali	91,350	Rinascente	3,920
Montedison	1,595	SNIA	2,931
Olivetti Comn	7,910		

FRANKFURT (in German marks)

AEG	225.50	Karstadt	443.00
Allianz Vrs	1,090.00	Mannesmn	130.80
BASF	254.10	Metallges	257.00
Bayer	267.50	Mnch Rvrs	2,080.00
Bayer Verns	340.00	RWE	219.50
BMW	466.00	Siemens	461.00
Commrzbnk	237.50	Suedzucker	300.00
Daiml Benz	742.00	Thyssen Hu	107.00
Deutsch Bk	486.00	Thyssen Ind	88.00
Dresdnr Bk	256.50	Veba	274.50
Hoechst AG	245.50	Volkswagen	264.00

PARIS (in French francs)

Air Liquide	528.00	Michelin	230.00
Beghin	391.00	Peugeot	1,086
LVMH	1,479	Radiotech	1,000
Mach Bull	38.00	Total CFP	334

BUENOS AIRES

(in old Argentine pesos)

NOT AVAILABLE

thinking had to be done if the market moved; the orders would simply be activated like mousetraps. But let's see what actually happened.

Portfolio "insurance" is not really insurance. It is a form of money management that makes use of stock index futures to protect the value of a portfolio. In theory, when the market value of the stock declines, managers offset most of the losses through short sales in the futures contract obligation. In practice, not all the losses are offset because stock index futures prices are expected to track actual stock prices closely but not exactly.

On October 19, several assumptions were proven wrong. For one thing, futures and stock prices were soon widely out of synchronization, and no one knew for sure exactly where stock prices were going. Most portfolio managers who were lulled into believing that the computers would do the right thing could not absorb, analyze, and act fast enough on this unexpected set of circumstances. Many, of course, did start selling futures contracts.

When they did, two things happened. First, with so many managers and other investors creating supply by selling, futures prices started to drop dramatically. Then the second thing started to happen. The abrupt decline in futures prices scared stock owners into selling, which added fuel to the selling flames in both the futures and the stock markets.

The basic error on the part of money managers was that they relied on the performance of the program, not on their assessment of the fundamentals. They got away from making up their own minds, depending instead on "the computer" to adjust to market conditions.

Arbitrageurs base their trading techniques on the same basic assumption: That the difference in prices between futures and stocks will be small and fleeting. Using sophisticated programs, arbitrageurs look for discrepancies between futures and stock prices. When they find such gaps, they simultaneously sell the higher-priced instruments and buy the lower-priced one. They thereby lock in guaranteed profits in what is known as "riskless arbitrage."

Under normal circumstances, arbitrageurs, who account for about 20 percent of stock market trades, tend to close such gaps very quickly.

As the market plunged, however, these gaps widened and should have become an arbitrageur's dream come true. But both markets were losing value too fast, orders were too difficult to get executed at all, much less simultaneously, and the conditions were changing far to quickly for most traders to react quickly enough. Consequently, arbitrage trading on October 19 is estimated to be only 9 percent, most of it probably in the morning, before the "arbs" bowed out and in many cases were blown out of the market. When they ceased trading, they further deflated the buy side of the market.

Like arbs, speculators represent buying pressure in a bear market because they often trade against the direction of the market. Yet speculators also rely on the same assumptions: close tracking of futures and stock prices, prompt order execution, a reasonably adequate demand side, and enough time to react to the market. When all of these requirements went out the window, speculators had to stand back, thus denying the market even more would-be buyers.

Program traders of all kinds were being frustrated by the raging bear market. Yet the widespread fear was that these participants would enter the market as a group and create a highly volatile witching hour that would knock the market on its ear. For a couple of months after the Crash, it was believed that program traders were in too great a disarray for any such thing to happen. Witching hours could occur only in relatively orderly markets, when all the day-to-day conventions hold. Under extreme conditions, they seemed to have no more or less effect than any other supply factors.

Yet, critics of program trading persist by saying that the percentage of trades is not as influential as their timing. Certainly the speed of events not only on October 19, but normally in today's stock market, is a factor: "We are learning," said Robert A. Brusca, chief economist at

Nikko Securities, "that when we compress the time in which things happen, they happen differently." So it was conceivable that a limited amount of concerted trading at a critical point might have a different effect than it would under normal circumstances.

In addition, computer technology, while making the market more efficient, also makes it all but impossible for traders to react to all the available information. "Overnight," said Allen Sinai, chief economist of Shearson Lehman Hutton, as the firm was then known, "the reaction time to market-influencing events dropped from months or days to minutes and seconds. Unless you could evaluate all this data instantly, you were out of business."

For a while after October 19, no one knew for sure what role program trading really played. The circumstances were just too chaotic for anyone to know. SEC Chairman Ruder stated that index futures trading "occurred in significant amounts" and even that various forms of index futures trading played an important role in the collapse on October 19 and 20. He went on to question whether there is enough capital behind index futures trading, for which you need to put up only 5 percent of the value of the contract. (Compare this with the Reg T 50 percent requirement on a stock purchase.) When calls go out to index futures traders for more money in a declining market, there is less of a guarantee that the obligation will be honored. Whatever its real effect, program trading was banned from the NYSE on October 20. Only on November 9 was it allowed to resume, with money-market watchers holding their breath. The effect of its return was barely noticeable.

In January of 1988, the task force appointed by President Reagan issued a report that placed the blame squarely on program trading. The report went on to make a number of suggested changes, including limits on stock price swings, trading halts, and giving the Federal Reserve Board overseer duties for both the stock and the futures markets (now regulated separately). There was little doubt that program trading would undergo regulatory changes.

THE STOCK MARKET AND THE ECONOMY

Many people equate the well-being of the stock market with that of the economy. Others regard the market as at least an all-important economic indicator. The underlying, almost instinctive, assumption is that the fate of one is inextricably linked with that of the other. This perception is prevalent enough that on Meltdown Monday, President Reagan felt compelled to state publicly that, while the stock market might be undergoing a correction, the economy was sound.

Given this linkage, fears of recession, inflation, unemployment, and worse were understandably heightened after the Crash. Suddenly the budget and trade deficits, the value of the dollar, and other economic factors were hyped in the news.

There is some basis for this view. The stock market has acted as an indicator eight times since World War II. In each instance, it has presaged recession by a sustained decline, with lead times of about eight months. What is a "sustained decline?" A month or even two of retreating prices is not necessarily significant—three, four, or more months are. But we hadn't had a crash since 1945, when these records were started, and so the cause-effect relationship between a stock market crash and a recession remains to be seen.

Suffice it to say that the Commerce Department uses an index of 11 economic indicators, of which the stock market is only one. For some reason, however, we do not become as exercised over a steady decline in the gross national product as we do a sudden drop in the stock market. Such is the visibility of the stock market that we regard it as a far more telling indicator than perhaps it really is. Yet, its significance, yesterday, today, and tomorrow can never be discounted.

Glossary

Account Executive (AE). A brokerage firm employee who advises clients and handles orders for them. The AE must be registered with the National Association of Securities Dealers (NASD) before taking orders from clients. Also known as registered representative (RR) or stockbroker.

Account Statement. A statement sent periodically (at least quarterly) to clients, showing the status of their accounts with a broker/dealer.

Adjusted Debit Balance. The net money borrowed by a brokerage customer in a margin account as a result of both settled and unsettled transactions. It includes Special Miscellaneous Account (SMA).

Advance-Decline Theory. A market theory that uses the relative number of advances versus declines in relation to total issues traded to make buying and/or selling decisions. Formula = A − D/V.

AE. See Account Executive.

Affiliated Person. Anyone in a position to influence decisions made in a corporation, including officers, directors, principal stockholders, and members of their immediate families. Their shares are often referred to as "control stock."

Aftermarket. A market for a security either over the counter or on an exchange after an initial public offering has been made.
See Free-Riding; Hot Issue; Stabilization; Withholding.

All-or-None (AON) Offering. A "best-efforts" offering of newly issued securities in which the corporation instructs the investment banker to cancel the entire offering (sold and unsold) if all of it cannot be distributed.

All-or-None (AON) Order. An order to buy or sell more than one round lot of stock at one time and at a designated price or better. It must not be executed until both conditions can be satisfied simultaneously.

Alternative (Either/Or) Order. An order to do either of two alternatives such as either buy at a limit or buy stop for the same security. Execution of one part of the order automatically cancels the other.
See One-Cancels-the-Other Order.

American Stock Market Value Index. A market index for all common stocks listed on the ASE, prepared daily and grouped by geographic locale and industrial category.

American Stock Exchange Price Change Index. An "unweighted" market index for all common stocks listed on the ASE, prepared hourly.

Amex. An acronym for American Stock Exchange, Inc.

Amex Rule 411. The American Stock Exchange's version of the "know your customer" rule of the NYSE.
See Rule 405.

AON Offering. *See* All-or-None (AON) Offering.

AON Order. *See* All-or-None (AON) Order.

Arbitrage. The simultaneous purchase and sale of the same or equal securities in such a way as to take advantage of price differences prevailing in separate markets.
See Bona Fide Arbitrage; Risk Arbitrage.

Arbitrageur. One who engages in arbitrage.

As Agent. The role of a broker/dealer firm when it acts as an intermediary, or broker, between its customer and another customer, a market maker, or a contrabroker. For this service the firm receives a stated commission or fee. This is an "agency transaction."
See As Principal.

As Principal. The role of a broker/dealer firm when it buys and sells for its own account. In a typical transaction, it buys from a market maker or contrabroker and sells to a customer at a fair and reasonable markup; if it buys from a customer and sells to the market maker at a higher price, the trade is called a markdown.
See As Agent.

Ask-Bid System. A system used to place a market order. A market order is one the investor wants executed immediately at the best prevailing price. The market order to buy requires a purchase at the lowest offering (asked) price, and a market order to sell requires a sale at the highest (bid) price. The bid price is what the dealer is willing to pay for the stock, while the ask price is the price at which the dealer will sell to individual investors. The difference between the bid and ask prices is the spread.
See Bid-and-Asked Quotation (or Quote).

At-the-Close Order. An order to be executed, at the market, at the close, or as near as practicable to the close of trading for the day.

At-the-Market. (1) A price representing what a buyer would pay and what a seller would take in an arm's-length transaction assuming normal competitive forces; (2) An order to buy or sell immediately at the currently available price.
See Market Order.

At-the-Opening (Opening Only) Order. An order to buy or sell at a limited price on the initial transaction of the day for a given security; if unsuccessful, it is automatically canceled.

Auction Marketplace. A term used to describe an organized exchange where transactions are held in the open and any exchange member present may join in.

Authorized Stock. The maximum number of shares that the state secretary permits a corporation to issue.

Average. A stock market indicator based on the sum of market values for a selected sample of stocks, divided either by the number of issues or by a divisor that allows for stock splits or other changes in capitalization. The most widely used average is issued by Dow Jones.

Away from Me. When a market maker does not initiate a quotation, transaction, or market in an issue, he says it is "away from me."

Away from the Market. An order where the limit bid is below (or the limit offer is above) the quote for the security. For example, if a quote for a security is 20 to 20½, a limit order to buy at 19 is "away from the market."

Backing Away. The practice of an OTC market maker who refuses to honor his or her quoted bid-and-asked prices for at least 100 shares, or 10 bonds, as the case may be. This action is outlawed under the NASD Rules of Fair Practice.

Back Office. An industry expression used to describe non-sales departments of a brokerage concern, particularly a firm's P&S and cashier departments.

Back Up. A reverse in a stock market trend.

Balance Orders. The pairing off of each issue traded in the course of a day by the same member to arrive at a net balance of securities to receive or deliver. The net difference between buyers and sellers on the opening of the market allows the specialist to open the market appropriately.

Bar Chart. In technical analysis, a chart used to plot stock movements with darkened vertical bars indicating all prices. Most charts are issued daily, weekly, or monthly.

Barron's Confidence Index. A market index that measures investors' willingness to take risks according to yields on rated bonds.

Base Market Value. In the construction of a market index, the average value of securities traded at a certain time. All movement is usually reported in terms of a dollar or percentage change from an original value, or "base."

Bearish. An adjective used to describe an opinion or outlook where one anticipates decline in price of the general market, of an underlying stock, or of both.
See Bullish.

Bear Market. A securities market characterized by declining prices.
See Bull Market.

Bear Raiders. Groups of speculators who pool capital and sell short to drive prices down and who then buy to cover their short positions—thereby pocketing large profits. This practice was outlawed by the Securities Exchange Act of 1934.
See Raiders.

Beneficial Owner. The owner of securities who receives all the benefits, even though they are registered in the "street name" of a brokerage firm or nominee name of a bank handling his or her account.

Best-Efforts Offering. An offering of newly issued securities in which the investment banker acts merely as an agent of the corporation, promising only his "best efforts" in making the issue a success but not guaranteeing the corporation its money for any unsold portion.
See All-or-None (AON) Offering.

Bid-and-Asked Quotation (or Quote). The bid is the highest price anyone has declared that he or she wants to pay for a security at a given time; the asked is the lowest price anyone will accept at the same time.
See Offer.

Big Board. A popular slang term for the New York Stock Exchange.

Block. A large amount of securities, generally a minimum of either 10,000 shares or $200,000.

Block Positioner. A broker/dealer who takes positions for his or her own account and risk in order to facilitate a large purchase or sale of securities by customers that would otherwise be disruptive to the market. A block positioner may be given relief under Regulation T to assist the financing of such positions.

Blowout. A securities offering that sells out almost immediately.

Blue-Chip Stocks. Common stocks of well-known companies with histories of profit growth and dividend payment, as well as quality management, products, and services. Blue-chip stocks are usually high-priced and low-yielding. The term "blue chip" comes from the game of poker in which the blue chip holds the highest value.

Blue Room. One of the small trading areas just off the main trading floor of the New York Stock Exchange.

Blue-sky Laws. State securities laws pertaining to registration requirements and procedures for issuers, broker/dealers, their employees, and other associated persons of those entities.

Blue-Skying the Issue. The efforts of the underwriters' lawyers to analyze and investigate state laws regulating the distribution of securities and to qualify particular issues under these laws.

Board Broker. A member of an options exchange appointed by that exchange to handle public limit orders left in his or her care by floor brokers. In performing this function, he or she is said to be running the "public book." These brokers' prime responsibility is to ensure that a fair, orderly, and competitive market exists in the classes of options to which they are assigned. *See* Market Maker; Specialist.

Board of Arbitration. (1) A three-to-five-member NASD board, appointed ad hoc by the Board of Governors, to arbitrate disputes involving transactions among members, nonmembers, and customers. *See* Code of Arbitration. (2) A board appointed by the chairman of the NYSE Board of Directors, comprised of members and allied members who serve in various ways and numbers to settle disputes arising among members or between members, allied members, and nonmembers.

Board of Governors. The governing body of the NASD, most of whom are elected by the general membership; the remainder are elected by the board itself.

Boiler Room Sales. The use of high-pressure sales tactics to promote purchases and sales of securities.

Borrowing Power of Securities. (1) The money invested in securities on margin, shown in the customer's monthly statement. The margin limit is usually 50 percent of their stock values, 30 percent of their bond values, and full value of their cash equivalent assets.

(2) The securities pledged to a lender as collateral for a loan.

BOT. (1) Industry abbreviation for "bought."
(2) Abbreviation for balance of trade.
(3) Abbreviation for board of trustees (mutual savings bank industry).

Bought Deal. A commitment by a group of underwriters to guarantee performance by buying the securities from the issuer themselves, usually entailing some financial risk for the underwriters (or syndicate).

Box. A section of a cashier department where securities are stored temporarily. The department's responsibilities are sometimes subdivided to monitor both an active box and a free box for securities held by the firm.

Breadth Index. The net securities advanced or declined for a given day's trading dividend by the total issues traded. For example:

Advances	500
Declines	600
Unchanged	200
	1,300

$$\frac{600 - 500}{1,300} = 7.69\%$$

Breakout. In technical analysis, the rise through a resistance level or the decline through a support level by the market price of a security.

Broker. An agent, often a member of a stock exchange firm or the head of a member firm, who handles the public's orders to buy and sell securities and commodities, for which service a commission is charged. The definition does not include a bank.
See As Agent; As Principal.

Broker's Broker. Also known as a municipal securities broker's broker, a person who deals only with other municipal securities brokers and dealers, not with the general public.

Bucket Shop. An organization that accepts customer orders but does not immediately execute them. It waits until, and if, the market acts contrary to the customer's expectations, then executes the order but confirms it to the customer at the price prevailing originally. This practice is outlawed by the National Association of Securities Dealers.

Bulk Identification/Segregation. A system for segregating customer securities in accordance with SEC Rule 15c3—3 in which all certificates and/or depository positions of an issue are identified as belonging to all customers. For example, a broker has ten customers each owning 100 shares, and the broker segregates one certificate for 1,000 shares.

Bullish. Describing an opinion or outlook that a rise in price is expected either in the general market or in an individual security.
See Bearish.

Bull Market. A securities market characterized by rising prices.
See Bear Market.

Bunching Odd-Lot Orders. The combination of several odd-lot orders into round lots so they can be handled by a commission house broker, specialist, or two-dollar broker, thereby eliminating the odd-lot differential.

Buy-In. On any day on or after a prescribed settlement date, the purchasing firm that has failed to receive the certificates can give written notice to the selling firm that the contract is in default, and (1) after giving notice, purchase the security in the marketplace, and (2) hold the seller responsible for any money loss that may be incurred.
See Sell-Out.

Buy Stop Order. The instructions with a buy order for a broker or specialist on the exchange floor to execute the order at the best available price when the market price touches the customer's price or when a transaction takes place above the price. Upon execution, the transaction activates (elects or triggers) the order, making it a market order to buy.

Buy the Book. An instruction to buy, at the current offer price, all available shares from the specialist in a security and/or from other broker/dealers. This instruction usually comes from traders or institutions.

Buying Power. The dollar amount of equity securities a customer could purchase without additional funds and continue to meet the initial margin requirements of Regulation T of the Federal Reserve. Computed as Reg T excess divided by Reg T initial margin requirements. For example: $10,000 divided by 50% = $20,000.

Cage (The). A slang expression used to describe a location where a brokerage firm's cashier department responsibilities are satisfied.

Calamity Call. *See* Catastrophe (Calamity) Call.

Call Loan. *See* Broker's Collateral (Call) Loan.

Call Money. *See* Broker's Collateral (Call) Loan.

Call Money Rate. The percentage of interest a broker/dealer pays on a broker's collateral loan.

Cancellation. Revocation of a buy or sell order, an action that is permissible at any time prior to execution. After execution, it is allowed only with the consent of the other party to the trade and with the approval of an NYSE floor official.

Capitalization. *See* Total Capitalization.

Capital Stock. A corporation's total equity capital. This is a synonym for the more popular term, "common stock."

Carrying Cost. Expense of the interest paid on a debit balance when a position is established.

Cash Account. An account in a brokerage firm in which all transactions are settled on a cash basis.

Cash Contract. A securities contract by which delivery of the certificates is due at the purchaser's office the same day as the date of the trade.
See Buyer's Option Contract; Regular-Way Contract; When Issued/When Distributed Contract.

Cash Cow. A colloquial term for any business that generates an ongoing cash flow. These businesses have well-known products and pay dividends reliably.

Cash Dividend. Any payment made to a corporation's shareholders in cash from current earnings or accumulated profits. Cash dividends are taxable as income.

Cash on Delivery (COD). See Delivery Versus Payment.

Cash Trade. A transaction involving specific securities, in which the settlement date is the same as the trade date.

Catastrophe (Calamity) Call. An issuer's call for redemption of a bond issue when certain events occur, such as an accident at a construction site that severely affects the completion of the project.

CCS. See Central Certificate Service.

Central Bank. (1) A Federal Reserve Bank situated in one of twelve banking districts in the United States.
(2) The Federal Reserve System.

Central Certificate Service (CCS). Former name of the Depository Trust Company.

Certificate. The actual piece of paper that is evidence of ownership or creditorship in a corporation. Watermarked certificates are finely engraved with delicate etchings to discourage forgery.

Certificated Security. A security whose ownership may be represented by a physical document. Also known as being available in "definitive form."

Charter. A document written by the founds of a corporation and filed with a state. The state approves the articles and then issues a certificate of incorporation. Together, the two documents become the charter and the corporation is recognized as a legal entity. The charter includes such information as the corporation's name, purpose, amount of shares, and the identity of the directors. Internal management rules are written by the founders in the *bylaws.*

Check Kiting. The illegal practice of drawing a check upon a demand deposit account that contains no money or has insufficient funds. It is so called even if the person deposits someone else's check into his account prior to clearance of the check previously drawn and presented as payment for an obligation.

Churning. A registered representative's improper handling of a customer's account: He or she buys and sells securities for a customer while intent only on the amount of commissions generated, ignoring the customer's interests and objectives.

Circle. See Indication of Interest.

Clean. When block positioners can match customers' buy-and-sell orders for a security, they don't have to take the security into inventory. This kind of trade is said to be "clean." If the transaction appears on the exchange tape, the term "clean on the tape" is often used. Also sometimes referred to as "natural."

Clearance. (1) The delivery of securities and monies in completion of a trade.
(2) The comparison and/or netting of trades prior to settlement.

Climax (Buying/Selling). A large increase or decrease in the price of a security accompanied by large volume. The price change should gap, indicating a completion of a price increase or decrease cycle.
See Gap.

Close. The final transaction price for an issue on the stock exchange at the end of a trading day.

Close-Out Procedure. The procedure taken by either party to a transaction when the contrabroker defaults; the disappointed purchaser may "buy in," and the rejected seller may "sell out" or liquidate.
See Reclamation; Rejection.

Closing Transaction. Any trade that reduces an investor's current position.
(1) Purchase: The purchase of a listed option so as to close or eliminate an existing short/written position.
(2) Sale: The sale of a listed option so as to close or eliminate an existing long position.
See Opening Transaction.

CNS. See Continuous Net Settlement.

Code of Arbitration. Rules established and maintained by the NASD Board of Governors to regulate arbitration of intramember and customer/member disputes involving securities transactions.
See Board of Arbitration.

COD Trade. Cash on delivery. A general term to describe a transaction in which a seller is obliged to deliver securities to the purchaser or the purchaser's agent to collect payment.

COD Transaction. A purchase of securities in behalf of a customer promising full payment immediately upon delivery of the certificates to an agent bank or broker/dealer.

Collateral. Securities and other property pledged by a borrower to secure repayment of a loan.

Commingling. The act of using various customer securities in the same loan arrangement with the firm's securities. This practice is prohibited.

Commission. A broker's fee for handling transactions for a client in an agency capacity.

Commission House Broker. A member of the NYSE executing orders in behalf of his or her own organization and its customers.

Committee on Uniform Security Identification Procedures (CUSIP). An agency of the NASD responsible for issuing identification numbers for virtually all publicly owned stock and bond certificates.

Common Stock. A unit of equity ownership in a corporation. Owners of this kind of stock exercise control over corporate affairs and enjoy any capital appreciation. They are paid dividends only after preferred stock. Their interest in the assets, in the event of liquidation, is junior to all others.

Common Stock Equivalents. (1) Debt and/or equity securities capable of subscription, exchange, or conversion into common stock of the company.
(2) Convertible bonds and convertible preferred stock may be so classified at the time of issuance, based on many factors. Once so classified, they must be considered as common stock when computing primary earnings per share.

Common Stock Ratio. The relationship of common stock outstanding to the total capitalization of a corporation.

Competitive Bidding. A sealed envelope bidding process employed by various underwriter groups interested in handling the distribution of a securities issue. The contract is awarded to one group by the issuer on the basis of the highest price paid, interest rate expense, and tax considerations.

Competitive Trader. A member of an organized exchange who may, subject to certain rules and restrictions, trade for his or her own account and risk while on the trading floor.

Congestion Area. In technical analysis, a period of trading during which the market reacts in alternating directions with great frequency. This area is characterized by small peaks and dips without any clear trend in either direction.

Consolidated Tape. A system of reporting all trades in New York Stock Exchange-listed securities on one tape, called Tape A, and all other exchange-listed securities on another tape, called Tape B, regardless of where the trade takes place.

Contingent Order. One order given to the trading desk of a brokerage firm to buy stock and then sell a covered call option. Also called a "net order" and a "not held" order.
See Market Not Held Order; Switch (Contingent or Swap) Order.

Continuing Commissions. The practice of paying commissions to registered representatives after they have left the employment of the broker/dealer or to their heirs after a registered representative has died.

Continuous Net Settlement (CNS). A procedure used by all clearing corporations to simplify processing daily transactions and correspondingly to reduce the number of certificate deliveries required. The clearing corporation interposes itself on each transaction, crediting or debiting each member's total holdings in each issue. The net balance is carried forward from day to day.

Contrabroker. A term used to describe the broker with whom a trade was made.

Contract Sheet. A complete list of each member's daily transactions arranged by issue and prepared by the clearing house for members to check for accuracy of detail and approval of settlement terms.

Cooling-Off Period. See Twenty-Day (Cooling-Off) Period.

Cornering the Market. A situation in which a party or group has acquired a substantial quantity of the available shares and, as a result, exerts considerable influence on the shares' market price.

Corporation. A business organization chartered by a state secretary as a recognized legal institution of and by itself and operated by an association of individuals, with the purpose of ensuring perpetuity and limited financial liability.
See Certificate of Incorporation; Charter.

Credit Balance. (1) In a customer's account of a broker/dealer, the credit balance indicates that the broker/dealer owes money to the customer either conditionally or unconditionally.
(2) The opposite of debit balance.

Credit Department. *See* Margin (Credit) Department.

Cross (Crossing Stock). A broker/dealer's pairing off of a purchase order with a sell order in the same security at the same time and price for different customers.

Crowd. *See* Trading Crowd.

Cum Dividend. A term applied to stock at a time when the purchaser will be entitled to a forthcoming dividend.

Cum Rights. A term applied to a stock trading in the marketplace "with subscription rights attached," which are reflected in the price of that security.

Cumulative Preferred Stock. A preferred stock that accrues any omitted dividends as a claim against the company. This claim must be paid in full before any dividends may be paid on the company's common stock.

Cumulative Voting. A voting privilege that allows a stockholder to multiply the shares he or she owns by the number of vacancies to be filled on the board (or proposals to be resolved). The stockholder can then apportion his or her total votes accordingly in the manner he or she prefers. This procedures is particularly advantageous for minority stockholders.

Curbstone Broker. A trader for the American Stock Exchange.

Cushion Theory of Investment. A theory of investment that views the short seller as a stabilizing influence on either a bull or bear market.

CUSIP. See Committee on Uniform Security Identification Procedures.

Cyclical Stock. Any stock, such as housing industry-related stock, that tends to rise in price quickly when the economy turns up and fall quickly when the economy turns down.

Daisy Chain. A series of purchases and sales of the same issue at successively higher (or lower) prices, by the same group of people. Its purpose is to manipulate prices and draw unsuspecting investors into the market, leaving them defrauded of their money or securities.

Date of Record. The date set by the corporate board of directors for the transfer agent to close the agency's books to further changes in registration of stock and to identify the recipients of a forthcoming distribution. Also known as record date.
See Ex-Dividend (Without Dividend) Date.

Day Order. A transaction order that remains valid only for the remainder of the trading day on which it is entered.

Day Trading. The act of buying and selling a position during the same day.

Dealer. An individual or firm in the securities business acting as a principal rather than as an agent.
See As Agent; As Principal.

Debit. Money paid out of an account. In a debit transaction, the net cost is greater than the net sale proceeds.

Debit Balance. The balance owed by a customer in his or her account as reflected on the brokerage firm's ledger statement of settled transactions.

Delayed Opening. The delay of the opening of trading in a security when buy and sell orders are grossly out of balance with each other

Delivery Date. The day delivery of securities is made, which may be on or subsequent to settlement date.

Delivery Versus Payment. The purchase of securities in a cash account with instructions that payment will be made immediately upon the delivery of the securities, sometimes to the contrabroker but usually to an agent bank. *See* COD Trade.

Depository Trust Company (DTC). An independent corporation owned by broker/dealers and banks responsible for: (1) holding deposit securities owned by broker/dealers and banking institutions; (2) arranging the receipt and delivery of securities between users by means of debiting and crediting their respective accounts; (3) arranging for payment of monies between users in the settlement of transactions. The DTC is generally used by option writers because it guarantees delivery of underlying securities if assignment is made against securities held in DTC.

Depth. (1) The amount of general investor interest in the market, comparing the number of issues traded with the number of issues listed: the more that are traded, the greater the "depth" of the market.
(2) The "depth" of a security depends on how large a buy or sell order it can absorb without its price changing greatly.

Descending Tops. In technical analysis, a chart pattern element in which each new high price for a security is lower than the preceding high—indicating a bearish trend.

Descending Triangle. A major chart pattern in technical analysis indicating consecutive highs until a leveling-off point is reached.

Designated Order Turnaround (DOT). A computerized order routing system used by the New York Stock Exchange to match and automatically execute small market orders that is located at the trading post location for the particular stock in the presence of the specialist.

Differential (Differential Return). The dealer's compensation for handling an odd-lot transaction. The dealer adds the differential to the price of the first possible round-lot sale and fills a customer's buy order at that somewhat higher price (or at a somewhat lower price for sell order). The differential is generally one-eighth of a point and is not itemized separately on the trade confirmation.

Dip. Any slight drop in security prices during an ongoing upward trend. It is advisable to buy on dips when the price is temporarily low.

Direct Placement. Any direct sale of securities to one or more investors, typically life insurance companies

Discount Broker. A broker/dealer whose commission rates for buying and selling securities are markedly lower than those of a full-service broker. These brokers usually provide execution-only services.

Discretion. See Limit Order; Market Not Held Order.

Discretionary Account. A customer's account in which an employee of a member firm has authority to act arbitrarily. This term does not authorize the use of judgment as to time or price of execution for an order prompted by a customer.

Discretionary Order. An order that empowers a registered representative or other brokerage firm employee to use his or her own judgment on the customer's behalf with respect to choice of security, quantity of security, and whether any such transaction should be a purchase or sale.
See Discretionary Account; Fractional Discretionary Order.

Distributor. See Underwriter.

Distribution. The sale of a large block of stock, through either an underwriting or an exchange distribution.

Distribution Area. In technical analysis, a relatively narrow price range for a security for a long period, typically a month or more.

Distribution Stock. Publicly sold stock offered by persons affiliated with the issuer pursuant to an effective shelf registration.

Diversification. (1) Spreading investments and contingent risks among different companies in different fields of endeavor.
(2) Investing in the securities of one company that owns or has holdings in other companies.
(3) Investing in a fund with a portfolio containing many securities.

Dividend Payout. The percentage of dividends distributed in terms of what is available out of current net income.

Dividends. Distributions to stockholders declared by the corporate board of directors.

DK. A slang expression for "Don't Know," as applied to a securities transaction on which transactional data are missing when the brokers exchange comparison sheets. Also called a "QT" for a "questioned trade."

DNR. See Do Not Reduce (DNR) Order

Do Not Reduce (DNR) Order. A limit order to buy, a stop order to sell, or a stop-limit order to sell that is not to be reduced by the amount of a cash dividend on the ex-dividend date because the customer specifically requested that it be entered that way.

Don't Fight the Tape. Colloquial expression meaning "don't trade against the market trend."

Don't Know. See DK.

DOT. See Designated Order Turnaround.

Double Bottom. In technical analysis, a chart pattern showing that the price of a security has twice declined to its support level and risen again. It indicates that there is a demand for securities at that level and that the security shouldn't drop any farther.

Double Top. In technical analysis, a chart pattern showing that the price of a security has twice risen to its resistance level and fallen back. It indicates that there is a supply of securities at that level and that the security, in trying to move higher, is running into resistance at that price.

Dow Jones Average. A market average indicator consisting (individually) of (1) 30 industrial, (2) 20 transportation, and (3) 15 public utility common stocks; the composite average includes these 65 stocks collectively.

Downgrade. Lowering a bond rating by a rating service, such as Moody's or Standard & Poor's.

Downtick. The sale of a listed security at a lower price than that of the last regular-way transaction. For example, if a stock last sold at 27, the next regular-way transaction at 267/8 is said to be a downtick.

Dow Theory. A theory predicated on the belief that the rise or fall of stock prices is both a mirror and a forecaster of business activities.

DTC. See Depository Trust Company.

Due Bill. A document evidencing the fact that one party owes another a dividend or other distribution.

Dumping. (1) In the securities market, the offering of large amounts of stock without regard for the effects on prices or the market.
(2) In international finance, the selling of goods overseas below cost to get rid of a surplus or to gain a competitive edge on foreign firms.

DVP. See Delivery Versus Payment.

E&OE. Errors and omissions excepted. This legend often appears on a customer's statement. It is intended to absolve the firm of liability if it makes a mistake in preparing that statement.

Early Warning System. A system of financial reports made by broker/dealers under various exchange and SEC rules designed to provide information on the broker/dealer's financial condition.

Effective Date. The date on which a security can be offered publicly if no deficiency letter is submitted to the issuer by the SEC. It is generally no earlier than the twentieth calendar day after filing the registration statement.

Efficient Market Hypothesis. A theory stating that market prices reflect the knowledge and expectations of all investors. Seeking undervalue stocks or forecasting any kind of market movement is futile because new developments are already reflected in the corporation's stock price, making it impossible to beat the market. Making the right investment is based purely on chance.

Efficient Portfolio. A portfolio, arrived at mathematically, with a maximum expected return for any level of risk or a minimum level of risk for any expected return.

Either/Or Order. See Alternative (Either/Or) Order.

Electing Sale. The round-lot transaction that activates (triggers) a stop order.

Exchange Distribution. The marketing of a large block of stock by one or two member organizations under special terms and conditions. Buy orders are solicited informally and then crossed with the large block of stock at the current market price on the floor of the exchange.

Ex-Clearing House. A term used to describe a transaction that is to be settled (i.e., paid for and delivered) without benefit of clearing corporation facilities.

Ex-Distribution. The security is trading so that the buyer will not be entitled to a distribution that is to be made to holders.

Ex-Dividend (Without Dividend) Date. A date set by the Uniform Practice Committee or by the appropriate stock exchange, upon which a given stock will begin trading in the marketplace without the value of a pending dividend including in the contract price. It is closely related to and dependent on the date of record. It is often represented as "X" in the stock listing tables in the newspapers.

Execution. Synonym for a transaction or trade between a buyer and seller.

Exercise Date. The date when the sale or purchase of an option takes place according to the contract.

Expiration Date. The date an option contract becomes void. The expiration date for listed stock options is the Saturday after the third Friday of the expiration month. All holders of options who wish to exercise must indicate their desire to do so by this date.

Ex-Rights. A term applied to stocks trading in the market-place for which the value of the subscription privilege has already been deducted and which therefore no longer bears such a right; it is literally trading "rights off."

Ex-Warrants. The security is trading so that the buyer will not be entitled to warrants that are to be distributed to holders.

Face Value. The redemption value of a bond appearing on the face of the certificate. Also sometimes referred to as par value, or the principal value.

Fail Contract. A transaction between brokerage concerns that is not completed by delivery and payment on a settlement date.

Fair and Reasonable. See Five Percent Guideline.

Fair Market Value. The price, based on the current market value determined by supply and demand, for which a buyer and seller are willing to make a transaction.

Fill-or-Kill (FOK) Order. An order that requires the immediate purchase or sale of a specified amount of stock, though not necessarily at one price. If the entire order cannot be filled immediately, it is automatically canceled (killed).

Financial and Operational Combined Uniform Single (FO-CUS) Report. A report required periodically of brokers by various regulatory authorities that gives vital statistics regarding the firm's capabilities to handle its business.

Firm Market (Price, Quote). In the OTC market, a quotation on a given security rendered by a market maker at which he or she stands ready and able to trade immediately.

Five Percent Guideline. A general guideline established by the NASD Board of Governors to define "fair" in a random trading transaction; it is not a rule or regulation and is used only as an approximate criterion for markups, markdowns, and commissions.

Flash Prices. When reporting falls six or more minutes behind activity on the stock exchange floor, transactions in 30 representative issues are periodically culled from their proper sequence and immediately published on the ticker tape.

Floor. The securities trading area of an exchange. *See* Trading Post.

Floor Broker. A person who is a member of the exchange and works on the exchange floor executing the orders of public customers or other investors who do not have physical access to the area.

Floor Brokerage. A fee paid to a specialist or to a two-dollar broker on the floor for executing a trade as agent.

Floor Department. The department of the NYSE responsible for the administration and supervision of trading rules and regulations on the floor of the exchange.

Floor Order Tickets. Abbreviated forms of order tickets, used on the floor of the exchange for recording executions.

Floor Trader. See Registered (Floor) Trader.

FOCUS. See Financial and Operational Combined Uniform Single (FOCUS) Report.

FOK Order. See Fill-or-Kill (FOK) Order.

Fourth Market. A term referring to the trading of securities between institutional investors without the use of broker/dealers.

Free Box. A bank vault or other secure location used to store fully paid customer securities. The depositories of the NCC and DTC serve as free boxes for many member firm customers.

Free-Riding. As used in credit activities within the securities industry, the illegal practice of purchasing and selling an issue without showing ability and intent to pay for the transaction. The penalty for this practice is to freeze the account for 90 days.

Free-Riding and Withholding. As defined by the NASD in distributions of hot issues, the failure of a member to make a bona fide offering of a security that the member is distributing as an underwriter or selling group member.

Free Securities. A term used to describe securities unencumbered by a lien.

Frozen Account. A special cash account in which a customer sells a security he or she had purchased but not paid for, and then either (1) fails to pay by the seventh business day after the transaction, or (2) withdraws any portion of the proceeds before payment for the purchase. Full payment is required before any further purchase executions for 90 days.

Full Disclosure Act. The Securities Act of 1933.

Fundamental Analysis. A method for analyzing the prospects of a security through the observation of accepted accounting measures such as earnings, sales, assets, and so on.
See Technical Analysis.

Futures. Short for "futures contract," which is an agreement to make or take delivery of a commodity at a specified future time and price. The contract is transferable and can therefore be traded like a security.

Gap. In technical analysis, a "break" between the trading ranges of a stock's price for two successive days. That is, the two ranges do not overlap. A gap usually signals a reversal because the market is overbought or oversold.

Garage. One of the small trading areas just off the main trading floor of the New York Stock Exchange.

Gather in the Stops. A tactic in stock trading in which enough stock is sold to drive its price down to a point where stop orders are known to exist. The stop orders become market orders, in turn creating movement and setting off more stop orders. This process is called *snowballing.*

General Account. See Margin (General) Account.

Give Up. The practice by the payer of a commission or fee directing the recipient to "give up" part of the fee to another broker. In some situations the practice may be illegal.

Going Away. A term applied to the purchase of one or more serial maturities of an issue either by institution or by a dealer.

Going Private. Moving a company's shares from public to private ownership, either through an outside private investor or by the repurchase of shares. A company usually decides to go private when it shares are selling way below book value.

Going Public. A private company is "going public" when it first offers its shares to the investing public.

Golden Handcuffs. A contract between a broker and a brokerage house, offering lucrative commissions, bonuses, and other benefits, as long as the broker stays with the firm. Upon leaving, the broker must return much of the compensation.

Good Delivery. Proper delivery by a selling firm to the purchaser's office of certificates that are negotiable without additional documentation and that are in units acceptable under the Uniform Practice Code.

Good Name. A slang expression used to denote the registration of securities so as to permit good delivery.

Good-till-Canceled (GTC or Open) Order. An order to buy or sell that remains valid until executed or canceled by the customer.
See Limit Order; Stop Limit Order.

Graveyard Market. A bear market in which selling investors are faced with large losses, while prospective investors keep their money in cash until the market gets better.

Greenmail. In response to a corporate takeover attempt, the "target" corporation buys back its shares from the potential acquirer at a premium. The would-be acquirer then abandons the takeover bid.

Green Shoe. In an underwriting agreement, a clause that allows the syndicate to purchase additional shares at the same price as the original offering. This lessens the risk for the syndicate.

Group Sales. Sales of securities by a syndicate manager to institutional purchasers from "the pot."

Growth Company (Stock). A company (or its stock) that has mad fast gains in earnings over the preceding few years and that is likely to keep on showing such signs of growth.

GTC. See Good-till-Canceled (GTC or Open) Order.

Guaranteed Stock. Preferred stock whose dividend is guaranteed by someone other than the issuer.

Gun Jumping. (1) Illegally soliciting orders before an SEC registration is effective.
(2) Buying a security based on information that is not yet public (that is, "inside information").

Haircut. The amount taken off the value of securities for the purpose of computing a broker/dealer's net capital. The range of percentages taken off—the "haircuts"—ranges from 0 percent for U.S. government obligations to 100 percent for fail contracts.

Hammering the Market. The intensive sale of stocks to drive prices down.

Hard Dollars. The dollars that a brokerage firm pays for analysis, research, or other client-related services.

Head and Shoulders. In technical analysis, a bar chart pattern of a stock's price movement marked by a shoulder line, a neck line, and a head line resembling a person's upper torso. As the price moves toward the shoulder line, the analyst considers the trend bearish. This is known as a *head and shoulders top.* The reverse pattern, with the head at the bottom, is called a *head and shoulders bottom.* This pattern is considered bullish.

Heavy Market. A market for a stock that contains many more sellers than buyers. This market is characterized by falling prices.

Hedge. Any combination of a long and/or short positions taken in securities, options, or commodities in which one position tends to reduce the risk of the other.

Hemline Theory. Theory stating that the trend in stock prices goes hand-in-hand with the trend in the hemlines of women's dresses: If hemlines drop, so do stock prices.

Highballing. The illegal act of swapping securities with a customer at price levels above that prevailing for those same issues under competitive conditions.

Holder of Record. The party whose name appears on a company's stockholder register at the close of business on the record date. That party will receive a dividend or other distribution from the company in the near future.

Hit the Bid. Term applied to the situation in which a seller accepts the buyer's highest bid. For example, if the ask price is 34¼ and the bid 34, the seller "hits the bid" by accepting 34.

Holding the Market. Going into the market with enough buy orders to generate price support for a security. The purpose is to offset a downward trend. Viewed by the SEC as a form of illegal manipulation (except in the case of a new issue cleared by the SEC).

Home Run. Any large gain by an investor in a short period, commonly the result of takeover bids.

Horizontal Price Movement. In technical analysis, a string of transactions in which the prices change little. This pattern, if sustained, indicates no trend.

Hot Issue. A security that is expected to trade in the after-market at a premium over the public offering price. *See* Withholding.

Hot Stock. (1) A security whose price rises quickly on the first day of sale.
(2) Stolen stock.

House Account. An account managed by a firm executive and/or handled at the firm's main office. No salesperson receives a commission on transactions in a house account.

House Call. Notification of the customer by the brokerage house that the equity in a margin account is below the maintenance level.

Hypothecation. The act of borrowing money to finance purchasing or carrying securities while using those securities as collateral for the loan.

ID System. See National Institutional Delivery System.

Immediate or Cancel (IOC) Order. An order that requires immediate execution at a specified price of all or part of a specified amount of stock: the unexecuted portion has to be canceled by the broker.

Inactive Market. See Narrow Market.

Index. A stock market indicator, derived in the same way as an average, but from a broader sampling of securities.

Index Options. Options on stock indexes.

Indication. On the ticker tape, an approximation of the current quotes.

Indicator. A unit of measurement used by the securities market analyst to help forecast market direction, volume of trading, direction of interest rates, or buying and selling by corporations.

Individual Proprietorship. See Proprietorhip (Individual).

Initial Margin Requirement. The minimum equity requirement (in 1993, $2,000) a customer must furnish his brokerage firm, as established by New York Stock Exchange Rules, at the time a margin account is opened.

Inside Market. The favorable, wholesale market price for a security available only to a market maker and other members of the NASD.

Insider. An officer, director, or principal stockholder of a publicly owned corporation and members of their immediate families. This category may also include people who obtain nonpublic information about a company and use it for personal gain.

Institution. A large organization engaged in investing in securities, such as a bank, insurance company, mutual fund, or pension fund.

Institutional Delivery. See National Institutional Delivery System.

In the Tank. Colloquial expression for a security or group of securities that is quickly losing value.

Intraday. Meaning "within the day," this term is most often used to describe daily high and low prices of a security or commodity.

Investment Advisor. A person, company, or institution registered with the SEC under the Investment Advisors Act of 1940 to manage the investments of third parties.

Investment Advisors Act of 1940. A federal law requiring those who charge a fee for investment advice to register with the SEC. Exceptions include banks, some brokers, and newspapers with broad-based readership.

Investment Banker. A broker/dealer organization that provides a service to industry through counsel, market making, and underwriting of securities.

Investment History. Under NASD interpretation with regard to a hot issue, certain customers must have made at least 10 purchases over a three-year period with an average dollar value equal to that of the hot issue allocated.

IOC Order. See Immediate or Cancel (IOC) Order.

Issue (Issuance). (1) Any of a company's class of securities. (2) The act of distributing securities.

Issued-and-Outstanding Stocks. That portion of authorized stock distributed among investors by a corporation.

Issuer. A corporation, trust, or governmental agency engaged in the distribution of its securities.

Joint Account. An account including jointly two or more people.

Last Trading Day. Options cease trading at 3:00 P.M. eastern standard time on the third Friday of the expiration month.

Late Tape. The exchange tape when it is late in reporting completed transactions. When the tape falls behind five minutes or more, the first digit of transactions is deleted. For example, 47½ becomes 7½.

Legal Delivery. A delivery of securities that is not a good delivery because of the way in which registration of the certificates was carried out.

Leveraged Buyout. Taking over a controlling interest in a company using borrowed money.

Leverage Stock. Any stock bought with credit, such as in a margin account.

Limit Order. An order in which a customer sets a maximum price he or she is willing to pay as a buyer and a minimum price he or she is willing to accept as a seller. *See* Market Order; Stop Order.

Limit Price. A modification of an order to buy or sell. With a *sell* limit order, the customer is instructing the broker to make the sale at or above the limit price. With a *buy* limit order, the customer is instructing the broker to make the purchase at or below the limit price.

Liquidation. The voluntary or involuntary closing out of security positions.

Liquidity. (1) The ability of the market in a particular security to absorb a reasonable amount of trading at reasonable price changes. Liquidity is one of the most important characteristics of a good market.
(2) The relative ease with which investors can convert their securities into cash.

Listed Stock. The stock of a company traded on a securities exchange and for which a listing application and registration statement have been filed with the SEC and the exchange itself.

Loan Value. The maximum permissible credit extended on securities in a margin account, presently 50 percent of the current market value of eligible stock in the account.

Locked Market. A highly competitive market in which the bids and prices are temporarily the same—that is, they are "locked."

Long Market Value. The market value of securities owned by a customer (long in his or her account).

Long Position. The ownership of securities.

Maintenance Call. A broker/dealer's notice to a customer to deposit additional equity in his or her account to meet either New York Stock Exchange or the broker/dealer's own minimum maintenance requirements.

Major Market Index. An index prepared by the American Stock Exchange and upon which futures contracts are traded.

Manipulation. Making securities prices rise or fall artificially, through aggressive buying or selling by one investor or in connection with others. This is a severe violation of federal securities laws.

Margin. (1) The amount of money or securities that an investor must deposit with a broker to secure a loan from the broker. Brokers may lend money to investors for use in trading securities. To procure such a loan, an investor must deposit cash with the broker.
(2) In futures, the amount of money deposited with the broker to protect both the seller and the buyer against default. To establish a position in commodities, a client must deposit cash with the broker; the amount, or rate of margin, depends on exchange regulations and other factors.

Margin Call. A demand on the customer to deposit money or securities with the broker when a purchase is made or when the customer's equity in a margin account declines below a minimum standard set by an exchange or the firm.

Margin (General) Account. An account in which a customer uses credit from a broker/dealer to take security positions.
See Margin.

Markdown. The fee charged by a broker/dealer acting as a dealer when he or she buys a security directly from a customer for themselves.
See As Principal; Five Percent Guideline.

Marketability. How easily a security can be bought and sold.
See Liquidity.

Market-If-Touched Order. An order allowable only on the Commodity Futures Exchange and also the CBOE. Such a buy order is activated when a series declines to a predetermined price or below. Such a sell order is activated when a series rises to a predetermined price or higher.

Market Index. A general measurement of market movement, that, unlike an average, includes weighting of prices in terms of outstanding shares.

Market Maker. (1) An options exchange member who trades for his or her own account and risk. This member is charged with the responsibility of trading so as to maintain a fair, orderly, and competitive market. He or she may not act as an agent.
(2) A firm actively making bids and offers in the OTC market.

Market Not Held Order. An order to buy or sell securities at the current market with the investor leaving the exact timing of its execution and the price up to the floor broker. If the floor broker is holding a "market not held" buy order and the price could decline, he or she may wait to buy when a better price becomes available. There is no guarantee for the investor that a "market not held" order will be filled.

Market Order. An order to be executed immediately at the best available price.

Market Price. (1) The last reported sale price for an exchange-traded security.
(2) For over-the-counter securities, a consensus among market makers.

Market Value. The price that would be paid for a security or other asset.

Marking. Manipulative action at the close by a trader during the execution of an option contract. The purpose of this action is to improve the equity position in the client's account, even if the transactions do not represent the fair value of the contract.

Mark to the Market. As the market value of a borrowed security fluctuates, the lender may demand more in cash collateral for a rise in value, or the borrower may demand a partial refund of collateral for a decline. The written notice for either demand is a "mark" to the market.

Markup. The fee charged by a broker/dealer acting as a dealer when he or she buys a security from a market maker and sells it to a customer at a higher price.
See As Principal; Five Percent Guideline.

Matched Orders. Sales and purchases by the same beneficial owner of the same security at the same time and price, giving the impression of extensive trading in that security. This is a violation of the Securities Exchange Act of 1934.

Member. A term used to describe a member of the New York Stock Exchange or other organized exchange or clearing corporation.

Member Firm. A term used to describe a company that has as an officer or partner a member of the New York Stock Exchange, another organized exchange, or clearing corporation.

Member Takedown. A situation in which a syndicate member buys bonds at the takedown (or member's discount) and then sells them to a customer at the public offering price.

Merger. The nonhostile and voluntary union of two corporations.
See Takeover.

Minimum Maintenance Margin. The minimum equity customers must have in their accounts as defined by various Federal Reserve regulations and New York Stock Exchange rules. In 1988, for example, 25 percent of long market value must equal equity.

Minimum Trading Variation. The minimum amount of variation allowable in the trading values in an exchange, usually one-eighth of a point.
See Point.

Minus Tick. A transaction on an exchange at a price below the previous transaction in a given security.

Missing the Market. The failure by a member of the exchange to execute an order due to his or her negligence. The member is obliged to reimburse the customer promptly for any losses due to the mistake.

Mixed Account. A margin account continuing both long and short positions in securities.

Moody's Investors Service. One of the best-known bond rating agencies, owned by Dun & Bradstreet.

Mutilation. A term used to describe the physical condition of a certificate, note, bond, or coupon when the instrument is no longer considered negotiable.

N. (1) "Newly listed" when used in lowercase with a stock transaction report in the newspaper.
(2) "New York Stock Exchange" when used as a capital next to a stock transaction report.

Narrow Market. Light trading and great price fluctuations with regard to the volume on a securities or commodities market. Also known as think market and inactive market.

NASD. See National Association of Securities Dealers.

NASDAQ. See National Association of Securities Dealers Automated Quotations.

NASDAQ OTC Price Index. See National Association of Securities Dealers Automated Quotations Over-the-Counter Price Index.

National Association of Securities Dealers (NASD). An association of broker/dealers in the over-the-counter securities organized on a nonprofit, non-stock-issuing basis. Its general aim is to protect investors in the OTC market.

National Association of Securities Dealers Automated Quotations (NASDAQ). A computerized quotations network by which NASD members can communicate bids and offers.

National Association of Securities Dealers Automated Quotations Over-the-Counter Price Index. A computer-oriented, broad-based indicator of activity in the unlisted securities market, updated every five minutes.

National Clearing Corporation (NCC). An NASD affiliate organization responsible for arranging a daily clearance of transactions for members by means of a continuous net settlement process.

Natural. See Clean.

Negotiability. In reference to securities, the ability to easily transfer title upon delivery.

Negotiated Marketplace. The over-the-counter market, in which transactions are negotiated between two parties. The opposite of auction marketplace.

Negotiated Underwriting. The underwriting of new securities issues in which the spread purchase price and the public offering price are determined through negotiation rather than through bidding.

Net Change. The last column in a listed stock or bond table showing the difference between the closing prices of that day and the last day of the security traded,

adjusted for dividends and other distributions.
See Listed Stock Table.

Net Price. The proceeds of a sale or the gross payment on a purchase after deducting or adding, respectively, all expenses.

Net Proceeds. The contract price less all expenses incurred on a sale execution.
See Net Price.

New Account Report. A mandatory document for broker/ dealers who conduct a customer business, this is a record of inquiry probing into the essential facts relative to the background, financial circumstances, and investment objectives of each customer.

New Issue. (1) Any authorized but previously unissued security offered for sale by an issuer.
(2) The resale of Treasury shares.

New York Stock Exchange Index. A "weighted" market index consisting of all common stocks listed on the Big board.

Next-Day Contract. A security transaction calling for settlement the day after trade date.

NH. See Not Held (NH) Order.

No-Action Letter. In response to a query as to whether an activity is in violation of securities regulations, the SEC may issue a letter stating that it will take no action, criminal or civil, if the activity is not in violation.

Nominal Quotation. A quotation that is an approximation of the price that could be expected on a purchase or sale, and that is not to be considered firm in the event that a purchase or sale is consummated.
See Numbers Only.

Noncumulative Preferred Stock. Preferred stock on which omitted dividends do not accrue and the shareholders have no claim to them in the future.

Nonpurpose Loan. A loan involving securities as collateral that is arranged for any purpose other than to purchase, carry, or trade margin securities.
See Purpose Loan.

Normal Market. In futures trading, a market with adequate supply. In this type of market, the price of a commodity for future delivery should be equal to the present cash price plus the amount of carrying charges needed to carry the commodity to the delivery date.

Normal Trading Unit. The accepted unit of trading in a given marketplace: On the NYSE it is 100 shares (round lot) for stocks and $1,000 par value for bonds. In some relatively inactive stocks, the unit is 10 shares. For NASDAQ traded securities it is 100 shares for stocks and $10,000 par value for bonds.
See Odd Lot; Round Lot.

Not Held (NH) Order. An order that does not hold the executing member financially responsible for using his or her personal judgment in the execution price or time of a transaction.

See Market Not Held Order.

NQB. *See* National Quotation Bureau, Inc.

NSCC. *See* National Securities Clearing Corporation.

Numbers Only. A dealer's response to a request for a quote with just numbers; the dealer is not obligated to make a transaction.
See Nominal Quotation.

Odd Lot. An amount of stock less than the normal trading unit, normally a trade of one to ninety-nine shares.
See Round Lot.

Odd-Lot Differential. Generally, the dealer who facilitates an odd-lot transaction will buy the securities ⅛ or ¼ point below the next round-lot trade, or *sell* the securities ⅛ or ¼ above the next round-lot trade.

Odd-Lot Theory. A theory of market activity stating that small (odd-lot) investors frequently become heavy buyers as the market peaks and that they sell heavily in a declining market, just prior to a rally.

Off-Board. An expression that may refer to transactions over the counter in unlisted securities or to transactions involving listed shares that were not executed on a national securities exchange.

Offer. The price at which a person is ready to sell.
See Bid-and-Asked Quotation (or Quote).

Offering (Asked) Price. The lowest price available for a round lot.

Offering Circular. (1) A publication that is prepared by the underwriters and that discloses basic information about an issue of securities to be offered in the primary market.
(2) Sometimes used to describe a document used by dealers when selling large blocks of stock in the secondary market.

Offering Date. When a security is first offered for public sale.

Offer Wanted (OW). Notation made, usually in the pink or yellow sheets, by a broker/dealer who wants another dealer to make an offer for a security.

Off-Floor Order. An order that originates off the floor of the NYSE and that has priority over on-floor orders.

Office Order Tickets. Transaction order forms filled out in great detail at each sales office of member firms.
See Floor Order Tickets.

One-Cancels-the-Other Order. Two or more orders to be treated as a unit. If one order is executed, the other is canceled.

On-Floor Order. An order originating on the floor of the exchange.

On-the-Quotation Odd-Lot Order. An odd-lot order that must be executed immediately; the price is therefore based on the existing round-lot quotation on the floor of the New York Stock Exchange or on some other exchange.

On the Tape. A trade reported on one of several ticker tapes.

OPD. Appearing next to a ticker symbol, these letters indicate an issue's initial transaction during a trading session or the ticker price of the transaction did not get published shortly after execution. The symbol is used to report the correct opening price.

Open Box. *See* Active Box.

Opening. (1) The price at which a security or commodity starts trading.
(2) A short period during which interest rates drop and corporations can issue bonds at reduced prices.

Opening Only Order. *See* At-the-Opening (Opening Only) Order.

Opening Transaction. Any trade that increases an investor's position.
(1) *Purchase:* An opening purchase transaction, so as to establish a new long position, adds long securities to the account.
(2) *Sale:* The writing or selling of a listed option, so as to establish a new short position, adds short securities to the investor's net position.
See Closing Transaction.

Open on the Print. Term used when a block positioner takes the contra side of the trade from an institution. The transaction is printed on the tape, but buyers and sellers are still needed to offset the risk.

Open Order. *See* Good-till-Canceled (GTC or Open) Order.

Option. A contract wherein one party (the option writer) grants another party (buyer) the right to demand that the writer perform a certain act.

OTC Margin Stock. A stock traded over the counter whose issuer meets certain criteria that qualify the stock for margined purchases or short sales, as governed by Regulation T.

Overnight Position. The inventory in a security at the end of a trading day.

Oversold. In technical analysis, a security that is expected to go down in price or that went down too fast. This situation usually manifests itself as a "gap" or a "selling climax," where the closing price of a security is much below the previous day's close.

Over-the-Counter (OTC) Option. (1) A market, conducted mainly over the telephone, for securities made up of dealers who may or may not be members of a securities exchange. Thousands of companies have insufficient shares outstanding, stockholders, or earnings to warrant listing on a national exchange. Securities of these companies are therefore traded in the over-the-counter market between dealers who act either as agents for their customers or as principals. The over-the-counter market is the principal market for U.S. government and municipal bonds and for stocks of banks and insurance companies.
(2) A market for options traded directly between buyer and seller, unlike a listed stock option. These options have no secondary market and no standardization of striking prices and expiration dates.
See Secondary Market.

Overtrading. A practice in violation of NASD principles. A broker/dealer overpays a customer for a security to enable the customer to subscribe to another security offered by that broker/dealer at a higher markup than the loss to be sustained when the firm sells the customer's first security at prevailing market prices.

Overvalued. (1) In securities trading, a security whose market price is higher than it should be in the opinion of fundamental analysts.

(2) In options trading, a security trading at a higher price than that indicated by the mathematical models. *See* Fair Market Value; Undervalued.

OW. See Offer Wanted.

P/E Ratio. See Price/Earnings (P/E) Ratio.

Painting the Tape. An individual or group making numerous transactions without any real change in ownership. The purpose is to dupe investors into thinking the security is being actively traded and joining in that activity.

Paired Shares. When the common stock of two companies that are run by the same management is sold as one unit, it is said to be "paired," "stapled," or "Siamese."

Paper Loss/Profit. An unrealized loss or profit on a security still held. Paper losses and profits become actual when a security position is closed out by a purchase or sale.

Parking. The practice by a dealer of selling a security to another dealer to reduce the seller's net capital. The securities are sold back to the first dealer when a buyer is found, and the second dealer recoups any carrying charges.

Partial Delivery. A delivery of fewer securities than the amount contracted for in the sales transaction.

Participate but Do Not Initiate (PNI) Order. On large orders to buy or sell, an instruction given to a broker from institutional buyers or sellers not to initiate a new price, but either to let the market create a new price or obtain a favorable price through gradual and intermittent transactions.

Participating Preferred Stock. A preferred stock that is entitled not only to its stated dividend, but also to additional dividends on a specified basis if dividends are declared after payment of dividends on common stock. Usually, extra dividends are shared equally by common and participating preferred stockholers.

Partnership. A type of business organization typified by two or more proprietors.

Par (Value). The face nominal value of a security.

(1) A dollar amount assigned to a share of common stock by the corporation's charter. At one time, it reflected the value of the original investment behind each share, but today it has little significance except for bookkeeping purposes. Many corporations do not assign a par value to new issues. For preferred shares or bonds, par value has importance insofar as it signifies the dollar value on which the dividend/interest is figured and the amount to be repaid upon redemption.

(2) Preferred dividends are usually expressed as a percentage of the stock's par value.

Pegging. Also known as stabilization. Keeping a security's offer price at a certain level by means of a bid at or slightly below the price. Pegging is legal only in underwriting.

Pennant. In technical analysis, a roughly triangular chart pattern whose apex points to the right. Pennants do not indicate any clear trends because the stock may rise or fall near the apex.

Penny Stocks. Colloquial term for—but not limited to—low-priced, high-risk stocks that usually sell for less than $1 per share. These shares usually require a special margin maintenance requirement, and purchases are often limited to unsolicited orders.

Perpetual Warrant. A warrant with no expiration date.

Picture. The prices at which a broker/dealer or specialist is ready to trade. For example, "The picture on XYZ is 18½ to 19, 1,000 either way."

Pink Sheets. A list of securities being trade by over-the-counter market makers, published every business day by the National Quotation Bureau. Equity securities are published separately on long pink sheets. Debt securities are published separately on long yellow sheets.

Place. A securities distribution to a buyer, either publicly or privately.

Plus Tick. A transaction on a stock exchange at a price higher than the price of the last transaction. Also known as an uptick.

Plus-Tick Rule. An SEC rule stating that a short sale of a round lot has to be made at a price that was an advance over the last different regular-way sale of that security. For example, if the last transaction was at 40, the next short sale must be at 40⅛ or higher. If the last sale was itself an advance, then a sale at the same price is a zero plus tick and legitimate for a short sale. For example, if the last two transactions were at 40 and 40⅛, then the next sale could be at 40⅛—a zero plus tick.

PNI Order. *See* Participate but Do Not Initiate (PNI) Order.

Point. (1) In stocks, $1.
(2) In market averages, it means simply a point—a unit of measure.

Point and Figure (P&F) Chart. In technical analysis, a chart of price changes in a security. Upward price changes are plotted as "X's," and downward prices are plotted as "O's." Time is *not* reflected on this type of chart.

Poison Pill. Any kind of action taken by a takeover target company to make its stock less palatable to an acquirer. Tactics include issuing new preferred stocks that give shareholders the right to redeem at premium price if a takeover does occur. This makes acquisition much more expensive for the would-be acquirer.

Portfolio. Holdings of securities by an individual or institution. A portfolio may include preferred and common stocks, as well as bonds, of various enterprises.

Portfolio Theory. A theory based on an investment approach that permits investors to classify, estimate, and control the kind and amounts of return and risk in their own portfolios.

POS. See Preliminary Official Statement.

Position. (1) The status of securities in an account—long or short.
(2) To buy or sell a block of securities so that a position is established.
See Facilitation.

Pot, The. A pool of securities, aside from those distributed amount individual syndicate members, that is allocated by the manager for group or institutional sales. When "the pot is clean," the portion of the issue reserved for institutional (group) sales has been completely sold.

Pot Is Clean. See Pot, The.

Preemptive Right. See Subscription Privilege (Preemptive Right).

Preference Stock. See Prior Preferred (Preference) Stock.

Preferred Stock. Owners of this kind of stock are entitled to a fixed dividend to be paid regularly before dividends can be paid on common stock. They also exercise claims to assets, in the event of liquidation, senior to holders of common stock but junior to bondholders. Holders of preferred stock normally do not have a voice in management.

Preliminary Agreement. An agreement between an issuing corporation and an underwriter drawn up prior to the effective date and pending a decision by the underwriter on the success potential of the new securities. *See* Indication of Interest.

Preliminary Official Statement (POS). Also known as the preliminary prospectus, the preliminary version or draft of an official statement, as issued by the underwriters or issuers and subject to change prior to the confirmation of offering prices or interest rates.

Preliminary Prospectus. See Preliminary Official Statement (POS).

Presold Issue. A completely sold-out issue of municipal or government securities prior to the announcement of its price or coupon rate. This practice is illegal with regard to registered corporate offerings, but it is not illegal in the primary distribution of municipals or Treasuries.

Price/Earnings (P/E) Ratio. A ratio used by some investors to gauge the relative value of a security in light of current market conditions.
Ratio = Market Price Divided by Earnings per Share.

Price Range. The range defined by the high and low prices of a security over a given period.

Primary Distribution (Offering). The original sale of a company's securities. The sale of authorized but unissued shares of stock is a primary sale, while the resale of Treasury shares is a secondary sale.

Primary Market. The new issue market as opposed to the secondary market.

Primary Movement. A long-term (one- to five-year) movement or direction in the market.

Principal, As. *See* As Principal.

Principal Trade. Any transaction in which the dealer or dealer bank effecting the trade takes over ownership of the securities.

Principal Transaction. *See* As Principal.

Principals (Stockholders). The investors in a corporation with an equity interest, entitled to voting privileges, dividends, access to books and records, ready transferability of stock, proportionate shares of assets in liquidation, and subscription privileges.

Principal Value. The face value of an obligation that must be repaid at maturity and that is separate from interest. Often called simply "principal."

Prior Preferred Stock. Preferred stock whose claim on corporate assets takes precedence over other issues of preferred stock should the issuer be dissolved. It also has priority on its claim on earnings when dividends are declared.

Prior Preferred (Preference) Stock. A kind of preferred stock entitling the owner to prior claim to forthcoming dividends or claim to assets in liquidation proceedings.

Private Placement. The distribution of unregistered securities to a limited number of purchasers without the filing of a statement with the SEC. Such offerings generally require submission of an investment letter to the seller by all purchasers.

Proceeds Sale. A secondary market sale whose proceeds are used for another purchase. The two transactions are considered as one transaction, and the total sales charges must be less than 5 percent.
See Five Percent Guideline; Switch (Contingent or Swap) Order.

Profit Taking. A dropoff in general market prices after a sharp increase, in the absence of any adverse socio-economic influence. Traders are assumed to be taking short-term profits.

Proprietary. A term applied to the assets of a brokerage firm and those of its principals that have been specifically pledged as their capital contribution to the organization.

Proprietary Account. An account used by broker/dealers for trading securities, options, or commodities for their own account and risk, as opposed to trading for their customers.

Proprietorship (Individual). A type of business structure consisting of one owner, who is personally responsible for all debt liabilities but who also can manage the business as he or she sees fit.

Prospectus. A document that contains material information for an impending offer of securities (containing most of the information included in the registration statement) and that is used for solicitation purposes by the issuer and underwriters.

Proxy. (1) A formal authorization (power of attorney) from a stockholder that empowers someone to vote in his or her behalf.
(2) The person who is so authorized to vote on behalf of a stockholder.

Proxy Contest. The situation in which a person or group of people, other than a company's management, attempts to solicit shareholders' proxies, usually to change the management of the company.

Proxy Statement. Material information required by the SEC to be given to a corporation's stockholders as a prerequisite to solicitation of votes. It is required for any issuer subject to the provisions of the Securities Exchange Act of 1934.

Prudent Man Investing. Investing in a fashion that is exemplified by the conduct of a conservative person managing his or her own assets. In certain cases this type of investing is limited to the "legal list." Some states use the "prudent man" rule as a legal guideline for investing others' money.

Public Book (of Orders). A book that contains the buy or sell orders entered by the public away from the current market and that is kept by the board broker or a specialist. Only the specialist knows at what price and in what quantity the nearest public orders are.
See Board Broker; Market Maker; Specialist.

Publicly Held. Term applied to a corporation whose shares are traded according to either SEC rules or New York Stock Exchange rules.

Public Offering (Distribution). The offering of securities for sale by an issuer.

Purchasing (Buying) Power. The amount of security value available in a margin account solely from the use of existing equity in excess of current federal requirements.

Pure Hedge. A buying hedge used to lock in an interest rate and thereby protect against a decline in interest rates.

Purpose Loan. A loan, using corporate securities as collateral, that is used to purchase, trade, or carry margin securities.
See Nonpurpose Loan.

Pyramiding. Using profit generated by a position to add to that position.

Questioned Trade. See DK.

Quotation or Quote. See Bid-and-Asked Quotation (or Quote).

Raiders. Persons or groups of persons who attempt to buy a controlling share in a company's stock for the purpose of voting in new management, not for investment purposes.
See Bear Raiders.

Rally. A brisk rise following a decline in the general price level of the market or in the price of an individual stock.

R&D. See Receive and Deliver (R&D) Section.

Random Walk Theory. A hypothesis stating that historical prices, because they react to random influences on the market, are of no use in forecasting price movements. Espoused in 1900 by the French mathematician, Louis Bachelier, and revived in the 1960s, this theory contradicts the principals used in technical analysis.
See Technical Analysis.

Range. A set of prices consisting of the opening sale, high sale, low sale, and latest sale of the day for a given security.

Rating Agencies. Organizations that publicly rate the credit quality of securities issuers, the most often cited being Moody's Investors Service, Inc. and Standard & Poor's Corporation.

Reading the Tape. Appraising a security's performance by monitoring the price changes on the ticker.

Reclamation. The privilege of a seller in a transaction to recover his or her certificates and return the control money, or of a buyer to recover his or her contract money and return the certificates, should any irregularity be discovered upon delivery and settlement of the contract. *See* Rejection.

Record Date. See Date of Record.

Registered Form. A term applied to securities that are issued in a form allowing the owner's name to be imprinted on the certificate and that allow the issuer to maintain records as to the identity of the owners. Opposite of bearer form.

Registered Representative. See Account Executive.

Registered Secondary Distribution. An offering of securities by affiliated persons that requires an effective registration statement to be on file with the SEC before distribution may be attempted.

Registered Security. (1) A certificate (stock or bond) clearly inscribed with the owner's name.
(2) A stock or bond that is registered with the SEC at the time of its sale. If such an initial registration does not take place, then the term also includes any security sold publicly and in accordance with the SEC's rules.

Registered (Floor) Trader. A member of the NYSE who buys and sells stocks for his or her own account and risk on the floor of the exchange.

Registration Statement. A document required to be filed with the SEC by the issuer of securities before a public offering may be attempted. The Securities Act of 1933 mandates that it contain all material and accurate facts. Such a statement is required also when affiliated persons intend to offer sizable amounts of securities. The SEC examines the statement for a 20-day period, seeking obvious omissions or misrepresentations of fact.

Reg T Call. A notice to a customer of a broker/dealer that additional equity is needed in his or her account to meet the minimum standards set by Regulation T of the Federal Reserve.

Reg T Excess. The amount of equity in a customer's account above the minimum requirements of Regulation T of the Federal Reserve.

Regular Specialist. A member of the NYSE who continually solicits and executes orders in listed stocks assigned to him or her. The specialist also maintains an orderly market and provides price continuity and liquidity by means of transactions for his or her own account and risk on those stocks assigned to them by the exchange.
See Associate Specialists; Relief Specialist.

Regular-Way Contract. The most frequently used delivery contract. For stocks and corporate and municipal bonds, this type of contract calls for delivery on the fifth business day after the trade. For U.S. government bonds and options, delivery must be made on the first business day after the trade.

Regulation T. A Federal Reserve Board regulation that explains the conduct and operation of general and special accounts within the offices of a broker/dealer firm, prescribing a code of conduct for the effective use and supervision of credit.

Rejection. The privilege of the purchaser in a transaction to refuse a delivery lacking in negotiability or presented in the wrong denominations, without prejudice to his or her rights in the transaction.
See Reclamation.

Repeat Prices Omitted. A ticker tape announcement to signify that the tape has fallen three minutes behind transactions on the trading floor. Sequential transactions at the same price are then purposely eliminated from the tape; only the first trade prices in a string of transactions appear.

Resistance. In technical analysis, an area above the current stock price where the stock is available in abundance and where selling is aggressive. This area is said to contain what chartists call a *resistance level.* For this reason, the stock's price may have trouble rising through the price.
See Support.

Resistance Level. See Resistance.

Restricted Account. (1) A margin account in which the equity is less than the current federal requirement.
(2) The cash account of a customer who has failed to pay for a purchase under Regulation T and must have cash in the account for a period of 90 days prior to executing a buy.

Reversal. In technical analysis, a substantial, and/or long-term, countermovement of a trend.

Reversal Arbitrage. A riskless arbitrage involving the sale of the stock short, the writing of a put, and the purchase of a call with the options all having the same terms.

Rigged Market. The manipulation of a security price in an attempt to attract buyers and sellers.
See Manipulation.

Right. See Subscription Right.

Rights Offering. A right that is granted by a corporation and that enables shareholders to purchase a number of shares of a new issue of common stock, usually at a lower price than the market price of the existing shares. The offer is made to the shareholders before the issue is offered to the public.

Rising Bottom. In technical analysis, a chart pattern, usually on a daily chart, indicating a rising trend in a security's price.

Risk Arbitrage. A purchase and short sale of potentially equal securities at prices that may realize a profit.
See Bona Fide Arbitrage.

Round Lot. A unit of trading or a multiple thereof. On the NYSE, stocks are traded in round lots of 100 shares for active stocks and 10 shares for inactive ones. Bonds are traded in units of $1,000.
See Normal Trading Unit; Odd Lot.

Rounding Bottom. In technical analysis, a chart pattern suggesting the shape of a saucer. Also called a saucer. The trend is considered upward.

Rounding Top. In technical analysis, a chart pattern suggesting the shape of an inverted saucer. A rounding top indicates a downward trend.

RR. See Account Executive.

Run. (1) A market maker's list of offerings, including bid-offer prices (and, for bonds, par values, and prices).
(2) In technical analysis, a quick movement of prices, usually in reference to an uptrend.

Running Ahead. An AE's entering a personal buy/sell order before entering a customer's order. This activity is not ethical.

Running Through the Pot. In a distribution, the syndicate manager can take securities back from the group members and put them into "the pot" for institutional sales. Usually this is done if institutional sales are doing better than retail sales.
See Pot, The.

RVP Trade. See Receive Versus Payment (Trade).

S. A symbol on the ticker tape meaning the actual quantity if preceded by more than one digit.

For example: T
2s50½
means 200 shares of AT&T at 50½

S .
S ˙ A symbol on the ticker tape meaning actual quantity in a security that trades in round lots of 10 shares.

S .
T ˙ A symbol on the ticker tape meaning "stopped."

Safekeeping. A protected condition maintained as a service by a brokerage firm for its customers' fully paid securities registered in the customers' own names. The practice entails use of vault space to store those certificates until they are withdrawn or sold.

Same Day Substitution. A provision of Regulation T of the Federal Reserve that allows a customer to sell securities and buy securities of a lesser or equal amount without having to deposit separate initial margin requirements on the purchase.

Saucer. *See* Rounding Bottom.

Scale Orders. Multiple limit orders entered by investors at various prices but at the same time. The purpose is to obtain an overall, or average, favorable purchase or sale price. Multiples of round lots may be either *bought* at prices scaled down from a given value or *sold* at prices scaled up from a given value.

Scalper. A market maker who puts heavy markups or markdowns on transactions.
See Five Percent

Screen (Stocks). To look for stocks that meet certain predetermined investment and financial requirements.

Scrip. Document evidencing the fractional share of a stock distributed by a company because of an exchange of stock, split, or spin-off. The owner can then buy the remaining fraction to make a full share.

Seasoned Issue. An issue, once distributed, that trades actively and that has great liquidity.

SEC. See Securities and Exchange Commission.

Secondary Distribution (Offering). A public offering of stock by selling it to stockholders.

Secondary Market. (1) A term referring to the trading of securities not listed on an organized exchange.
(2) A term used to describe the trading of securities other than a new issue.

Secondary Movement. A short-term movement in the market in the opposite direction from the primary movement.

SEC Rules. See Rule plus specific number.

Securities Act of 1933. Federal legislation designed to protect the public in the initial issuance and distribution of securities by providing to prospective purchasers full and accurate information about an issue. The law that governs the primary market.

Securities Analysis. The historical study of stock movements and trends by means of charting. Most brokerage firms now employ an analyst to aid them in predicting the financial condition of a company or group of companies.

Securities and Exchange Commission (SEC). A government agency responsible for the supervision and regulation of the securities industry.

Securities Exchange of Act of 1934. Federal legislation designed to protect the public against unfair and inequitable practices on stock exchanges and in over-the-counter markets throughout the United States. The law that governs the secondary market.

Securities Investor Protection Corporation (SIPC). Formed by the Securities Investors Protection Act of 1970, a government-sponsored, private, nonprofit corporation that guarantees repayment of money and securities to customers in amounts up to $100,000 cash equity and $500,000 overall per customer in the event of a broker/dealer bankruptcy.

Security. A transferable instrument evidencing ownership or creditorship, such as a note, stock or bond, evidence of debt, interest or participation in a profit-sharing agreement, investment contract, voting trust certificate, fractional undivided interest in oil, gas, or other mineral rights, or any warrant to subscribe to, or purchase, any of the foregoing or other similar instruments.

Seek a Market. Look to make a buy or sale.

Segregate. To keep customer securities physically separate from those owned by the broker/dealers.

Segregated Securities. Customer-owned securities fully paid for or representing excess collateral in a margin account that are locked away and cannot be used in the conduct of the firm's business.

Segregation. A protected condition maintained by a brokerage firm for its customers' fully paid securities and those representing excess collateral in margin accounts.

Sell the Book. An instruction to the broker/dealer to sell as many shares as possible at the best available bid.

Selling Concession. A fraction of an underwriter's spread granted to a selling group member by agreement. It is payment for services as a sales agent for the underwriters.

Selling Dividends. The unfair and unethical practice of soliciting purchase orders for mutual fund shares solely on the basis of an impending distribution by that fund.

Selling Group. Selected broker/dealers of the NASD who contract to act as selling agents for underwriters and who are compensated by a portion of the sales charge (selling concession) on newly issued stocks. They assume no financial liability for the unsold balance, but they do not share in profit from syndicate residuals.

Selling Off (Sell-Off). Selling commodities or securities to avoid losses from continued drops in price.

Selling on the Good News. Practice of selling a stock right after good news has pushed the stock price very high. The investor thinks that the stock has reached its top price.

Sell-Out. Upon failure of the purchasing firm to accept delivery of the security and lacking the proper rejection form, the seller can without notice dispose of that security in the marketplace at the best available price and hold the buyer responsible for any financial loss resulting from the default.
See Buy-In.

Sell Plus. A market or limit order to sell a security at a price higher than the previous differently pried transaction for that security.

Sell Stop Order. A memorandum that becomes a market order to sell if and when someone trades a round lot at or below the memorandum price.

Separate Account. A specialized legal entity created by an insurance company to incorporate contracts offered by the company under a variable annuity plan.

Separate Customer. As defined by SIPC, the accounts of a given customer at a single brokerage firm. Different types of accounts held by the same person do not constitute "separate customers."

Settlement (Delivery) Date. The day on which certificates involved in a transaction are due at the purchaser's office.

Shadow Calendar. Forthcoming issues that are registered with the SEC but that are not offered yet, usually because of a backlog at the SEC.

Share. A stock certificate—a unit of measurement of the equity ownership of a corporation.

Share Broker. A discount broker who charges a commission that decreases as the number of shares traded increases.

Shareholder. See Principals (Stockholders); Stockholder (Shareholder).

Shark Repellant. Any step taken by a "target" corporation to discourage a takeover. Also called a porcupine provision. *See* Poison Pill.

Shark Watcher. A company whose business is to detect takeover attempts by watching trading patterns in a client's stock.

Shelf Distribution. A privilege written in a registration statement enabling an affiliated person to dispose of sizable amounts of securities from his or her portfolio (shelf) over a nine-month period following the effective date. For OTC transactions, order tickets must be marked "distribution stock"; for exchange sales, "Dist."

Shop/Shopping the Street. (1) "Shop" is slang for the broker/dealer's office.
(2) "Shop" or "shopping the street" means a broker/dealer's gathering quotations from OTC market makers to form a basis for negotiating a transaction. *See* Firm Market (Price, Quote); Subject Market (Price, Quote); Workout Market.

Short-Against-the-Box. A situation in which a person is both long and short in the same security at the same time in his/her account, a practice usually employed to defer tax liability on capital gains. Although the customer sells the stock short, he/she actually owns the security, which is held in the broker's "box." The aim is to protect a capital gain in owned shares, while deferring the taxes due if the shares were actually sold and the capital gain reported. This way, the investor can wait until he or she is in a more favorable tax situation to sell the securities.

Short Interest Theory. Short interest positions are reported each month as of the fifteenth. The theory postulates that an increase in the short interest is bullish since those customers who are short must buy back that position, causing a demand for securities. A decline in short interest would be bearish.

Short Market Value. The market value of security positions that a customer owes to a broker/dealer (short in the account).

Short Position. (1) The number of shares in a given security sold short and not covered as of a particular date.
(2) The total amount of stock sold short by all investors and not covered as of a particular date.
(3) A term used to denote the writer of an option.

Short Sale. The sale of a security that is not owned at the time of the trade, necessitating its purchase some time in the future to "cover" the sale. A short sale is made with the expectation that the stock value will decline, so that the sale will be eventually covered (i.e., repurchased) at a price lower than the original sale, thus realizing a profit. Before the sale is covered, the broker/dealer borrows stock (for which collateral is put up) to deliver on the settlement date.

Short Selling Power. The dollar amount of equity securities a customer may sell short without additional funds and continue to meet the initial margin requirements of Regulation T of the Federal Reserve. Short selling power is equal to the Reg T excess divided by the Reg T initial margin requirements. For example, $10,000/50% = $20,000.

Short-Stop (Limit) Order. A memorandum that becomes a limit order to sell short when someone creates a round-lot transaction at or below the memorandum price (electing sale). The short sale may or may not be executed since the rules then require that it be sold at least one-eighth above the electing sale as well as high enough in value to satisfy the limit price.

Short-Term Capital Transaction. The sale of securities held for six months or less, or a short sale and a purchase to cover at a profit within any time period.

Siamese Stock. See Paired Shares.

Silent Partner. A member of a partnership represented only by capital and not entitled to a voice in management, a limited partner.

Simultaneous (Riskless) Transaction. A transaction in which the broker/dealer takes a position in a security only after receipt of an order from a customer, and only for the purpose of acting as principal so as to disguise his or her remuneration from the transaction.

Sinker. Slang for a bond with a sinking fund.
See Sinking Fund.

Sinking Fund. (1) An annual reserve of capital required to be set aside out of a current earnings to provide monies for retirement of an outstanding bond issue and, sometimes, preferred stock. Such a feature has a favorable effect on the market value of that issue.
(2) A separate account in the overall sinking fund for monies used to redeem securities by open-market purchase, by request for tenders or call, or in accordance with the redemption schedule in the bond contract.

SL. Stockbroker shorthand for "sold."

Snowballing. See Gather in the Stops.

Soft Market. The market for securities with low demand.

Soft Spot. Term used to describe the weakness in a select stock or group of stocks during a generally strong and advancing market.

Sold Last Sale. A ticker tape identification for a transaction that has volatile fluctuations between sales. It appears for an issue that has moved one or more points if its previous sale was 197⅞ or below, two or more points if its previous sale was 20 or above.

Sold-Out Market. In commodities trading, the futures contracts of a particular commodity are hard to come by due to contract liquidations and limited offerings.

Sold Sale (SLD). A transaction appearing on the ticker tape out of its proper sequence.

Sold to You. Term used by over-the-counter traders to confirm the acceptance of their offer.

Special Bid. A New York Stock Exchange procedure for facilitating bids for a large block of stock. Regulations are similar to those regarding a special offer.

Special Cash Account. An account in which the customer is required to make full payment on the fifth business day after the trade date, and in no case later than the seventh calendar day, or arrange for COD payment on the fifth business day. The account is defined in Regulation T.
See Frozen Account.

Specialist. A member of the NYSE with two essential functions: First, to maintain an orderly market, insofar as reasonably practicable, in the stocks in which he or she is registered as a specialist. To do this, the specialist must buy and sell for his or her own account and risk, to a reasonable degree, where there is a temporary disparity between supply and demand. To equalize trends, the specialist must buy or sell counter to the direction of the market. Second, the specialist acts as a broker's broker, executing orders when another broker cannot afford the time. At all times the specialist must put the customer's interest before his own. All specialists are registered with the NYSE as regular, substitute, associate, or temporary.

Specialist Book. The chronological notebook of NYSE specialists used to keep a record of the buy and sell orders they receive for execution at specified prices. It also includes their own inventory of securities. The book is *not* public information.

Special Offering. The disposal of a large block of stock in accordance with certain terms and conditions, by inviting members of the exchange to place buy orders on the floor to be executed by crossing in the normal procedure. The seller pays a special commission.

Special Units. Units of three or more fully qualified specialists who have banded together in a partnership or corporation for the purpose of maintaining an orderly market in specific stocks.

Spectail. A combination of "speculator" and "retail." A broker/dealer who does more speculative trading for his or her account than handling of client orders.

Speculation. The employment of funds in high-risk transactions for relatively large and immediate gains in which the safety of principal or current income is of secondary importance.

Spin Off. A distribution of stock in a company that is owned by another corporation and that is being allocated to the holders of the latter institution.

Split. A division of the outstanding shares of a corporation into a larger number of shares, by which each outstanding share entitles its owner to a fixed number of new shares. Individual shareholders' overall equity remains the same, but they own more stock, since the total value of the shares remains the same. For example, in a two-for-one split, the owner of 100 shares, each worth $100, would be given 200 share, each worth $50.

Split Commission. When one AE executes a transaction that was brought in by another AE, they split the commission between them.

Split Down. A corporate reorganization whereby the holder of a security must return the certificate to the issuer and receive proportionately fewer shares in the exchange.

Split Offering. (1) An offering combining both a primary and secondary distribution.

(2) A municipal bond offering part of which consists

of serial bonds and part of which is made up of term bonds.

Split Order. The periodic purchase or sale of small parts of a large block of securities to avoid market upset and price fluctuations.

Split Rating. A term used to describe the situation in which a corporation has been given different credit ratings by different services.

Split Up. A corporate recapitalization in which the holder of a security receives proportionately more shares from the issuer in relation to his or her current ownership in the company.

Sponsor. See Underwriter.

Spot Secondary Distribution. A secondary distribution that does not require an SEC registration statement and may be attempted on the spot, without delay.

Spread. (1) The difference in value between the bid and offering prices.
(2) Underwriting compensation.

Stabilization. The syndicate manager is empowered by the members of his group to maintain a bid in the after-market at or slightly below the public offering price, thus "stabilizing" the market and giving the syndicate and selling group members a reasonable chance of successfully disposing of their allocations. This practice is a legal exception to the manipulation practices outlawed by the Securities and Exchange Act of 1934.

Stag. A speculator who buys and sells stocks rapidly for fast profits.

Stagflation. The combination of sluggish economic growth, high unemployment, and high inflation.

Stagnation. (1) A period of low volume and inactive trading on a securities market.
(2) The economic doldrums resulting from retarded economic growth.

Standard & Poor's (S&P) Corporation. A source of investment services, most famous for its *Standard & Poor's
Rating* of bonds and its composite index of 425 industrial, 20 transportation, and 55 public utility common
stocks, called *Standard & Poor's Index.*

Standby Commitment. *See* Standby Underwriting Agreement.

Standby Underwriting Agreement. An agreement between
an investment banker and a corporation whereby the
banker agrees for a negotiated fee to purchase any or
all shares offered as a subscription privilege (rights
offering) that are not bought by the rights holders by
the time the offer expires.

Stapled Stock. See Paired Shares.

Statutory Voting. A means by which a stockholder is given the
right to cast one vote for each share owned in favor of or
against each of a number of proposals or director/nomi-
nees at a formal meeting convened by the corporation.

Stickering. Changing the official statement of a new issue
by printing the altered information on adhesive-backed
paper and "stickering" onto the statement.

Sticky Deal. An underwriting that, for one reason or another, will be hard to market.

Stock Ahead. An expression used on the floor of the New
York Stock Exchange to signify that one or more
brokers had made a prior bid (or offer) at the same
price as an order you had entered. Sometimes a
customer's order remains unexecuted for this reason. In other words, there is "stock ahead" of the
order.

Stock Dividend Distribution. A distribution to shareholders made upon declaration by a corporation's board of
directors. This distribution differs from the usual
disbursement in that it is given in the form of additional shares of stock instead of money.

Stockholder (Shareholder). The owner of common or preferred stock.

Stockholder of Record. Person named on the issuer's stock
books as the owner.

Stocks. Certificates representing ownership in a corporation and a claim on the firm's earnings and assets;
they may yield dividends and can appreciate or decline
in value.
See Authorized Stock; Common Stock; Issued-and-
Outstanding Stocks; Preferred Stock; Unissued Stock.

Stock Watcher. A computerized service in the stock watch
department of the NYSE that keeps track of the trading activity and movements of listed stocks.

Stop Limit Order. A memorandum that becomes a limit (as
opposed to a market) order immediately after a transaction takes place at or through the indicated (memorandum) price.

Stop Loss Order. A customer's order to set the sell price of
a stock below the market price, thus locking in profits
or preventing further losses.

Stop Order. A memorandum that becomes a market order only if a transaction takes place at or through
the price stated in the memorandum. Buy stop orders
are placed above the market, and sell stop orders are
placed below it. The sale that activates the memorandum is called the electing (activating or triggering) sale.
See Buy Stop Order; Market Order; Sell Stop Order.

Stop-Out Price. The lower dollar price at auction for which
Treasury bills are sold.

Stopped Out. An expression reflecting a broker's unsuccessful attempt to improve upon the price of a transaction after having been guaranteed an execution
price by the specialist.

Stopping Stock. A specialist's guarantee of price to a broker, thus enabling the broker to try to improve upon that price without fear of missing the market.

Street. "Wall Street"—that is, the New York financial community, as well as the exchanges throughout the country.

Street Name. When securities have been bought on margin or when the customer wishes the security to be held by the broker/dealer, the securities are registered and held in the broker/dealer's own firm (or "street") name.

Subject Market (Price, Quote). In the OTC market, a range of buying or selling prices quoted by market makers at which they are unable to trade immediately. Such prices are subject to verification by the parties whose market they represent.

Subscription. An agreement to buy a new issue of securities. The agreement specifies the *subscription price* (the price for shareholders before the securities are offered to the public). This right is called the *subscription privilege or subscription right.*

Subscription Privilege (Preemptive Right). A shareholder's right to purchase newly issued shares or bonds (before the public offering). It must be exercised within a fixed period, usually 30 to 60 days, before the privilege expires and becomes worthless.

Subscription Ratio. The ratio of old stock to new stock offered as a subscription privilege.

Subscription Right. A privilege granted to owners of certain stocks to purchase newly issued securities in proportion to their holdings, usually at values below the current market price. Rights have a market value of their own and are actively traded. They differ from warrants in that they must be exercised within a relatively short period of time.

Subsidiary. A company 5 percent of whose voting shares are owned by another company.

Substantial Net Capital. Each member of the New York Stock Exchange is required to maintain "substantial net capital."

Substitution (Swap). The sale of one security in an account to use the proceeds to pay for the purchase of another security on the same trade date.
See Switch (Contingent or Swap) Order.

Suitability. The appropriateness of a strategy or transaction, in light of an investor's financial means and investment objectives.

Sunshine Law. Law giving the public access to the meetings and records of government agencies (such as the SEC and the Commodities Futures Trading Commission).

Super-Restricted Account. An old term no longer in use. A margin account in which the equity is less than 30 percent of the market value of the adjusted debit balance in the account.

Support. In technical analysis, an area below the current price of the stock where the stock is in short supply and where the buyers are aggressive. The stock's price is likely not to go lower than this level, which is called a *support level.*
See Resistance.

Support Level. See Support.

Suspended Trading. The temporary ceasing of trading of an issue.

Suspense Account. A record maintained by a broker/dealer to reflect unreconciled money and securities differences in its business activities.

Swap Order/Transactions. See Switch (Contingent or Swap) Order.

Sweetener. A special feature in a securities offering, such as convertibility, that encourages the purchase of the security.

Switch (Contingent or Swap) Order. An order to buy one security and then sell another at a limit, or to sell one security and then to buy another at a limit. The transaction may also be called a proceeds sale if, as is usually the case, the proceeds of the sell order are applied against the expenses of the buy order.

Syndicate. A group of investment bankers who purchase securities from the issuer and then reoffer them to the public at a fixed price. The syndicate is usually organized with one or more members acting as *syndicate manager,* to ensure the successful offering of a corporation's securities.

Tailgating. An account executive's purchase of a security for his/her own account right on the heels of a purchase of the same security for a customer.

Take a Bath. Slang meaning to incur a large loss.

Take a Flier. Slang meaning to enter into a highly speculative investment.

Take a Position. (1) To hold stocks or bonds, in either a long or short position.
(2) To purchase securities as a long-term investment.

Take Delivery. In securities, accepting a receipt of stock or bond certificates after they have been purchased or transferred between accounts.

Takedown. In an underwriting, the number of securities that a syndicate member is supposed to sell.

Take Off. The summary of daily changes in a security that is posted to the stock record.

Take Out. The money that an investor "takes out" from an account when there is a net credit balance.

Takeover. The assumption of control over a corporation by another corporation, through acquisition or merger. *See* Poison Pill; Shark Watcher; Tender Offer.

Tape. A financial news service that reports the prices and sizes of transactions. Although this information was once reported on a paper tape from a "ticker tape" machine, it is now displayed on electronic screens. The name "tape," however, persists.

Tape Racing. An account executive's executing personal orders before executing a sizable customer order, to take advantage of the large order's effect on prices.

Technical Analysis. An approach to market theory stating that previous price movements, properly interpreted, can indicate future price patterns.

Technical Sign. A movement in a security's price that, under certain circumstances, indicates a short-term trend.

Telephone Booths. Booths or cubicles ringing the stock exchange trading rooms that are used by member organizations to (1) receive orders from their offices, (2) distribute orders to brokers for execution, and (3) transmit details of the executed orders back to their offices.

Temporary Specialist. An experienced member of the exchange appointed by a floor official to act as a specialist only in an emergency situation. His or her responsibilities are the same as those of a regular specialist. *See* Associate Specialists; Relief Specialist.

Tenants by Entirety. A form of ownership by which assets legally transfer to the surviving spouse upon the death of either party in a marriage. If a securities account were so owned jointly by husband and wife, it would transfer to the surviving spouse upon the death of either tenant.

Tender Offer. A formal proposition to stockholders to sell their shares in response to a large purchase bid. The buyer customarily agrees to assume all costs and reserves the right to accept all, none, or a specific number of the shares presented for acceptance.

Thin Market. See Narrow Market.

Third Market. Transactions in exchange-listed stocks by broker/dealers.

Third-Party Account. A brokerage account carried in the name of a person other than a customer. The practice is prohibited by NYSE regulation.

Third-Party Check. A check drawn to the order of one person who endorses it to another person, who subsequently presents it to someone else in satisfaction of an obligation.

Throwaway Offer. A nominal (approximate) bid or offer that should not be considered final.

Tick. A transaction on the stock exchange.
See Minus Tick; Plus Tick; Zero Minus Tick; Zero Plus Tick.

Ticker Tape. A trade-by-trade report in chronological order of trades executed, giving prices and volumes. Separate tapes exist for various markets. The mechanism used to be mechanical, but it is now some sort of electronic display.

Tight Market. An active, vigorous market with narrow bid-offer spreads.

Tight Money. An economic condition characterized by scarce credit, generally the result of a money supply restricted by the Federal Reserve.

Tip. A suggestion as to what to buy or sell.

Tombstone. The type of newspaper advertisement used for public offering. The ad simply and drably lists all the facts about the issue. Also called the offering circular.

Total Capitalization. The aggregate value of a corporation's long-term debt, preferred, and common stock accounts—or, put another way, funded debt plus shareholders' equity.

Total Cost. The contract price plus all expenses incurred on the purchase execution.

Total Volume. A column in the listed stock tables showing total shares of stocks traded (omitting the last two zeros).

Trade Date. The date a trade was entered into, as opposed to settlement date.

Trader. A person or firm engaged in the business of buying and selling securities, options, or commodities for a profit.

Trading Authorization. The legal right conferred by a person or institution upon another to effect the purchase and/or sale of securities in the former's account.

Trading Crowd. Members of an exchange involved in the purchase and sale of a particular issue. They gather the specialist's position.

Trading Floor. The location at any organized exchange where buyers and sellers meet to transact business.

Trading Post. Twenty-three locations on the floor of the NYSE that were 7-foot-high, horseshoe-shaped structures with an outside circumference of from 26 to 31 feet. The one exception is a tablelike structure, Post 30, in the garage, where most inactive preferred stocks are traded in multiples of 10 shares. The posts have been replaced by a round structure with a lot of electronics display.

Transfer and Ship. Customer instructions to have securities transferred into his or her name and sent to his or her address.

Trend. Movement, up or down, in a security's market price, or in the market itself, for a period of six months or more.

Trendline. The line superimposed by technical analysts on price plottings to indicate a price trend. Drawn beneath the prices, the line reflects an upward trend; above the prices, it means the trend is downward.

Triangle. In technical analysis, a chart pattern of stock price movements with the base at the left and the apex at the right. Also called a flag, coil, wedge, or pennant, depending on the price movements.

Triggering Sale. See Electing Sale.

TTV. See Trading to Total Volume.

Turkey. A security that is not doing an investor any good.

Twenty-Day (Cooling-Off) Period. A period of 20 calendar days following the filing of a registration statement with the SEC, during which (1) the SEC examines the statement for deficiencies; (2) the issuing corporation negotiates with an underwriting syndicate for a final agreement; and (3) the syndicate prepares for the successful distribution of the impending issue. The final day of the period is normally considered the effective date.

Two-Dollar Broker. A member of the New York Stock Exchange who executes orders in any security for any organization, in return for which he receives a brokerage fee. Their fee, which is negotiable, is actually larger than $2 per trade. They are also known as independent brokers or agents.

Underlying Security. The security that an investor has the right to buy or sell according to the terms of a listed option contract.

Undervalued. A term used to describe a security that is trading at a lower price than it should.
See Overvalued; Fair Market Value.

Underwriter. Also known as an "investment banker" or "distributor," a middleman between an issuing corporation and the public. The underwriter usually forms an underwriting group, called a syndicate, to limit risk and commitment of capital. He or she may also contract with selling groups to help distribute the issue—for a concession. In the distribution of mutual funds, the underwriter may also be known as a "sponsor," "distributor," or even "wholesaler." Investment banker also offer other services, such a s advice and counsel on the raising and investment of capital.

Underwriter's Retention. The percentage of total issue to which each member of an underwriter's group is entitled and which he or she distributed to customers. The retained amount is usually equal to about 75 percent of the member's total financial commitment. The syndicate manager decides, on behalf of the other members, how to distribute the rest of the issue (or "the pot") and how it is to be sold to institutional investors (group sales) or reserved for handling by selling groups.

Underwriting Compensation (Spread). The gross profit realized by an underwriter equal to the difference between the price he paid to the issuing corporation and the price of the public offering.

Undivided Account. In an underwriting agreement, an arrangement for the sharing of liability in which each member of the syndicate is liable for any unsold portion of an issue. The degree of liability is based on each member's percentage of participation.
See Syndicate.

Unissued Stock. That portion of authorized stock not distributed among investors.

Unlisted Security. A security that is not traded on an exchange. Usually called an over-the-counter security.

Unwind a Trade. (1) To undo a transaction, such as "unwinding" a short sale with a purchase.
(2) To correct an erroneous transaction.

Upgrade. Raising a security's rating by improving the credit quality of the issue or issuer.

Uptick. See Plus Tick.

Uptrend. Any generally upward movement in a security's price.

Vault Cash. All the cash in a bank's vault.

Venture Capital Company. An investment company whose objective is to invest in new or underdeveloped companies.

Volume. Number of bonds or shares traded during specific periods, such as daily, weekly, or monthly.

Volume Deleted. A ticker tape announcement to signify that quantities of less than 5,000 shares per transaction will not appear until the ticker tape can stay abreast of trading activity on the stock exchange floor. It appears when the tape falls two minutes behind.

Volume Resumed. The volume-deleted condition is no longer in effect.

Voluntary Underwriter. An individual or corporation that purchases a security from an issuer or affiliated person and offers it for public sale under an effective registration statement.

Wallflower. A stock that investors are, by and large, just not attracted to.

War Babies. Securities of corporations engaged in defense contracts. Also known as war brides.

Warehousing. The illegal sale of a corporate security with a provision for its repurchase by the seller at some future date and at a prearranged price.

Warrant. An inducement attached to new securities in distribution giving purchasers a long-term (usually a five- to ten-year) privilege of subscribing to one or more shares of stock reserved for them by the corporation from its unissued or Treasury stock reserve. *See* Subscription Right.

Wash Sale. (1) For regulatory purposes, the purchase and sale of the same security at the same time and price without any real change of ownership. This practice is outlawed under the Securities Exchange Act of 1934.

(2) For tax purposes, a sale at a loss and repurchase of the same or a similar issue, within 30 days before or after the first transaction, while intending to use that loss to offset capital gains or taxable income in that year. The loss is generally not allowed as a tax deduction.

See Manipulation.

Watch List. A list of securities, established by a broker/dealer or an exchange, that is under scrutiny for evidence of illegal or unethical practices.

Watered Stock. A corporation's issuance of additional shares without increasing its capital. Also called diluting the shares.

WD. See When Issued/When Distributed Contract.

Weak Market. A market characterized by a greater number of sellers than buyers, which creates a general downtrend in prices.

Wedge. See Triangle.

W Formation. *See* Double Bottom.

When Issued/When Distributed Contract. A delivery contract involving securities (stocks or bonds) that have been proposed for distribution but not yet issued. The date of delivery is set for some time in the future by the NASD Uniform Practice Committee or the appropriate stock exchange, as the case may be.

White Knight. Colloquial expression for a person or firm who blocks a hostile takeover attempt by taking over the target company itself.

Wholesaler. See Underwriter.

WI. See When Issued/When Distributed Contract.

Window Settlement. Transactions that are not cleared through the SCC or NCC and that are completed in the office of the purchasing firm by means of certificate delivery versus immediate payment.

Wire House. Any large exchange member firm.

Wire Room. An area in each branch office and in the home office where messages may be received and sent using machinery that creates a printed copy of the messages. Message traffic normally consists of order data, reports of order executions, trade settlement information, and other sales data.

With or Without a Sale Order (WOW). A odd-lot limit order to buy or sell either at a price derived from an effective round-lot quotation (with a sale) or at the existing round-lot quotation plus differential (without a sale),whichever occurs first in accordance with the customer's limit.

Withholding. A failure by a broker/dealer to make a bona fide distribution of a hot issue, thus encouraging demand at a premium price. This practice is a violation of the NASD Rules of Fair Practice.
See Free-Riding.

Without Dividend. See Ex-Dividend (Without Dividend) Date.

Wooden Ticket. Confirming execution of a customer's order without actually executing it.

Workout Market. In the OTC market, a range of prices quoted by a market maker who is not certain that a market is available, but who feels he or she can "work one out" within a reasonable period of time.

WOW Order. See With or Without a Sale Order.

Wrinkle. Colloquial term for a feature in a security that could benefit the holder.

Write. The process of selling an option. The writer is the investor who sells the option.

Write-Out. An exchange floor procedure by which special- ists are allowed to buy stock for themselves from a customer's offering in their books, or sell from their accounts to a customer's bid. They must, however, allow the broker who entered the order to execute and "write out" the confirmation of the transaction and earn the contingent brokerage fee.

X. *See* Ex-Dividend (Without Dividend) Date.

XCH. *See* Ex-Clearing House.

XD. Shorthand notation meaning "ex-dividend." *See* Ex-Dividend (Without Dividend) Date.

X Dis. *See* Ex-Distribution.

XRT. *See* Ex-Rights.

XW. *See* Ex-Warrants.

Yo-Yo Stock. A stock whose price rises and drops often and quickly.

Zero Minus Tick. A transaction on the exchange at a price equal to that of the preceding transaction but lower than the last different price.

Zero Plus Tick. A transaction on the exchange at a price equal to that of the preceding transaction but higher than the last different price.

Index

A

Account executive (AE), 61,
  68-73, 233
  selecting, 68-73
Accounting department,
  167-69
Account statement, 233
Activity sale, 86
Adjusted debit balance, 233
Advance-decline theory, 234
Advisory and voting solicita-
  tions, 173

Affiliated person, 234
Aftermarket, 234
After-tax loss, 209
Agents, 80
All-or-none offering, 89, 234
Alternative order, 90, 234
American Stock Exchange:
  floor, 81
  history, 33-35
  Market Value Index, 182,
  234